ThinkingThrough

Thinking Through
New Literacies for Primary
and Early Years

ThinkingThrough Education

Thinking Through New Literacies for Primary and Early Years

Jayne Metcalfe, Debbie Simpson,

Ian Todd and Mike Toyn

⑤SAGE | **m** LearningMatters

Los Angeles | London | New Delhi
Singapore | Washington DC

Learning Matters
An imprint of SAGE Publications Ltd
1 Oliver's Yard
55 City Road
London EC1Y 1SP

SAGE Publications Inc.
2455 Teller Road
Thousand Oaks, California 91320

SAGE Publications India Pvt Ltd
B1/I 1 Mohan Cooperative Industrial Area
Mathura Road
New Delhi 110 044

SAGE Asia-Pacific Pte Ltd
3 Church Street
#10-04 Samsung Hub
Singapore 049483

Editor: Amy Thornton
Development editor: Clare Weaver
Production controller: Chris Marke
Project management: Deer Park Productions,
Tavistock, Devon
Marketing manager: Catherine Slinn
Cover design: Toucan
Typeset by: PDQ Typesetting Ltd
Printed and bound by CPI Group (UK) Ltd,
Croydon, CR0 4YY

Library of Congress Control Number: 2013936978

British Library Cataloguing in Publication data

A catalogue record for this book is available
from the British Library.

ISBN 978 0 85725 875 5
ISBN 978 0 85725 809 0 (pbk)

Contents

About the authors

Jayne Metcalfe is a senior lecturer in the Faculty of Education at the University of Cumbria. She is interested in the use of ICT to support learning across the curriculum, and in particular the use of ICT in the Early Years. E-safety training is another area of interest and Jayne is involved in e-safety training of student teachers. Prior to joining the university she worked as a primary teacher and held the role of ICT coordinator.

Debbie Simpson is a senior lecturer in the Faculty of Education at the University of Cumbria. She is currently the acting Programme Leader for the Primary PGCE course. Her academic interests lie in technology enhanced learning in higher education, ICT/ computer science educational policy and curriculum, and new literacy studies. She is currently working on a PhD in Technology Enhanced Learning. Prior to joining the university she worked as a primary teacher in a number of local schools.

Ian Todd is a senior lecturer in the Faculty of Education at the University of Cumbria, with a specialism in English and an interest in the teaching of ICT. Prior to joining the university he taught in a number of primary schools across the north west of England and was head teacher of a large primary school in Lancashire. He has at various times been subject leader for both English and ICT.

Mike Toyn is a senior lecturer in the Faculty of Education at the University of Cumbria where he also coordinates the teaching of primary ICT. He has a Masters in the use of digital technologies in education. His teaching interests are in the use of digital media to promote creative learning and using ICT to support interaction between learners. Prior to joining the university he worked as a primary teacher and held the role of ICT coordinator.

Introduction

This book, which is part of a series called Thinking Through Education, explores new literacies in relation to teaching and learning in primary schools. New literacies as a concept have grown in academic standing since the late 1990s following the work of the New London Group (1996). However, there has been little impact that is explicitly focused on the teaching of new literacies in primary schools despite the ever widening range of literacies that children encounter in their lives. Indeed, much of the emphasis on literacy in schools is closely linked to 'traditional' literacy and its relationship with SATs and school league tables.

This book considers a wide spectrum of new literacies and the role that they play in children's development, learning and lives. Each chapter is focused on a different literacy or aspect of such and offers a discussion of how the literacy can be best defined as well as thoughtful consideration of its impact on teaching and learning. Like the other books in this series, it is not meant to be a guide to a collection of activities that are proven to work in the classroom. Rather, it is meant to help develop a deep understanding of new literacies in order to provide reflective practitioners with the tools needed to provide well-reasoned teaching and learning activities that will develop children's literacy in a wide sense of the word.

Who is this book for?

This book is primarily for those training to gain Qualified Teacher Status (QTS) to work as a teacher in primary schools, so that it refers to the Teachers' Standards (DfE, 2012).

However, you may already work in a school in one of many roles such as a teaching assistant or classroom teacher. Whatever your role, you may find the book valuable to help you think through the pedagogy behind new literacies in order to support your ongoing professional development.

The team of authors who have written this book share many years of experience in teaching in primary schools ranging from Early Years to Key Stage 2 and incorporating roles such as subject leaders and coordinators to headships. All now work in higher education as teacher educators and share a passion for the use of ICT in teaching and learning. It is this passion for the flexible approaches that ICT can offer which provided the catalyst to write this book and you will find many references to the close relationship that technology and new literacies share.

Critical thinking skills

In common with the other books in this series, this one makes use of a number of different thinking skills, which are integrated into the various chapters. These include:

Consider – the factors that influence these decisions

Interpret – people's motivation and the consequences of these actions

Compare – different actions, people and contexts

Articulate – your beliefs and assumptions (in speech and writing)

Discuss – with other people – tutors, other students, teachers – the issues raised

Identify – what you have to do, or to avoid, to make your plans successful

Analyse – the reasons there may be for these actions

Each chapter begins with an overview of the key points that will be considered along with a short section that highlights the Teachers' Standards that relate to the chapter. Each chapter contains a number of critical thinking exercises, which will draw on the list of skills identified above to help you to focus your thoughts and develop your understanding of the issues in a structured way. They are accompanied by a commentary that provides some feedback on your likely responses to the critical thinking activity. Each chapter also includes at least one case study, which will be used to illustrate, in a practical manner, some of the key themes from the chapter.

Chapter 1 is focused around an overview of new literacies. It does this by considering what is meant by literacy and how understanding of this has changed over time. This provides a justification for why our understanding of it needs to be broadened to incorporate the range of new literacies which are part of our lives. Chapter 1 explores different models of literacy, which go beyond the confines of being able to decode words that are written on a page and provides an example of the text from a SATs paper in order to elaborate on the social and cultural aspects that are bound up in the words that we read. It provides examples ranging from the use of language forms in text messages sent via mobile phones to the use of tablet computers in education.

Chapter 2 has as its focus the role of technology in supporting early reading and writing. It begins with an exploration of the impact that TV can have on the literacy development of young children and the importance of parental views and support in this. It then progresses to use Postman Pat as an example of how familiarity with a popular TV character can provide a context for the development of a range of literacy skills that can be supported by a wide range of technologies. This then develops into a discussion that analyses the potential of using film and visual images as a vehicle for developing many key early literacy skills.

Chapter 3 concerns verbal literacy and particularly its links to online technologies. The use of blogging tools is an example of this where writing is similar in format to verbal forms of language so it is used as the basis of a case study. Other online strategies include 'quad' blogging, fan fiction and the use of Twitter with a Year 2 class. The problems that can be raised by seemingly simple internet searches is discussed in depth and forms a useful introduction to Chapter 4.

Chapter 4 explores what is meant by information literacy and makes connections between the definitions of literacy that were discussed in Chapter 1 and the way in which information literacy is defined. It builds on the examples provided in Chapter 3 to argue that information literacy is an essential and multi-faceted skill. It offers some frameworks through which to consider what is meant by information literacy and how it might be applied in classroom environments. The way in which information is filtered is used to start the chapter and ideas develop through to a section in which the importance of creating information, rather than simply consuming it, is emphasised.

Chapter 5 considers oral and aural literacy through the medium of music and the role that digital technologies play in music. It will encourage you to consider how widely you use music in the classroom and if the genre of music you use would match that listened to by children outside of the classroom. It goes on to explore the links between music and literacy and as such it emphasises the important role that music can plan in children's wider learning of literacy. It considers the emotional impact of particular pieces of music and the effect that music can have in films and so on. It progresses on to outline some practical ICT tools that can be used to bring music making and remixing into the classroom.

Chapter 6 starts with a case study that outlines the vast array of visual information that is available to us as we go about our daily lives. This is used to discuss the point that literacy is concerned with understanding, not simply decoding words, and that understanding of visual signs and symbols is part of the literacy of our daily lives. It moves on to look at the links between visual literacy and reading; writing; and speaking and listening. It concludes with an example that looks at how a form of critical media analysis can tie all of these together.

Chapter 7 is a discussion of identity in cyberspace. Many of the chapters in this book make reference to the role of technology in supporting new literacies and literacy development and this chapter explores the issues that arise when personalities are represented online. It offers an insight into the differences between 'digital natives' and 'digital immigrants' and develops this into a study of the amount of personal information that digital natives frequently make available online. This leads on to a discussion of the vital role that e-safety plays in making use of technology to support the development of new literacies before considering how avatars can be used to help represent personalities online.

Chapter 8 looks at new literacies and inclusion. It begins by highlighting that access to literacy has been historically used as a means of withholding information and power from large sections of society. This is used to set the scene for an exploration of the role of inclusion and new literacies. This covers two perspectives: first, the way that new literacies can support inclusion and second, special steps that might be needed to ensure that all children are included when working with new technologies. There are sections on new literacies and inclusion, children with English as an additional language, children with special educational needs and new literacies from a feminist perspective.

Chapter 9 looks at the important area of ethics, particularly in relation to the 'remix culture'. A salutary story about the use of materials sourced online is used to start the chapter as well as to introduce many of the key ideas that are subsequently discussed. Of course, these matters are not clear-cut or there would be no need to debate them and there would be no grey areas; this is highlighted through a discussion of the role of imitation in art. Sampling, mashups, ownership and the law are all discussed in order to help you develop an understanding of this complex area.

1

What's new about new literacies?

Debbie Simpson

Chapter Focus

This chapter will introduce you to some definitions of what it means to be literate, and encourage you to take a critical approach to the ways in which the term 'literacy' is used in education policy documents, in the media, in school and in everyday conversations.

The critical thinking exercises in this chapter focus on:

- **analysing** widely held assumptions about what it means to be literate, including your own;
- **identifying** the key features of The New Literacy Studies;
- **considering** the relationship between literacy and technology;
- **articulating** the implications for educators.

The key ideas discussed are: **literacy definitions, literacy models, 'new' literacies, texts, technology** and **pedagogy**.

This chapter is particularly relevant to the following Teachers' Standards (2012):

Part 1: Teaching

A teacher must:

1 **Set high expectations which inspire, motivate and challenge pupils**
   - set goals that stretch and challenge pupils of all backgrounds, abilities and dispositions
2 **Promote good progress and outcomes by pupils**
   - plan teaching to build on pupils' capabilities and prior knowledge
   - demonstrate knowledge and understanding of how pupils learn and how this impacts on teaching
3 **Demonstrate good subject and curriculum knowledge**
   - demonstrate a critical understanding of developments in the subject and curriculum areas, and promote the value of scholarship
   - demonstrate an understanding of and take responsibility for promoting high standards of literacy, articulacy and the correct use of standard English, whatever the teacher's specialist subject.

Introduction

This chapter begins with a case study that introduces themes of literacy, technology and pedagogy, which will be explored in greater detail in this and subsequent chapters. In this chapter we explore ideas about what it means to be literate, and how definitions of literacy have changed over time. We identify some of the assumptions that lie behind these definitions and consider how our own ideas about literacy have been influenced by background, education, experience and training.

We turn then to the field of New Literacy Studies (NLS) from which the term 'new literacies' emerges, and identify its key features. We consider how sociocultural perspectives encourage us to think of literacy as a social practice rather than as a set of skills to be mastered. We critically evaluate the old literacy/new literacy dichotomy, and discuss whether there is room for both perspectives in the primary classroom. Finally we consider the role of digital technologies in the teaching of literacy, and consider key pedagogical issues and implications for practitioners.

CASE STUDY

At a primary school in Blackpool, in the north west of England, children and teachers gather for the first ever *KidsMeet* event, where children take the place of teachers and present to each other (and to the world via video-link) something they have learned in class that inspires them, has made a difference to them or that they think is worth sharing with everyone else.

There are 12 presentations from children aged 5 to 11 years old, on a range of topics from drama games to *Twitter*. Most children speak in small groups, although one pupil does a presentation all on her own.

Year 6 pupils talk about their 'digital pencil-cases' (known in 'teacher talk' as *ipods* and *ipads*), which are great for publishing their writing straight to a blog and for responding to comments from their world-wide audience. They are also keen to show off how the audio features of their digital pencil-cases make their ideas accessible to all ages. The youngest presenters, from Year 1, demonstrate outstanding ICT expertise as they provide a live demonstration of audio and image editing, and explain how this has inspired and enriched their retelling of *Cinderella*.

The presentations in the hall break off as a live video conference call is received from Birmingham, where four Year 4 boys introduce the series of video tutorials they have created, demonstrating how to write 'exciting sentences'. Back in the hall, children from a school in Bradford demonstrate how to make computer mini-games with a program called *Kodu*, while pupils from a primary school in Liverpool show how they use *Google Apps* to work collaboratively when

/continued

CASE STUDY – continued

researching, creating and presenting their topic work on evacuees. A Year 6 pupil recommends the use of *Popplet* to organise topic work, and last but not least, Year 5 children talk about their play scripts, and show a mini horror movie they have made based upon the *Brainpop Moby* series. They talk about how they learned to edit, act, script, write, direct and produce their movie.

This KidsMeet event (since followed by others around the country) provides a snapshot into some of the inspiring work taking place in primary classrooms every day. You can read more about this first meeting at **http://lordlit.com/2011/ 06/17/741/**. However, if you enter the phrase *Blackpool Kidsmeet* into a search engine you can browse the pupil and teacher blogs, videos and photos to get a full flavour of the event directly from its participants.

Kidsmeet is a pupil-focused event designed by teachers to provide children with opportunities to showcase their learning. The primary focus is on literacy, including speaking and listening, and the use of new technologies to support and enhance learning. During this chapter we will analyse some ideas about literacy and technology in order to better understand the rationale behind this and similar initiatives.

Key idea: **Literacy**

Isn't literacy just about learning to read and write?

Few educational practices have greater ability to prompt passionate debate than the teaching of reading and writing.

No educational practice is neutral. All learning is based on some assumptions and the process of becoming literate is no exception. Even arriving at a definition of what it means to be literate is not straightforward, as you will discover in this chapter. Each day-to-day practice that you perhaps take for granted in our schools is the product of sometimes fiercely contested social and political processes. Few educational practices have greater ability to prompt passionate debate than the teaching of reading and writing.

Today we regard 'literacy' as a highly desirable condition and 'illiteracy' is portrayed as a scandal, disease or epidemic to be eliminated at all costs. Prior to the twentieth century, however, it was feared that mass literacy might lead to social unrest, by raising the expectations of the poor through access to subversive and radical literature and encouraging them to question the political and social status quo. The notion that literacy should be acquired in early childhood, and that an individual's failure to do so would have calamitous consequences for them personally and for society as a whole, is a relatively recent phenomenon.

Three main reasons are usually offered for the importance of mass literacy. These are linked to the economic and social well-being of the state, and to personal advancement. It is now held to be self-evident that a literate workforce is a productive workforce; essential to a nation's economic well-being. The performance of UK pupils, relative to those from other countries in international league tables of literacy, is watched anxiously, and slippage 'down the international tables' is a matter for media comment and political concern. Secondly, literacy is seen as a social good. Links have been made between childhood poverty and low literacy levels, and there is particular anxiety regarding the high levels of illiteracy among inmates of prisons and Young Offenders Institutions. Young white males from lower socio-economic classes in particular are believed to be marginalised through their poor literacy skills and resulting exclusion from employment and education. Finally, literacy is valued as a route to self-actualisation. Personal fulfilment is held to be a direct consequence of literacy, and is linked to an individual's ability to read and write fluently for pleasure, for personal empowerment, to express creativity and to engage fully in a world dominated by print.

Critical thinking exercise 1: exploring definitions of literacy

Consider the following tests of literacy that have been used separately at different times and by different people to assess literacy capability in populations and individuals. Do any of them surprise you?

A literate person can:

1. read and write his or her own name;
2. read, write and speak in English at levels of proficiency necessary to function on the job, in the family of the individual and in society;
3. with understanding both read and write a short, simple statement on his everyday life;
4. understand, interpret and deduce information from a given text;
5. name one person by name or title who is part of the judicial branch of government in Alabama;
6. communicate proficiently, including with technology.

Variously, these 'literacy tests' have been used: to assess historical [1], national [2] and global [3] rates of literacy in populations; to select children at age 11 for grammar school education [4]; as a test applied to people of African American

/continued

> **Critical thinking exercise 1 – continued**
> ethnicity in order for them to be granted voting rights [5]; to assess suitability for
> an administrative post [6].
>
> **Discuss** which, if any, of these definitions seem to you to be reasonable tests of
> literacy. What assumptions or hidden agendas can you detect in the statements?
> Which of the three priorities for literacy, economic, social and self-actualisation, do
> you think are prioritised in these statements?

Comment

Definitions of what it means to be literate have changed over the years as society itself
has changed. Being recognised as a literate person depends upon who is measuring
literacy, and how, and why. Organisations that devise tests of literacy often go into
detail about the results of their testing and the conclusions that can be drawn from
their results, but they rarely spell out the assumptions that underlie their models of
literacy.

To further illustrate the contentious nature of literacy and literacy tests, consider the
dispute focusing on recent proposals in the UK (2011) for a reading assessment test for
children aged six. Proposals by the Department for Education (DfE, 2010) aim to
'eliminate illiteracy' through *assessing reading at age six to make sure that all children
are on track.* The proposed test will focus on the ability of children to decode words,
using a *'non-word reading test'.* This is a test that includes nonsense words such as
mip, glimp or *zog* to assess children's ability to pronounce straightforward spelling
patterns.

This proposed reading test has been criticised strongly by a number of prominent voices
from politics, education and literacy studies, among them an all-party parliamentary
group for education and the UK Literacy Association (UKLA). To understand the
background to the debate and how some of the tensions arise, you will need to
examine contrasting theoretical models of literacy.

Key idea: **Models of literacy**

> Understanding the polarised views of literacy helps to gain an insight into the way
> that literacy is defined and how it can be developed.

Models of literacy can be classified into two main types: autonomous models and social
models. An autonomous, or individual, model of literacy identifies a person as 'literate' if
they have mastered a set of discrete skills, of which foremost is the ability to relate
spoken sounds (phonemes) with symbols (graphemes) or such as alphabetic characters.
All writing is a visual representation of language and all languages which have a writing

---

system (orthography) rely on a shared agreement that symbols and sounds stand in a systematic relationship to each other. Some languages, such as modern Turkish, have a stable, one-to-one correspondence between letters and sounds; others, such as English, have a more complex system with many exceptions and irregular forms. For example, consider the sound which is pronounced 'ay' (as in 'day') in the following words: *way, maid, save, great, rein, reign, eight, fete, straight, champagne, grey*. It has been found (Seymour *et al.*, 2005) that it takes children roughly two years longer to read English than to read Finnish which has a more regular system. This relationship of sounds to letters has been likened to a 'code'. Children are said to have 'cracked the code' when they can reliably encode and decode common patterns of sounds and symbols; however, as we have seen, there are many exceptions to the common patterns and there is much more work for children and their teachers to do before they can be described as fully literate. For example, the many words in the English language which have irregular, inconsistent and unique patterns (such as '*yacht*') need to be memorised during repeated exposure to print.

The autonomous model of literacy identifies learning to read as a technical and neutral skill, based on memorisation and application of phonic patterns, and the irregular exceptions, in order to crack the reading code. Literacy is essentially an individual cognitive process that takes place within the learner's own head.

Critics of the autonomous model of literacy raise a number of problems with it. Firstly, they suggest that the model makes it easy for failure to read and write to be blamed on the learner, through lack of ability, application or motivation; or on the teacher, through lack of 'correct' teaching and remediation. They suggest we need to look much more widely into the complex reasons for some children failing to learn to read. A further criticism is that reliance on over-simplified definitions of literacy can result in disadvantaging already marginalised groups in society, through a muddled process of cause and effect. If poor literacy levels are most often identified among deprived socio-economic groups, then is poverty a cause of illiteracy or a result of it? If illiteracy is deemed to be a cause of poverty then resources may be unevenly directed towards raising school literacy scores, at the expense of other policy initiatives to tackle deprivation.

Supporters of social models of literacy argue that literacy is much more than the ability to encode or decode text. Paolo Freire is a key figure in proposing socially and culturally inspired alternatives to autonomous models of literacy. Reading (and writing) must be accompanied by critical reflection developed through social interaction, before it can truly be defined as 'literacy'. Freire is particularly critical of the notion of *functional literacy*; the ability to read and write sufficiently well to play a part in the social environment and contribute to economic growth, but not well enough to critique, challenge or change the existing social order. Freire would regard a reading test that includes sounding out groups of letters, without regard for meaning and context, as an inadequate indicator of literacy. For him, encoding and decoding alphabetic print must be integrated into a far wider context; one that encourages learners to collaboratively make sense of their world.

During the 1990s an integrated model of literacy emerged, that took into account both autonomous and social perspectives. This approach was perhaps most clearly described by Freebody and Luke (1990) as *The Four Resources Model* of literacy, which defines literacy as a linked repertoire of capabilities (see Figure 1.1).

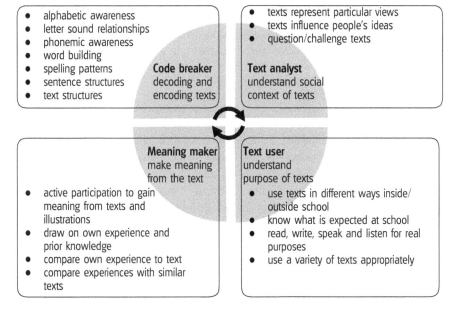

Figure 1.1 Model based on Freebody, P. (1992). A socio-cultural approach: Resourcing four roles as a literacy learner. In A. Watson and A. Badenhop (Eds.) Prevention of Reading Failure (pp. 48-60). Sydney: Ashton-Scholastic.

It is important to note that Freebody and Luke do not intend their model to be developmental; the roles of the learner described in the model are not learned in any particular order but develop alongside each other. All four resources are equally important and each should be systematically integrated into planned learning sequences at all levels of schooling.

> **Critical thinking exercise 2:** linking theory to practice
>
> **Consider** a recent literacy lesson that you have taught or observed. Reflecting on what you have read in this section about models of literacy, can you **identify** any features of the lesson that reflect autonomous, socio-cultural or integrated approaches to literacy development?

Comment

It may seem a long step from debates about which type of reading test should be taken by six-year-olds to discussions of power in society, but it is the political and ideological roots of many of the key features of literacy teaching that we now take for granted, that leads to such fierce debate about the literacy curriculum and teaching approaches. Understanding the theoretical background of these debates and examining our own assumptions about what literacy is and how it is developed supports us in making informed choices between different approaches to teaching. The next section introduces you to the field of New Literacy Studies and discusses how the ideas that lie behind it are already influencing the way that literacy is, and could be, taught in our schools.

Key idea: **Discourses**

The field of 'The New Literacies' is based on a socio-cultural perspective of what it means to be literate in our society and builds on the ideas of Freire (above) and also those of James Paul Gee (1996). Gee's work is based on the assumption that each individual first acquires a primary 'Discourse'[1] a particular way of talking, listening, valuing, behaving and interacting with others. Children absorb a primary Discourse long before they begin formal education. *Primary Discourses are those to which people are apprenticed early in life during their primary socialization as members of particular families within their sociocultural settings* (Gee, 1996, page 137).

Gee suggests that we adopt a number of secondary Discourses as we develop, through the influence of education, work and social groups. We each have only one primary Discourse but we can adopt many secondary Discourses. Gee defines literacy as the mastery (or fluent performance) of a secondary Discourse. The more dissimilar any secondary Discourse is from our primary Discourse, then the more effort and resources will be needed to learn it. Therefore a child who begins school with a primary Discourse that is very different to the school Discourse is, at least potentially, disadvantaged. 'Literacy', for these children, will be harder to achieve. Not all Discourses are equal, according to Gee, and some are associated with greater social power and status than others. These are known as dominant Discourses. Gee argues that dominant groups in society apply various tests and filters to identify individuals who have developed fluency in the dominant Discourse, and these tests are often focused on 'superficial' features of language such as spelling, grammar and accent.

---

1 Gee distinguishes between Discourse (with a capital D) and discourse (lower case d) to differentiate between different concepts in his work.

Critical thinking exercise 3: primary and secondary Discourses: Michael Rosen's critique of the 2011 English SATs test

Former children's laureate Michael Rosen recently critiqued the 2011 English SAT paper which included a comprehension exercise of an article from the Travel Section of the Sunday Times (16 February 2003) entitled: *'Caves and Caving in Davely Dale – Visitors' Guide'*. Rosen's full critique can be found online on the *Times Educational Supplement* forum at **http://community.tes.co.uk/forums/p/ 488574/6732581.aspx.6732581**

Here is a sample of text from the SATs paper, quoted by Rosen.

'And I was struck by the beauty you can only see underground. Etched on a wall, as big as my hand, are the delicate fronds of a soft coral. Further on, a long expanse of wall seems to have been covered in melted candle wax: in fact it's rock, and the surreal effect is produced by the same process that makes stalactites.'

Rosen analyses the SATs sample text and accompanying comprehension questions in detail; commenting as follows:

What kind of child is this booklet easy for? What kind of child is this booklet difficult for and why? I'll tell you what kind of child this booklet is easy for? The child I once was. And this is why:

1. *I was read to every night from the time I was one or two, till I was about seven or eight.*

2. *One or other of my parents still read to me regularly and on appropriate occasions until my father stopped writing at the age of about 85.*

3. *With a combination of library books, bought books, comics, annuals, magazines, sports programmes, catalogues, I and my brother were surrounded with print material – texts, if you like – for the whole of our lives in our parents' house.*

4. *Most of these texts were talked about and argued about, performed and played with almost every day.*

5. *Though we didn't go caving before I was 11, we were taken for most of the holidays on the kind of outdoor camping holidays which brought us into contact with people who talked about landscape in terms very similar to the ones used in this booklet.*

6. *We had a very same hinterland of art, history, zoology, architecture being talked about in our house or on trips that would have made most of the passage …fairly comprehensible.*

/continued

Critical thinking exercise 3 – continued

My parents were both teachers who would go on to become teacher trainers, (my father a professor) but who were also committed to the process of learning about human beings in the environment which this passage and the whole booklet exemplifies.

Rosen concludes:

> In other words, the eleven year old me (and of course there is a tiny minority of eleven year old 'me's' in the cohort who've just done this SAT paper), would have been at a fantastic advantage tackling this paper.

Consider your reactions to Rosen's critique. If you agree with his analysis, what do you think the likely reaction might be of a child taking this examination whose primary Discourse is very different to that of the writers of the article (or that of the young Rosen)?

Discuss what type of literacy text might be a more appropriate choice in this context than an extract from a broadsheet newspaper, in order to provide a fair assessment of reading and comprehension skills.

If you disagree with Rosen (and plenty of people do), **articulate** the arguments you would make in response to his critique.

Comment

You may agree with some of the criticisms offered by Rosen of the SATs test paper above, but still consider that it is an appropriate test of literacy for 11 year olds. You might argue that even if the style of the extract is not a close match to a child's primary Discourse it does nevertheless represent the dominant Discourse, and it is important that schools teach children how to interpret and use this Discourse to help them get on in life.

On the other hand, you might feel that this Discourse represents a narrow view of our society and that success in life can be achieved by many routes. You might believe that children with backgrounds that differ enormously from that of Michael Rosen will be so daunted by this Discourse that they become alienated and unable to access the benefits of education at all.

The position you take on this argument is less important than your ability to identify underlying assumptions and critically evaluate the different perspectives in order to arrive at your own point of view.

So far you have considered the socio-cultural ideology behind the concept of new literacies, and thought about the extent to which educational practice is influenced by events and ideas beyond the classroom. In the following section you will begin to identify just what else is *new* about *new literacies.*

Key idea: **Texts: range and meaning**

You have already come across a number of definitions of literacy drawn from a variety of sources, and here is one more: Lankshear and Knobel (2010) define literacies as *socially recognized ways of generating, communicating and negotiating meaningful content through the medium of encoded texts within contexts of participation in Discourses* (page 64).

By this definition, they explain, three concepts are implied. Firstly, individuals can be said to engage in literacy when they apply their knowledge and skills to accomplish tasks in purposeful and socially recognised ways. This includes through the use of technology, as well as via the printed word. Secondly, texts are defined as consisting of any idea which is encoded in a form which allows it to be retrieved even when the 'encoder' is not present in person. So, for example: *someone who 'freezes' language as a digitally encoded passage of speech and uploads it to the Internet as a podcast is engaging in literacy* (page 225).

Thirdly, they emphasise the discursive nature of literacy. Literacy is not a standalone skill but is dependent upon meaning, and meaning is always socially negotiated. You are probably familiar with 'textese', the abbreviated form of writing used on mobile phones and in instant messaging, designed originally to fit long messages into limited character sets. An example is 'CU l8tr 2nt m8' which can be decoded as 'see you later tonight, mate'. If you are a confident texter, you will not only know at once what the message means, but also will probably be able to tell straightaway that it has been written by someone who is not entirely at ease with *textese*. If you come across *textese* in a socially inappropriate context such as a job application or examination paper then you will draw conclusions about the writer, without even having met them. If a teacher uses *textese* in your assignment feedback or when marking a child's homework you will draw conclusions about them too.

> **Critical thinking exercise 4:** texts and meaning
>
> **Think** of an occasion when you have misinterpreted a message or been misinterpreted by someone else. This might be an occasion when the actual words used convey a message that is different to the literal meaning. For example, a parent asking 'What time will you be home tonight?' to a young teenager might really be saying 'Please take care while you are out because I am worried about you'. Think about what the meaning 'received' by the teenager might be.
>
> /continued

Critical thinking exercise 4 – continued
Discuss how many different meanings may be intended or received, depending on context, by the simple question 'Would you like a coffee?' You might also consider whether there is any cultural or contextual significance in being offered a coffee, rather than 'a nice cup of tea'.

Discuss examples, from your experience in schools, of 'socially constructed meaning'. In the classroom teachers often say things like 'I'm looking for someone who is being sensible'. What do they mean by that? What do you think children think they mean?

Comment

The point is that 'texts', in the sense of encoded messages, always carry meaning embedded in their style, presentation and context that goes beyond the literal (e.g. see you later tonight), and that meaning will be interpreted differently by different people. Differences between intended meaning and received meaning can cause problems for children not yet fully 'encultured' into the secondary Discourse of their school or classroom. Their misunderstandings may be attributed to a range of causes, such as lack of ability or lack of application.

Key idea: **New technologies, new thinking**

Lankshear and Knobel divide the concept of the 'new' in new literacies into two parts, which they call 'new technical stuff' and 'new ethos stuff'.

New technical stuff

Literacy is no longer solely about print, we are surrounded by information in many varied forms, and the term 'literacy' itself has become associated with skills that are far removed from encoding and decoding text. Visual literacy, information literacy, emotional literacy, digital literacy; no doubt you can find many more examples of the ways that the word 'literacy' has been invoked to describe competencies with which we are sometimes told we should equip ourselves in order to succeed. New literacies researchers are interested in exploring these new modes of literacy and especially in analysing the impact of digital technologies on literacy practices.

Digital technologies can support us to do existing tasks in new ways. For example, a few years ago you might have bought a train ticket by calling at the railway station or ringing the ticket office, now you can book online and pay by credit card. You might have met up with friends in person or sent letters and postcards to them, now you can use text (SMS) and social networking to catch up on news and gossip in your social circle. Equally, digital technologies can be integrated into social practices that in some significant sense represent *new things to do*. The podcasting example from earlier in the chapter is a good example of this. It is important to note, however, that *new*, when applied to technology, does not necessarily mean the most up-to-date technology, for example email is already considered to be an *'old'* new technology.

New ethos stuff

The ethos of a society has been described as its distinctive character and the set of fundamental values that is accepted by the majority of its members. New Literacy Studies theorists argue that the contemporary world is different in important ways than how it was even 30 years ago, and that the difference in part is related to developments in technology. They identify two distinct opinions about the impact of technology.

One view is that essentially things are the same and that technology is merely an 'add on' that helps us to do the same types of tasks more quickly and efficiently, such as buying a train ticket. The opposing view is that technology has fundamentally changed the way we think about things, as well as the way we behave. This view holds that, because of technology, society itself is now more participatory, collaborative and less hierarchical in nature. For example, making your views heard in public was, 30 years ago, a very difficult thing to do. The 'gateway' to public media: books, newspapers, television and radio, was in the hands of a very few people. Now anyone can reach a wide audience through self-publishing their blog on the internet, starting a Facebook group or having their video 'go viral' on YouTube.

To summarise, the new in new literacies takes into account the new skills, strategies and practices prompted by the introduction of new technologies, and acknowledges that as technology changes other new practices are invented and old ones are modified. The *literacy* in new literacies implies that being able to deal with and adapt to technology is central to full participation in our global community, just as reading and writing print has been central for previous generations. In other words, the emphasis of 'new literacy studies' does not reject the 'print-centric' skills of reading and writing but seeks to *provoke new skills as well* (Baker et al., 2010). New literacies are multifaceted: they take into account multiple Discourses, multiple methods of communication and multiple points of view.

Critical thinking exercise 5: considering your own use of Web 2.0 technologies

Whether or not you have come across the term *'Web 2.0' technology*, you almost certainly use it in your everyday life. Web 2.0 technologies combine the *new technology* stuff and the *new ethos stuff* discussed by Lankshear and Knobel. Web 1.0 technology has been used to describe (in retrospect) internet-based services that support distribution of information, for example, web-pages published

/continued

Critical thinking exercise 5 – continued

by individuals and organisations that allow only 'one-way' interaction with the content. What one 'gets' from the website is what the publisher(s) put there. In contrast, Web 2.0 applications enable interactive and collaborative engagement; content is contributed and controlled as well as merely consumed by its users.

Compare the Web 1.0 and Web 2.0 activities and resources in the following table. (Locate on the internet and explore any terms or resources which are unfamiliar to you.)

Articulate the extent to which Web 2.0 services provoke new skills by offering us new things to do, as well as new ways of doing existing things.

Web 1.0	Web 2.0
Image gallery	Image sharing (e.g. *Flickr*)
Reference encyclopaedia	Collaborative encyclopaedia (e.g. *Wikipedia*)
Personal website	Blog
Downloading music	Social music sharing (e.g. *Spotify*)
Personal website	Social networking (e.g. *Facebook*)
Word-processing	Collaborative real-time text editing (e.g. *Google docs/PrimaryPad*)
Video archive	Video sharing (e.g. *YouTube*)

Key idea: **Pedagogy and the new literacies**

In the Independent Review of the Primary Curriculum (Rose, 2009) literacy was explicitly defined as four strands of language – reading, writing, speaking and listening. According to the National Literacy Trust (**literacytrust.org.uk**) while this may not seem a radical idea it is incredibly important: *Literacy has tended to be defined by reading and writing skills, while assuming speaking and listening will develop organically.* Children's reading skills cannot be developed in isolation but are underpinned with their understanding about language, which is *developed through conversation and interaction with others.* This is a *socio-cultural* approach to literacy.

For an example of where an *autonomous* theory of literacy has an impact on day-to-day practice in the classroom, we can turn to the current emphasis of the Department for Education on *synthetic phonics* as the favoured approach to teaching reading. This system breaks down the sounds of words into discrete units (phonemes) and links them with their written symbols (graphemes). These phonic units are then 'synthesised' or linked together to make words. The context of the words themselves is not emphasised, indeed some synthetic phonics schemes discourage children from interacting with actual books for the first few weeks of tuition. Most teachers and schools will not apply one approach or another rigidly, no matter how much they are encouraged to do so. They will make decisions and choose approaches that take account of the needs of their individual pupils.

As literacy commentator Henrietta Dombey (2006, page 6) observes,

> *The most successful schools and teachers focus both on phonics and on the process of making sense of text. Best practice brings these two key components together, in teaching that gives children a sense of the pleasures reading can bring, supports them in making personal sense of the texts they encounter and also shows them how to lift the words off the page.*

To summarise, the examples above are not intended to demonstrate that one literacy approach is always right and one is always wrong. The key idea is for you to be able to **identify** when one method is chosen over another, to **interpret** why this may be so, and to **evaluate** the assumptions behind these choices. To engage in this process is to engage with pedagogy and to exercise your responsibility as a teacher to make informed decisions on behalf of the children you teach.

Reading this book

Tony Eaude (2011) points out that many parents and politicians believe that teaching is just a matter of common sense, and are suspicious of educational theory. However, what seems to be 'common sense' may not be supported by experience or research evidence. Eaude describes pedagogy as far more complicated than rocket science (page 13). The pedagogical ideas underpinning this book are set out below. We encourage you to identify our assumptions, and to question and challenge them as you go along.

We consider that teachers should recognise and value the Discourses that children bring to school, even where these are very different to their own. This includes children's literacy development in areas that are important to the children but that are not traditionally encountered in school, for example texts mediated through the use of technology.

Children from a young age are already engaging with technology for education, entertainment, and social activities, yet relatively little if any time in school is spent exploring these literacies. If it is, then it tends to be negative attention, as part of a 'cyber-safety' or 'e-safety' programme. While we wholeheartedly agree that it essential to teach children how to keep safe when encountering the challenges and complexities of the online world, we do not believe that this should be the dominant discussion. Raising children's and teachers' awareness of e-safety is a theme addressed continuously throughout this book, but it is approached in the context of encouraging 'critical literacy'. Online texts are real-world texts, not reading primers. They are subject to hidden (and open) agendas, some of which may be damaging to children whether they are deliberately ill-intentioned or not, through bias, inaccuracy, advertising, and provenance and mutability of content, and so on. We do not believe, however, that a critically literate approach to online content can be achieved without engaging with it, and where better for children to do this than within the secure environment of the classroom?

There is a further reason why we believe that widening the curriculum in schools to include the 'new literacy' approach is a good idea. As Gee notes, children need to learn to interpret 'multimodal' texts critically in order to operate successfully in society. This can have a number of benefits. Jennifer Stone (2007) analysed the 'literacy level' of popular children's websites, and found that in terms of complexity of ideas, vocabulary, sentence length and grammar many are at least equivalent to school texts. She suggests that children are motivated to read online texts related to their interests and will persevere when they would have given up on school texts. The Literacy Association considers that if teachers include in their lessons the types of web based material that children engage with outside school, they can increase children's engagement and improve their comprehension of more conventional texts.

 Where reading is in daily competition with the allure of digital gaming, on hand-held consoles and mobile telephones as well as computer screens, we have to work doubly hard to demonstrate its rewards. We cannot expect children to defer gratification until they have mastered the techniques.
Children certainly need instruction in the techniques, but they only become effective and committed readers through reading texts that interest them.

UK Literacy Association (UKLA): *Teaching Reading*

Conclusion

To return to the case study at the beginning of this chapter, you will now be able identify in it some of the key ideas discussed in this chapter. The teachers involved in Kidsmeet are taking a child-centred approach that is inspired by some of the technologies and practices that children are engaging with outside school, for example, the use of handheld 3G mobile phones, tablet computers and online gaming. They are making use of the collaborative and interactive nature of Web 2.0 technologies to promote social approaches to literacy. These technologies and practices are skilfully drawn into the classroom and integrated into what might be regarded as more traditional literacy skills, such as sequencing sets of instructions, or publishing writing to a real audience. Children are challenged in ways that seem relevant to them, for example where a group of Year 4 boys create instructional videos to demonstrate to other children how to make their sentences more exciting. There is also recognition of children's primary Discourses through celebrating their naturalistic presentation style, compared by the children to 'a bit like hanging out on the playground'.

The chapters that follow this will provide further case studies of how new literacies, together with new technologies, are broadening the horizons of both teachers and children, and will, we hope, prompt you to think further about the pedagogies involved and inspire you to try out some of the ideas in your own practice.

Further Reading

Classroom pedagogy is discussed in detail in Eaude, T. (2011) *Thinking Through Pedagogy for Primary and Early Years*. Exeter: Learning Matters.

Writing systems and the development of reading are explained clearly in Flynn, N. and Stainthorp, R. (2006) *The Learning and Teaching of Reading and Writing*. Chichester: John Wiley & Sons, from which some examples in this chapter are taken.

Paolo Freire's best-known work about socio-cultural approaches to literacy is Freire, P. and Macedo, D. (1987) *Literacy: Reading the word and the world*. South Hadley, MA: Bergin & Garvey.

For an overview of new literacies, together with examples drawn from classroom practice, see Lankshear, C. and Knobel, M. (2006) *New Literacies: Everyday practices and classroom learning*. Maidenhead: Open University Press.

For further details about models of literacy, particularly socio-cultural approaches, see Street, B.V. (1995) *Social Literacies: Critical approaches to literacy in development, ethnography, and education*. London: Longman.

For a fuller discussion of systematic synthetic phonics as an approach to teaching reading see Joliffe, W., Waugh, D. and Carss, A., *Teaching Systematic Synthetic Phonics in Primary Schools*. Learning Matters/SAGE: London.

2

Technological interventions in early literacy

Jayne Metcalfe

Chapter Focus

This chapter investigates some current and prospective technological interventions to support early reading and writing (everyday technologies, moving image media, framework programs such as Clicker and online tools) from a sociocultural perspective. Classroom practice and the interaction of both the emergent reader and writer and their teacher with technology are examined critically.

The critical thinking exercises in this chapter focus on:

⊙ **considering** the role that popular culture, new technologies and media play in the lives of young children today;

⊙ **identifying** how children's early experiences and new ways of learning with popular culture and new technologies can be built upon in the classroom;

⊙ **exploring** ways in which moving image media texts can support children's communication, language and literacy development;

⊙ **comparing** writing on paper with writing on screen and reflecting on the implications for early years educators.

The key ideas discussed are: **young children, popular culture, media and new technologies, moving image media texts** and **on-screen writing.**

This chapter is particularly relevant to the following Teachers' Standards (2012):

Part 1: Teaching

A teacher must:

1 **Set high expectations which inspire, motivate and challenge pupils**
   ⊙ establish a safe and stimulating environment for pupils, rooted in mutual respect
2 **Promote good progress and outcomes by pupils**
   ⊙ be aware of pupils' capabilities and their prior knowledge, and plan teaching to build on these
   ⊙ demonstrate knowledge and understanding of how pupils learn and how this impacts on teaching

/continued

Chapter Focus – continued

- ⊙ have a secure knowledge of the relevant subject(s) and curriculum areas, foster and maintain pupils' interest in the subject, and address misunderstandings

3 Demonstrate good subject and curriculum knowledge
- ⊙ demonstrate a critical understanding of developments in the subject and curriculum areas, and promote the value of scholarship
- ⊙ demonstrate an understanding of and take responsibility for promoting high standards of literacy, articulacy and the correct use of standard English, whatever the teacher's specialist subject

4 Plan and teach well-structured lessons
- ⊙ impart knowledge and develop understanding through effective use of lesson time
- ⊙ promote a love of learning and children's intellectual curiosity
- ⊙ contribute to the design and provision of an engaging curriculum within the relevant subject area(s)

5 Adapt teaching to respond to the strengths and needs of all pupils
- ⊙ have a clear understanding of the needs of all pupils, including those with special educational needs; those of high ability; those with English as an additional language; those with disabilities; and be able to use and evaluate distinctive teaching approaches to engage and support them.

Key idea: **Technology in the home**

Research shows that most young children are growing up in media-rich homes where they actively engage in a wide range of digital practices and develop an array of digital skills, knowledge, and understanding from birth (Marsh *et al.*, 2005; O'Hara, 2011).

Critical thinking exercise 1

A Consider the role that new technologies and media play in the lives of pre-school children today. **Discuss** your ideas with someone from the 'older generation' and then **compare** these with your own experiences as a child.

/continued

Critical thinking exercise 1 – continued

Examine your own attitudes to children's use of media and new technologies; **consider** the influence of your own upbringing on your views of the role of technology in young children's lives.

B Identify the educational opportunities afforded by children's engagement with media and new technologies in the home, and in particular how it contributes to the development of children's emergent literacy skills.

C Recall ways in which you have seen media and new technologies used in early years settings to promote children's learning in literacy.

CASE STUDY

Paige and Aidan are twins, they are four years old. They spend a great deal of their time playing with their toys, sharing books and they both love to go to the park to play on the swings. They both also really enjoy watching television and DVDs on the large TV set in the living room, they have a vast collection of DVDs. Family visits to the cinema, to see the latest film, are always well received too.

Paige's favourite TV programmes are *Dora the Explorer* and *Peppa Pig* and she has watched her *Beauty and the Beast* DVD many times. Sometimes she watches the TV alone, at other times Mum watches with her. There are many shows on CBeebies and Nickelodeon that she enjoys too and she can often be found flicking through the channels using the remote control to select her preferred programme.

Aidan's TV show of choice is *Ben 10*, a cartoon all about a 10-year-old kid who has a watch-like device that allows him to turn into different alien species and adventures abound as a result. Aidan is also a big fan of the more adult show *Dr Who*. He likes to watch this with his older brother Frankie who is 9 years old. Mum and Dad enjoy the programme too and so they often all watch as a family, *X Factor* is another family favourite.

Both children happily sit quietly and watch the TV, but most of the time they take a more active role. Paige loves to sing and dance around to the music and songs from the shows; she also has a number of toys that relate to the TV programme, such as her miniature pig family or her princess wands and tiaras. She likes to play with these on the carpet while the TV is on, or later when the show has finished. Aidan on the other hand really identifies with the characters

/continued

CASE STUDY – continued

and is keen to dress up and re-enacts part of the narrative while the programme or film is playing, or after viewing. He is keen to make props and create costumes to wear as well as use some shop-bought items. Mum often becomes involved in this creative process and in the ensuing role play sometimes, often under the direction of Aidan.

The family is regularly reminded of the children's TV and film preferences. Paige has Peppa Pig pyjamas and a Peppa Pig quilt and Aidan has a toy watch, just like Ben 10, which he loves to wear and incorporate into his role play, he also has a Ben 10 lunch box for Nursery. Paige and Aidan both like to listen to music and story CDs and have a number of books and comics relating to their favourite TV and film programmes or characters.

Both the children also enjoy playing games on the CBeebies website, Mum helps navigate to the site and the children move between games and use the mouse with growing confidence. Mum prefers the games designed to help with early literacy and numeracy skills, but recognises the value of the games in developing their knowledge and understanding in a number of areas. Aidan also watches intently when Frankie plays games on his Play Station with his Dad or friends. He has had a few turns, but Mum says he is too young; she would rather they play games designed for their age group and so happily lets them interact with the Peppa Pig and Ben 10 apps that Dad has downloaded for them on his iPad.

Comment

It is evident that popular culture, media and new technologies play important roles in the lives of Paige and Aidan and are a clear source of enjoyment for the children and their wider family. Both children have clear preferences in terms of what they like to watch on screen, in addition their favourite popular culture characters are linked to these TV shows and films, as are many of their toys and other artefacts such as clothing, bedding and books. They spend most time watching TV compared to other activities; however, it can be seen that their engagement with this media tends to be active rather than passive as they act out and imitate the characters on screen, either by themselves, with toys or props, or with other family members who are frequently involved in the role play. Through their play and roles as both audience and performers Paige and Aidan can be seen to be making sense of these on-screen narratives as they relate them to and draw upon their own experiences. Although the children sometimes watch TV and play games alone their engagement with media tends to take place in family spaces, such as the living room and tends to be social, rather than solitary.

On the whole the parents are supportive of their children's interest in popular culture, media and new technologies and feel they have a positive impact on their lives. This is evident when they purchase toys and other popular culture merchandise or become involved in their children's play linked to, for example, their favourite films and TV shows. They clearly recognise the role new technologies play in supporting the social aspects of family life, in developing their children's skills, for example social and linguistic, as well as the pleasure they clearly bring.

Research (O'Hara, 2011; Marsh, 2005) confirms that high incidences of technologies such as TV, DVDs, mobile phones, PCs, games consoles and digital cameras are to be found in young children's homes and parents are generally positive about the role of ICT in their children's lives. Parents are keen for their children to develop their technological literacy as they recognise the importance of these skills in the future, both for their children's education and the world of work. In a recent study (O'Hara, 2011) parents were proud of their children's developing skills and consistently reported that children from 18 months to two years of age were able to operate the TV independently, and that by the time they started nursery at four they were capable of using a range of ICT applications in the home, such as DVD players, computer websites and games, with confidence. This included switching on PCs and monitors, using the correct shut down procedures and locating games on the desk top; using facilities such as zoom, widescreen and fast-forward on DVD players; navigating children's websites and games by using familiar icons and symbols, scrolling down menus and selecting options from lists despite their underdeveloped reading skills (Marsh, 2004).

It is well recognised that children can also learn through ICT as well as about ICT and that this has an impact on children's achievements. A review of studies (Lieberman et al., 2009), that researched the effectiveness of various digital technologies on young children's (three to six years) learning, found that the use of, for example, software, programmable toys, interactive TV and games resulted in improvements in transferable skills such as planning, observation, problem solving, collaboration, thinking and reasoning. In addition, they found that well-designed products which aim to promote language learning in a fun and interactive way can develop children's knowledge and understanding of language. This included boosting children's vocabulary as well as their early reading and writing skills, through for example enhanced knowledge of the alphabet, phonics and word recognition and building. Parents also report increased motivation and concentration (Marsh et al., 2005; Marsh, 2004).

The role of parents is also seen as key to children's use and the affordances of different media and technologies in the home. While parents recognise the benefits of ICT, they are anxious about health and safety risks posed by ICT to their children. Fears mainly centre on children's potential access to inappropriate content or behaviour by third parties on the internet. Consequently, parents act as gatekeepers to their children's use of technology. This includes imposing restrictions such as time limits and on occasions blocking their children's access to technology altogether (O'Hara, 2011). Nevertheless, parents and other family members are also seen, either implicitly or explicitly, to scaffold children's learning, through for example, the purchase of technological toys and resources, encouraging and modelling their use, as well as interacting with their children when they engage with such devices.

A range of studies have shown that children's interest in and engagement with media and technology in the home is embedded in social practice and plays a key role in their early literacy development. Marsh (2004) uses the term 'techno-literacy' to refer to these practices and believes the early years curriculum needs to recognise and build upon children's existing funds of knowledge and experiences with ICT in the home: *It is no longer appropriate to focus on literacy as a paper-based activity when children access text in a range of modes, e.g. on computers, television and mobile phones* (page 52). Despite this, literacy practices in school primarily remain print based, and where new technologies are being incorporated into early years practice, there is a tendency, for them to be used to teach decontextualised skills such as phonics, rather than to generate multimodal texts and to transform practice through new ways of doing things (Lankshear and Knobel, 2007).

Reasons suggested are that educators only have a limited understanding of children's engagement with technology in the home and its contribution to early literacy development. Consequently, the digital knowledge understanding and skills that children bring with them is undervalued. In addition, the use of new technology is not always viewed by early years educators as aligned to play-based philosophies, and government policy and curriculum demands as well as resistance to change are also seen as key barriers (Davidson, 2009). Next we examine further some of the barriers to children's use of ICT in the early years to support language and literacy development. Finally, approaches to improving practice are explored.

Key idea: **The power of Postman Pat**

The Digital Beginnings report (Marsh et al., 2005) found that both parents and practitioners were generally positive about the use of popular culture, media and new technologies in early years settings. They acknowledged their contribution to children's learning in literacy and reported increased levels of motivation and engagement in children. Findings also showed that the majority of early years practitioners did make some use of children's popular culture to support children's learning generally, and more specifically their literacy development. This often involved the use of resources featuring popular TV or popular culture characters in role play areas and small-world play; however, their use of technology was more limited. Poorly equipped settings, practitioners' weak subject and pedagogical knowledge of media and new technologies often resulted in low level use of ICT. The need for adequate resourcing of settings with a range of technologies, which are relevant to the lives of today's young children, was thus highlighted, as was the importance of professional development for practitioners.

> **Critical thinking exercise 2**
>
> **A Reflect** on your own knowledge, skills and understanding of popular culture, media and new technologies and their use in the EYFS. Identify any personal professional development that is required and how this can be addressed.
>
> **B Consider** how you might link children's popular culture with different media and new technologies to support language and literacy in the EYFS curriculum.
>
> **C Discuss** additional ways in which children's early experiences and new ways of learning with popular culture and new technologies can be built upon in the classroom.

Comment

The previous case study and research cited serve to highlight the close relationship between popular culture and children's use of technology. Favourite characters, TV programmes and films play key roles in the lives of today's young children. Despite often being labelled as the latest 'fad', children's interest in media icons and the associated merchandise provides a commonality between children and as such a way of building relationships with other children. In addition, these media texts and artefacts can play an important part in children's identity construction as they take on different identities and explore their associated roles (Marsh, 2005). While there can be accompanying commercial and peer pressures, parents and practitioners should not underestimate the power of popular culture and media that now permeates children's lives.

The table on pages 29 and 30 illustrates how a popular culture character such as Postman Pat can be introduced to not only support children's literacy learning, but to include 'media literacy' approaches such as work involving moving images and the production of digital texts. Some of the latter are explored in more detail in the remaining parts of this chapter. As can be seen, many of the ideas are generic and could be applied to different characters. Identify other popular culture characters and consider how you might use them as a stimulus for similar work. Using the table as a model, try planning a half term theme based around your chosen popular culture character that incorporates the use of a range of digital technologies.

Building on children's funds of knowledge

Where children are engaged in rich media experiences it is important that these experiences are built upon and children's new ways of learning recognised. The packing of a **digital suitcase** and the importance of **building collaborative professional relationships** were two key strategies recommended by Harrison *et al.* (2009) to promote continuity between educational settings, i.e. preschool and more formal schooling.

Postman Pat theme	
Technology in the environment	Create Post Office role play area
	Suggested technological/ICT resources, these can be real, toy, or made
	<ul><li>Electric till</li><li>Cash machine</li><li>Computer/keyboard and printer</li><li>Telephone/fax machine/mobile phone</li><li>Scanning equipment</li><li>Franking machine</li><li>Digital weighing scales</li><li>Digital currency display</li><li>Photocopier</li><li>CCTV</li><li>Digital cameras for Passport photographs/driving licences</li><li>Microphone for tannoy</li><li>At the Post office software – designed to support children's role play. Available at http://shop.sherston.com/sherston/subject/ict/poff-mlt-cdrm-1.html</li></ul>
	Post office role play resources available at:
	www.earlylearninghq.org.uk/role-play-resources/post-office/
	www.sparklebox.co.uk/topic/roleplay/shops/post.html
	www.teacherspost.co.uk/free-resources-to-download.html also includes videos of the journeys of Lenny the letter
	www.tes.co.uk/teaching-resource/POST-OFFICE-ROLE-PLAY-RESOURCES-3011649/
	Outdoor area linked to theme of Postman Pat <ul><li>Post Office van with Satellite Navigation system</li><li>Road layout with traffic lights, pedestrian crossing, digital speed signs, speed camera, remote controlled cars...</li></ul>
	Visit to a post office/sorting office. Focus on technology and media
Digital cassette/CD players and recorders	Listen to stories on tape/CD
	Listen and sing along to the *Postman Pat* theme tune
	Tell and record stories
	Interview the postman or other post office worker, customers

Digital still cameras	Make own video to accompany the theme tune. See example at www.youtube.com/watch?v=WAYVfmSig0I. Take photos using digital still cameras and combine with audio file of song to make video using e.g. Windows movie maker or Photo story
	Create simple stop motion animation using digital cameras, toy figures and models and scenery made by the children
	Suggested software: Zu3D www.zu3d.com/
	I Can Animate from Kudlian software www.kudlian.net/products/icananimate/
TV, DVD and film	Episodes of *Postman Pat* on TV, DVD or on BBC iPlayer www.bbc.co.uk/iplayer/cbeebies/episode/b0078s0g/Postman_Pat_Series_3_Postman_Pat_and_the_Great_Greendale_Race/
	Postman Pat the Movie www.postmanpat-themovie.com
	Watch and discuss excerpts of films
	Use British Film Institution (BFI) material 'Starting Stories' to analyse films http://filmstore.bfi.org.uk/acatalog/info_3946.html
Multimedia software/web tools	Use software/web tools to create multimedia stories/texts
	Little bird tales www.littlebirdtales.com/
	2 Create a story http://www.2simple.com/
	Clicker 6 www.cricksoft.com/uk/products/tools/clicker/home.aspx
Digital messaging area	Provide computer and writing frames for children to:
	• write letters, cards, postcards, complete forms • receive and send messages e.g. by email
	Talk time postcards – recordable postcards
	http://www.tts-group.co.uk/shops/tts/Products/PD1727028/Talk-Time-Postcards-A6-30-Second/
Programmable floor robots	Programmable floor robots e.g. Bee Bot, Pixie, Roamer
	'Dress up' the robot as Postman Pat's van. Programme the robot to deliver letters and parcels to different locations
	Bee Bot App available from iTunes via www.tts-group.co.uk/shops/tts/content/view.aspx?cref=PSGEN2293277
Google Maps	Plan journeys for Postman Pat. Children identify where they live on the digital map and plan journeys to different locations in their locality
Online games	CBeebies Postman Pat www.bbc.co.uk/cbeebies/postman-pat
	Postman Pat website www.postmanpat.com/
	Postman Pat App availble from iTunes http://itunes.apple.com/gb/app/postman-pat-sds/id458116091?mt=8

The suggestion is that each child has an individual digital suitcase which provides a record of their ICT knowledge, skills and experiences. This may be in the form of learning stories from parents and preschool teachers, digital photographs or examples of their work. The digital portfolio is compiled by the child's current teacher and then travels with the child when they move settings to aid the transition process. The evidence can be used as a focus for discussion between teacher and child, but perhaps more importantly it enables teachers to plan a curriculum and implement pedagogical approaches which compliment those of the previous setting. This in turn should mean that teachers are more able to build upon a child's existing funds of knowledge and their preferred modes of communication to support their learning in literacy, and other areas of the curriculum.

Developing collaborative relationships with colleagues can also provide complimentary information to support this process. This could involve children's new and existing teachers visiting and observing children in their setting as well as using children's digital suitcases as a focus for professional dialogue. Both these strategies can help build shared understandings of teaching and learning approaches and expectations, especially with regard the use of new technologies to support literacy in the classroom.

It is important that teachers do find time to reflect on the changing nature of literacy and the implications for the classroom. Literacy is about language and communication, but the influence of new technologies means that new social practices are emerging and with that new ways of exchanging and sharing information (Merchant, 2005a). Today's children increasingly make meaning and communicate their ideas through visual, audio or multimodal 'texts' which are often shared via digital means such as the internet. Consequently, children have new purposes for communication and audiences that extend beyond the classroom. The remainder of this chapter explores in more detail some of the ways in which early years practitioners can provide meaningful and relevant literacy experiences for young children in educational settings.

Key idea: **Lights, camera, action! Film as texts**

The key roles TV and film play in children's lives and their skills and confidence operating the technology associated with this media has already been highlighted. The development and marketing of relatively inexpensive cameras, which enable young children to take photos and shoot movies with ease, combined with the relative simplicity of camera features on mobile phones has resulted in increased access and use of these technologies by children. Consequently, children are increasingly becoming creators of moving image media as well as consumers. Email and internet sites such as YouTube also means that with adult support their films can be made and shared with wider audiences.

Despite children's engagement with contemporary communicative practices out of school, research (Burn and Leach, 2004, cited by Marsh, 2008) shows provision and opportunities to work with moving image media in early years classrooms is limited.

A number of reasons have been put forward:

- Government policy and long-established approaches which result in a skills-based approach to language, and an emphasis on traditional print-based literature (Nixon and Comber, 2005).
- Moving image media is often excluded from the classroom and simply viewed as popular culture despite other 'new technologies' being recognised and brought into schools as learning tools (Nixon and Comber, 2005).
- A lack of work which explores the affordances of film and TV plus a lack of professional development opportunities to develop teachers' competence in using film in the classroom to support learning (Marsh, 2008).
- Developmental discourses which view such literate practices as too complex for young children, and as such are only suitable at later stages of schooling when children are competent with alphabetic print (Marsh, 2008; Grant and Lord, 2003 in Nixon and Comber, 2005).
- In more recent years, the need to build on young children's rich experiences of film and TV in the home and its potential value in the literacy curriculum, including the EYFS, is beginning to be recognised.

Critical thinking exercise 3

Consider the value of moving image media in supporting children's communication language and literacy development.

Comment

Work on film, television and video has potential to enhance teaching and learning across the Early Years Foundation Stage (EYFS) curriculum, but in particular, the use of moving image media can help develop children's knowledge, skills and understanding in communication, language and literacy. The British Film Institute (BFI) (2003) suggest that providing opportunities for children to watch and then talk about, discuss and debate TV, films and video they have already seen, as well as create simple videos and stop motion animations (SMAs), can help promote a range of skills which include:

Acquisition and development of language and vocabulary

This is especially true for children for whom English is an additional language and particularly for boys who may need encouragement in this area. While work on moving image media generates interest for both boys and girls it has been shown to motivate boys who are seen to more readily draw on their out of school experiences of film and TV in school and shows they enjoy sharing this expertise with others. Teachers can usefully draw on this enthusiasm and knowledge to extend aspects of their language and literacy, particularly their emergent writing practices. Music and songs which are so often an important feature of TV and film are also key tools for the development of children's language. Speaking and listening skills are also developed as children learn to work collaboratively.

Appreciation of the wide variety of audiences
Children could watch a collection of short clips from different genres and identify the intended audience and justify their reasons, i.e. films /TV for grown-ups and children, stories and information.

Understanding of narrative structure, characterisation, plot and so on
Discussing similarities and differences between the same story presented in paper-based form and as a film, for example, can serve to highlight the many links between reading printed and moving image texts. Children could talk about how soundtracks, sound effects, lighting and the position of the camera are used to create atmosphere and to present characters in different ways.

Identification of different genres and their associated features
Children's understanding could be developed by setting up the role play area as a film, news or weather studio where children have opportunities to become familiar with a particular genre and then to explore production and filming. The superhero theme is a good one to explore. This use of socio-dramatic play can also provide opportunities for reading a range of texts in different media (page 24) as well as emergent writing as children create and film their own stories.

Working with moving image media also provides opportunities for developing children's ICT knowledge, skills and understanding in this area. This can include:

- naming favourite TV programmes and films;
- identifying different genres, e.g. news, weather reports and intended audiences;
- appreciating the differences between still and moving images;
- recognition of various production roles, e.g. scriptwriter, director, camera operator;
- understanding and using elements of film language, e.g. cartoon animation, soundtrack, special effects, camera shot (close-up, long shot);
- knowing how to operate simple equipment and use it safely;
- planning and shooting short sequences of digital video and recognising they can be edited;
- recognising the role of soundtracks and exploring how sounds can be changed;
- understanding of how films have changed over time, e.g. use of colour, special effects.

> **Critical thinking exercise 4**
>
> Watch the Elmer SMA available at www.zu3d.com/gallery/elmer.
>
> **A Consider** the processes involved in the production of this short animation by young children and whether it is something you feel confident to carry out with children. **Identify** technological skills, resources and classroom organisation and management strategies that would be required.
>
> **B Identify** the literacy and wider learning taking place.

Comment

The animation is a retelling of the much loved story of *Elmer* by David McKee. It is evident that the children have been involved in the creation of the scenery and making the elephant models, did you spot they were old milk containers cut up and painted? The animated sequence has been created by moving the models slightly, taking a photograph and then repeating this process until the required action and sequence of events has been captured. The use of percussion instruments to create sound effects and carefully selected music to add mood (some of which, according to the credits, has been composed by the children) are both used successfully to accompany particular parts of the story.

Individual children have also taken turns to narrate the story and there is some coordinated speaking from a small group of children. It is clear from the credits that the whole class has been involved in this production and yet it is often assumed that this process is too complicated for young children. In addition, some early years practitioners feel that they do not possess the technological skills to support children in making a short film, you may even be feeling this yourself. So what are the steps involved in creating a SMA sequence?

Step 1: The idea

First, an idea is needed. This may be generated by the children or you as the teacher and could be linked to current thematic work in the classroom or be inspired by something an individual child or groups of children have experienced or seen, for example on the TV. Simply adapting a story that the children are familiar with is also a good starting point.

Step 2: Brainstorm ideas and develop a plan

Second, clear consideration needs to be given to the availability of time, materials and equipment. SMA can be time consuming, teachers and children often don't realise that working at 12 frames per second it takes 60 photographs to create a short sequence of around 5 seconds. Although the number of frames per second can be easily reduced for younger children it is important to consider what is realistically achievable.

Decisions also need to be made as to whether the children will be involved in designing their own scenery and models, or whether existing materials and resources such as Lego, PlayMobil or Plasticine, or a combination of both will be used. Making models and sets can be a highly rewarding process and contribute to children's learning across the curriculum.

Step 3: Storyboarding

The storyboarding process ensures that ideas are represented and the sequence of events planned; this only needs to be done with simple drawings and notes. With young children, this is best modelled by the teacher, incorporating children's suggestions on a simple template. It is best to keep the story simple and the number of characters relatively small.

Step 4: Models and sets

A wide range of materials can be used as already mentioned for sets and models. These can include:

- natural materials such as rocks, sticks, shells and leaves;
- small-world characters, which are readily available in EY classrooms, such as plastic animals, toy cars, dinosaurs and dolls;
- construction toys such as Lego and Stickle Bricks;
- clay or Plasticine (although beware in warm weather!);
- coloured card, fabric, paint, junk materials such as bottles and cardboard tubes can all be used to create characters or simple dioramas and backgrounds.

Step 5: Taking the photographs

You will need:

- a webcam, or digital camera with fully charged batteries and sufficient memory to take a large number of images – the flash is best turned off so as to avoid light variations;
- a tripod to help keep the camera in one place, alternatively use sticky tac or tape.

The process now involves children setting up the frame, taking a photograph, moving the models slightly, taking a photograph and so on until the required action and sequence of events has been captured. The frame should remain unchanged for each scene so it is important that the camera is not moved during this process. A good tip is to start and end each scene with 12 shots of the scenery with no action and then work on one shot per movement, and 6 shots to pause the action. The more shots and the smaller the movements the smoother the action will look. It is important, however, to note the skills of the children involved and work accordingly.

Film making is a team activity and it can be a good idea when children are working collaboratively for them to take on different roles such as the director, the model mover and the photographer so that each person is clear as to what they are going to be doing, this also avoids too many unwanted hands and shadows in the action!

Step 6: Stitching the animation sequence together

Once all the photos have been taken they need to be stitched together to create the animation sequence; titles and credits can also be added, as well as narration, sound effects and music.

The Elmer animation was created using Zu3D software www.zu3d.com/ which is very simple to use even for the youngest children. The interface is very intuitive and there are no complicated instructions to read or understand so that children can concentrate on the creative process rather than technical aspects hindering the realisation of their ideas. Other software that can be used includes Windows Movie Maker which is free with Windows http://windows.microsoft.com/enID/windows7/products/features/movie-maker, and iMovie for use on Macs www.apple.com/uk/apps/imovie/?cid=wwa-uk-kwg-features-00532.

Tutorials for creating SMAs in these software packages can be found at:

www.cleo.net.uk/resources/displayframe.php?src=321/consultants_resources/teknical/flashideas/ButtonTemplate2.html,

www.iherr.com/?page_id=6 and http://www.zu3d.com/tutorial-video respectively.

Other software available includes, I can Animate www.kudlian.net/products/icananimate/, MonkeyJam http://monkeyjam.org/ and JellyCam.

Step 7: Sharing your work

Once the file has been successfully saved as a movie it can be shared. There is potential for the animation to have a global audience, for example by uploading it to the school website, or even YouTube. Some software sites such as Zu3D also provide this facility.

Key idea: **Writing on screen**

It is well recognised that early literacy learning involves children developing awareness that print is used to carry meaning. Children's early mark making demonstrates an understanding that symbols carry meaning and as such this emergent writing is valued by early years educators. Unstructured opportunities to experiment with writing are normally provided through the provision of writing tables or in the context of children's role play; however, these are essentially paper based. Where technology is linked to writing the focus is often on the development of children's ICT skills or key literacy skills such as letter recognition. New technologies, however, are changing the nature of writing and as such there is a need for practitioners to provide meaningful experiences in the classroom that reflect these changes.

Critical thinking exercise 5

A Compare writing with pen and paper to writing on screen. What are the key similarities and differences? **Consider** the tools and how they are used as well as the process and end product. **Reflect** on the implications for early years educators.

B Describe the activities and experiences that you have provided, and that you have observed early years practitioners using to encourage children to write. **Consider** the role technology has played.

C Outline ways in early years practitioners could provide meaningful opportunities for children to 'write' on screen.

Comment

Merchant (2005b) identifies three key defining characteristics of on-screen writing, these include the use of new surfaces and media for writing, new tools and devices and ways of using or acting on these tools. These are explored below.

New surfaces and media

- Symbols appear on screen in response to physical actions such as typing on a keyboard or selecting options from with the click of a mouse or the use of a touch screen.
- Texts are often read as a scroll and subdivided with page breaks.
- Digital texts can be changed and copied, but cannot be touched in their original form. Changes are easily made, for example font colour, style and size.
- Visual and audio material is easily incorporated to create multimodal texts.
- Hyperlinks can be inserted to link between documents or to provide access to the internet.
- Screens, especially larger ones, are often seen as more public surfaces for writing which help/promote encourage collaboration/collaborative work.
- Power, connectivity is required.
- Compared to pen and paper the screen is a very different surface for writing.

Writing tools and ways of using them

- Various electronic writing devices with differing levels of portability are available, ranging from mobile handheld devices to desktop PCs, these make writing 'on the move' and in a range of locations possible.
- Different tools are used to write, or 'act on' screen writing, such as touch screen technology, mouse, stylus, keyboard, roller ball and joystick.
- Writing tools may have multiple functions, for example, keys on a keyboard or buttons on a mobile phone can perform a variety of actions.

- The physical actions for text production on screen i.e. the use of fingers and thumbs differ from those required to control a pencil.
- Different holding and carrying actions as well as different physical positions are used when using new technologies to write on screen.
- The physical handling and use of material objects associated with traditional paper-based writing tasks, such as paper and scissors, differs considerably when writing on screen.

Merchant (2005b) found that young children demonstrated a growing understanding of what it is like to write on screen. They needed little encouragement to engage with technologies such as computers and mobile phones and confidently carried out basic operations such as pressing keys and deleting text. The development of keyboard skills is helpful, especially as children's confidence with technology grows and the following links to online games are useful for developing such skills:

www.bigbrownbear.co.uk/keyboard/index.htm

http://annrymer.com/keyseeker/

http://primarygamesarena.com/Dance-Mat-Typing2012 Level 1

www.powertyping.com/rain.shtml

Purposeful writing on screen

However, in order to reflect the kind of experiences children encounter in their everyday lives, children need meaningful and purposeful reasons to write on screen. The provision of technology such as laptops and mobile phones (toy or defunct) in the 'writing area' or the 'writing table' is one possible way forward. However, Merchant (2005b) highlights the importance of capitalising on children's interests and popular culture as a stimulus for children's on-screen writing. Incorporating digital technology into children's socio-dramatic play, e.g. role play areas, provides opportunities for children to *act out everyday literacy practices combining their knowledge of popular culture with the technology (provided)* (page 193).

Role play

Children's role play areas provide an ideal opportunity to raise children's awareness of how, when and why technology is used in everyday life. It is therefore important that the role play area is equipped with resources that mirror the technological world in which the children live. While the inclusion of real technologies gives children the opportunity to further their knowledge and understanding of these tools, real items of technology that no longer work, for example, mobile phones; toy technologies, for example, toy tills; and ICT resources made by the children, for example, photocopiers and scanners, all have value and can enhance children's learning.

Children's understanding of the various technologies can be enhanced through adults modelling their use and using appropriate questioning while children are using the various technologies in their play. Perhaps more importantly adults can model on-screen writing within the play situation. For example, in Postman Pat's post office this may involve the adult in role as the customer creating their online driving licence www.kenttrustweb.org.uk/kentict/content/games/drivingLicence_v2.html or passport www.kenttrustweb.org.uk/kentict/content/games/memaker_v2.html. They may also model entering text on screen as they key in figures on the electronic till, cash machine or mobile phone. Consequently, children see adults writing for a real purpose and audience and in turn begin to imitate the adults, and use the technology resources more spontaneously and independently.

Twitter

Each morning at 11.30 in Giraffe class it's 'Twitter time'. The children start thinking about what they want to share with their audience and who is going to write it. The teaching assistant, and the 'star of the day' who chooses a writing buddy to help are involved in producing the daily tweet. The children think carefully about what they want to share with their audience and then they are encouraged to orally rehearse the sentence and then the spelling of each word before they type. This provides opportunities for talk for writing and application of phonic knowledge. While the children are encouraged to consider the various options, the teaching assistant does not correct or change anything that is typed.

Over time the use of Twitter has been developed. The daily tweet is now supplemented by independent tweets from a number of pupils; their tweets are always checked by an adult before sending. The children now also add Twitpics http://twitpic.com/ to show what they have been working on in class; this includes examples of their work from different areas of the curriculum.

Giraffe class now has an increasing number of followers, from family and friends to teachers and academics, although these are vetted first using True Twit (http://truetwit.com/truetwit/signUp/index). The children have also started building relationships and communicating with children in other schools from around the globe. The children love this, as it gives them a real audience and meaningful reasons for writing and sharing their work and achievements. It has also strengthened home–school links as increasing numbers of parents are following the Giraffe class.

This project highlights the motivating effect of writing with a purpose and an audience in mind, but also the role of technology in supporting this process and the immediacy of response that can be achieved. Read more at http://lordlit.com/2009/10/18/twitter-as-a-key-tool-in-year-one-literacy-vit/ or visit the Giraffe class at https://twitter.com/GiraffeClass.

Clicker

Clicker from Crick software www.cricksoft.com is a talking word processor which enables children to write and make meaning in a number of ways. They can type words using the keyboard or can select words, phrases and pictures from Clicker Grids, which sit below the writing document. Children can listen to the words and phrases in the grids by right clicking on them, this promotes confidence, greater independence and the use of more adventurous vocabulary. Sentences are automatically read back as they are completed enabling children to review their writing before progressing; this feature also helps reinforce simple sentence construction and the need for full stops. Words are also highlighted as they are spoken, this enables children to follow the text as it is read, and helps them make connections between the spoken and written word.

The latest version of Clicker has built-in painting tools, which enables children to create their own pictures which can act as a stimulus for writing or an alternative means of expression for struggling or reluctant writers. The built-in web cam also means children can instantly incorporate their own photographs into documents. Writing frames to scaffold the writing process are also available, this includes talking book templates where children can easily select pictures from the vast picture bank, add or create their own images and videos, as well as text and voice recordings. These tools are all highly motivating for children and encourage creative, multimodal ways of working.

Little Bird Tales

Little Bird Tales (http://littlebirdtales.com/) is a free online tool designed to let younger children create high-quality multimodal digital stories using a very simple interface. Users are able to combine their voice with images and text (although this is not required) to create multimedia stories. Audio can be added using a microphone or webcam. Pictures can be created online using the built-in art pad; photographs or images that have been created offline can also be uploaded. Finished books can be saved and accessed online. They can also be made public on the Little Bird Tales website or for example by embedding them into a class blog or school website. They can also be sent via email to friends and family.

It is clear that today's young children are creating and sharing their ideas in new ways, the transformative nature of technology now means that children are increasingly using images and audio as well as text to convey meaning, or a combination of these to create multimodal texts and are able to share these with local and more global audiences.

Conclusion

In this chapter you have considered the role that popular culture, new technologies and media play in the lives of young children today and the importance of building upon these early experiences and new ways of learning in early years educational settings, this has included strategies for the classroom. You have explored ways in which moving image media texts, including SMA, can support children's communication language and literacy development. Finally, you have compared writing on paper with writing on screen and are aware of pedagogical interventions that can support children's digital writing such as purposeful interaction and the use of technology in role play areas, the use of software such as Clicker, and online tools such as Little Bird Tales and Twitter.

Further Reading

British Film Institute (2003) *Look Again: A teaching guide to using film and television with three to eleven-year olds*. London: BFI Education. Accessed at: www.unicef.org/magic/resources/bfi_Education_LookAgain_TeachingGuide.pdf.

Marsh, J. (ed) (2005) *Popular Culture, New Media and Digital Technology in Early Childhood*. London: RoutledgeFalmer.

Marsh, J., Brooks, G., Hughes, J., Ritchie, L., Roberts, S. and Wright, K. (2005) Digital Beginnings: Young children's use of popular culture, media and new technologies. Accessed at: http://www.digitalbeginnings.shef.ac.uk/ DigitalBeginningsReport.pdf.

Marsh, J. and Hallet, E. (2008) *Desirable Literacies: Approaches to Language and Literacy in the Early Years* (2nd edition). London: SAGE.

Useful resources/websites

Animation for Education, a resource for schools www.animationforeducation.co.uk

Film Education www.filmeducation.org/

3 Verbal literacy

Ian Todd

Chapter Focus

This chapter focuses on verbal literacy, in particular the skills needed to read online. We invite you to consider whether reading online is different from reading print-based texts, whether any new skills are needed and therefore whether we need to alter our teaching to accommodate this. We also look at whether online writing, such as blogging and internet projects, can enhance writing skills and if the use of social media can play a role in teaching Literacy.

The critical thinking exercises in this chapter focus on:

- **analysing** the skills that are needed to read online;
- **reflecting upon** your own habits as a reader and how these might be transferred to the classroom;
- **discussing** the ideas described in the case studies with what you have already seen of classroom practice;
- **considering** any advantages that might be brought by new approaches to reading and writing.

The key ideas discussed are: **online versus print-based reading, reading for the modern world, online writing** and **social media in the classroom.**

This chapter is particularly relevant to the following Teachers' Standards (2012):

Part 1: Teaching

A teacher must:

2 **Promote good progress and outcomes by pupils**
   - demonstrate knowledge and understanding of how pupils learn and how this impacts on teaching
   - have a secure knowledge of the relevant subject(s) and curriculum areas, foster and maintain pupils' interest in the subject, and address misunderstandings
4 **Plan and teach well-structured lessons**
   - promote a love of learning and children's intellectual curiosity

/continued

CHAPTER FOCUS – continued

    ⊙ contribute to the design and provision of an engaging curriculum within the relevant subject area(s)

5 **Adapt teaching to respond to the strengths and needs of all pupils**

    ⊙ have a clear understanding of the needs of all pupils, including those with special educational needs; those of high ability.

Introduction

This chapter begins with a case study showing how much reading takes place online on a daily basis and how this is different from print-based reading. It goes on to explore how children might struggle in an online world if they are not explicitly taught the skills to access it and finishes by considering ways in which the teaching of writing can be complemented by online media. The critical thinking exercises explore the skills used at each stage and invite you to consider how traditional methods of Literacy teaching fit with new approaches.

Key idea: **Is online reading different from print-based reading? Are there any new skills that are needed?**

The profusion of digital media that has found its way into our daily lives means that many of us spend much of our time accessing information, for both work and pleasure, from a whole host of sources: desktop computers, laptops, tablets, smart phones, netbooks, as well as more traditional paper-based media such as books, newspapers and magazines. But are we actually 'reading' when we navigate through these digital 'pages' and, if so, are the skills we use any different from those traditionally taught in the classroom?

CASE STUDY

The time has come to choose the next family holiday. Following a brief, informal, conversation with household members (in which most choices were ruled out on the grounds of being 'too hot', 'too cold' or 'too expensive') I decide to log on to a well-known holiday website and search for ideas. My eyes scan across the information bar at the top to 'destinations' and, as I roll the mouse over this, a menu of countries appears. Selecting the one of my choice (Tunisia) I immediately scroll down to the bottom of the page where there is a map of the

               /continued

CASE STUDY – continued

country and a box on the right detailing the weather and climate. Satisfied that I won't 'fry' if I go at the right time of year I then scroll up to the top left where I enter a series of details into a filter so that I can find my 'ideal holiday'. Sometimes this requires writing in an empty box, other times negotiating a series of choices from a drop-down menu and, on other occasions, ticking a series of smaller boxes. Armed with these details, the computer flashes up 27 holiday possibilities over three 'pages'. The price is on the right of the page, a picture of the resort on the left and, in the middle, a description of the resort above a 'trip advisor traveller rating'. My eyes move immediately to the price, then back to the resort picture and over the rating, before resting on the description. Not satisfied, I scroll down, noticing of course that the page is far longer than the size of the screen. Realising that the hotel choices have been sorted 'highest to lowest', I remedy that using another drop-down menu and, having narrowed my choice to three possible hotels, hit the 'More details' button. Initiating the 'slideshow' of resort pictures, I glance around for further information, allowing myself a wry smile that 'today's special online price' actually turns out to be more than the price that first caught my eye on the last page. In a little under 15 minutes (less than the time it would have taken to drive to the travel agent on the high street) I have narrowed my choice to four hotels, which I can now argue over with my family for days to come.

The following morning I am back at my desk, but for very different reasons. I am marking essays that have been submitted to me electronically. I read them left to right and top of the page to bottom, occasionally using the 'new comment' tab to insert questions, comments or opinions. Three hours, and some rather tired eyes later, I have lunch and read the newspaper (as a sports fan, I always start with the back pages) scanning the headlines for interesting articles, missing out complete sections on 'Business', 'The Economy' and 'Entertainment' but feeling as though I have the gist of what is going on in our country and elsewhere in the world.

Much later, after a long day of teaching, meetings, marking then taxiing children to cubs and scouts, I sit in bed with the novel I have been struggling through for three weeks. It is a murder mystery and, while I am determined that I will not flick to the back page to find out who the murderer was, I keep forgetting who the main characters are, since I can only manage three or four pages before falling asleep. This means I have to flick back a few pages to remind myself of what has happened.

Today I manage just two pages…

Critical thinking exercise 1

A **Consider** the case study above. In which of the four scenarios am I actually reading? In each case what do you think is the purpose of my reading?

B **Analyse** the skills I am using when interacting with each different 'text'. Can you make a list of the main skills I am using? Do they differ according to whether I am using print-based or electronic texts?

C **Compare** the skills I was using above with the requirements of the current National Curriculum in terms of reading. Are there any differences?

D **Reflect upon** the variety of reading sources you use in an average week. Is that variety reflected in the breadth of reading opportunities we offer the children in the classroom? Does it need to be?

Comment

The four scenarios above are all, of course, examples of reading and they all had similarities in terms of purpose and the skill set needed to carry them out. In all of them, I was extracting information (whether it be about family holiday destinations, sports news or the characters from my novel). They each required me to be able to decode text and assign meaning to what I read. It could be argued that each had an element of deduction or evaluation about it: assessing the best holiday resorts; gauging the level of understanding of my students; deciding which sections of the newspaper I felt to be most relevant, and even prioritising the order in which to read them; and finally using the clues from the novel to try to work out who the murderer was. Three of the examples were clearly about reading for pleasure (directly, in the case of the novel and the newspaper, more indirectly with the holiday) while the fourth was linked directly to work. Each of the scenarios uses skills that can be linked directly to the National Curriculum. I am using my knowledge of phonics, word recognition, grammatical structures and context to make sense of what I have read. I am also using deduction, making connections to different parts of texts and using my knowledge of other texts to help comprehension. The skills of skimming, scanning and detailed reading are all evident as are links to plot and character. In the course of a fairly normal day I am, then, using most of the reading skills outlined in the National Curriculum and there are similarities in terms of purpose and skill set between the reading I did online and that which used print-based literature.

There are, however, significant differences as well. Coiro (2003, page 458) points out that the internet *provides new ways to interact with information*. The essentially non-linear nature of websites means that traditional, left to right, top to bottom reading is replaced by a much more varied, complex approach. Consider how I navigated the holiday website above. My eyes and mouse were moving in all sorts of directions, assessing information as I went and using the results of these decisions to take me to the part of the page that I felt to be most useful or appropriate, rather than just following the course set out by the writer. In this way, readers *navigate their own paths through the information that may be different than the path of other readers or the intended path of the author* (Coiro, 2003, page 459). This idea is built on by Miners and Pascopella (2007) who point out that using the internet requires us to be able to navigate as well as read. Compare this with how I read the novel, from beginning to end, taking great care not to jump forward to another point, lest it give away the identity of the murderer. There are, of course, overlaps between the two. While I read the novel in a traditional, linear fashion I did, however, flick back to a previous chapter to remind myself of earlier events. Similarly, with the newspaper, I was much more in charge of my own 'reading pathway' by eliminating what I did not want to read at the beginning and then starting at the back pages to read about the sport. Equally, one could argue that my online marking was actually an example of traditional, linear reading that just happened to be on a screen. However, these examples aside, the extent to which online reading requires us to navigate backwards and forwards, through a plethora of sound and images, and to work towards so-called 'self-directed text construction' (Coiro and Dobler (2007)) is generally far greater than with traditional print media.

With the above in mind, are there any skills that specifically relate to reading on the internet that may need to be taught in addition to, or instead of, traditional reading skills? The following case studies will investigate separate yet related issues. Firstly, the sheer number of websites that exist on any given topic makes finding the required information a far harder task than it might have been for previous generations. Henry (2006, page 615) points to *new reading comprehension skill sets to effectively search for information* and various authors warn of the dangers of information overload if *students do not possess adequate reading skills to sort through large amounts of information* (Brandt, 1997; Nachmias and Gilad, 2002; Yang, 1997, cited in Henry, 2006, page 615). Secondly, because *anyone can publish anything on the Web* (Henry, 2006, page 620) the need for pupils to be able to sift, evaluate and critically analyse what they are seeing becomes a vital skill. As Tapscott (1998, page 63, cited in Coiro, 2003) puts it: *It's not just point and click. It's point, read, think, click.* Finally, the fact that students are able to interact with what they read (often instantly) presents an enormous opportunity for all involved in the learning process but perhaps brings a new dynamic to the classroom. Larson (2009), citing earlier studies by Carico *et al.* (2004) and Grisham and Wolsey (2006), differentiates between *'the traditional literacy classroom'* where *'knowledge is mainly transmitted'* (page 646) and the opportunities for asynchronous, socially constructed learning that blogs, discussion boards, etc. can bring about.

Key idea: **Is the current way of teaching reading equipping children for the modern world?**

If we accept, from the last section, that while there are similarities between reading on paper and online, there are also some important differences, it should lead us to question whether these differences are being recognised in the curriculum and the classroom and whether, as teachers, we are taking steps to teach children the skills they need to navigate through the wealth of information that the internet holds. According to Henry (2006, page 616), *the process of searching for information on the Internet is a complex procedure that uses new literacy skills.* If this is the case, what are they and how can we help our pupils develop them?

CASE STUDY

Jenny, a teacher in her third year, sets the following as homework for some of her Year 4 class, as part of their RE topic on 'Founders and Leaders':

'Research a famous world leader. Find out what makes them special. If possible, do this in pairs.'

She only gives this homework to her top Literacy group, all of whom have a reading age at least 1 year above their chronological age. She decides to allow them to use the ICT suite to complete the homework after school, so that they can more easily work in pairs, but gives them no help with it, reasoning that they are very able readers and that 'all children are really computer savvy these days, aren't they?' She does, however, watch Kirsty and Jessica attempting theirs and notes the following.

The girls enter the word 'Leaders' into Google, which immediately displays 583,000,000 results. Kirsty reads the results on page 1 from top to bottom, one at a time (including entries from an English letting agent, an Australian newspaper and the Chinese communist party). They do this for another two pages, coming across entries that include the national college for school leadership and the NHS, but nothing that seems to help them. Eventually, they look at the headings at the bottom of page 3 and come to one that says 'famous leaders'. This 'narrows' the search to just over 100 million hits and includes images of Gandhi, George Washington and Mother Teresa, none of whom they recognise. However, they do find an entry entitled 'Biographies for kids, Famous leaders for young readers' which Jessica clicks on. This brings up a

/continued

CASE STUDY

copy of a painting of George Washington with a list of ads either side. After clicking on a couple of the ads and realising they are not helping in the search, they go back to Google and click on an entry entitled 'Famous Leaders'. This gives them a notable quote or saying from a list of well-known world leaders but nothing else. After reading the first six, they realise that, again, this will not aid their search. Eventually, they go back to the 'Biographies for kids' website, as this seems to be the only one they can find for children. They now scroll down to a list of American presidents. They begin with George Washington and read through this section, as well as the sections on John Adams and Thomas Jefferson before noticing the headings that say '1st president of the United States', etc. 'I know!' says Kirsty, 'Why don't we scroll down and find Barack Obama?' Having done this, they again read, word for word, the whole section on Obama's life before pasting the complete article into a word-processing document. They have now run out of time so they quickly print off what they have and write a sentence at the bottom saying why they think Obama is special.

Critical thinking exercise 2

A Consider why it took the girls so long to find any information on a world leader, when they are both very able readers.

B Discuss what skills they needed to have to be able to carry out this exercise more effectively.

C Analyse your own thoughts and pre-conceptions about children's ability when searching the internet. Do we make assumptions about their capability? Does their confidence sometimes mask the efficiency with which they can carry out the tasks we want them to complete? Do our own assumptions mean that we do not provide the support they perhaps need?

D Reflect upon how we might link our traditional teaching of reading to ways that would prepare the pupils for 'internet reading'.

Comment

Internet searches (usually as part of a longer project and often linked to a history or science topic) are very common tasks that children are asked to perform. Because we often assume that pupils will be both experienced in and adept at using the internet (and because they often find the idea of such a task really enjoyable) this activity is regularly given either as homework or as an independent activity while the teacher focuses on another group. What can often emerge is frustration on the part of the pupils, as they fail to find what they are looking for quickly enough, overwhelmed by the mass of information that exists on the web (sometimes resulting in them either starting to drift off-task or giving up). Those who do manage to complete the task may do so ineffectively: in the case of Jessica and Kirsty, two intelligent girls who remained on-task throughout, they essentially printed off a large chunk of somebody else's work, which they had not really considered or interacted with in any meaningful way (it certainly wasn't their own work) and then added one line of their own to it. In the case of homework, it can often result in hours of patient work on the part of parents (where the interest and expertise exists) to point their child in the right direction. The reason for this, according to Henry (2006, page 616) is that *the process of searching for information on the Internet is a complex procedure that uses new literacy skills.* Coiro points to the need for *clarification of the comprehension processes necessary for reading on the Internet* (2003, page 459). The first hurdle that the girls faced was that putting in a generic word such as 'leaders' brings up millions of results. Nowhere in the traditional teaching of reading do we really prepare the children for being bombarded by such a wealth of information. We would never, for instance, let them loose in a public library, with no help, and just one word as guidance (in this case 'leaders') and expect them to come up with a project, in their own words, in a relatively short space of time. Granted, access to the internet is quicker than sifting through books but the sheer number of options leaves many children not knowing where to start. This really leaves the teacher with two options: either provide the children with a list of websites that have already been filtered (in the same way that a teacher might provide a selection of books from the school library or loaned from another source) or give them the skills to narrow down or filter a search themselves. In the case of more able children, they will relish the freedom and independence to do their own research and we might argue that to deny children the opportunity to look for information on the web using search engines is to deny them an important life skill in the modern world. So how could we go about it? Henry (2006) outlines an approach called the SEARCH model, which looks like this:

1. **S**et a purpose for searching

2. **E**mploy effective search strategies

3. **A**nalyse search-engine results

4. **R**ead critically and synthesise information

5. **C**ite your sources

6. **H**ow successful was your search?

In the case of Jessica and Kirsty, the purpose had already been set by the class teacher, but it was very general. A series of guiding questions can narrow down the search process considerably, for instance asking the children to look for biographical details (when were they born, how old were they when they first became a leader, in what year did they die) and even giving a choice of leaders to look for from which the children could choose (e.g. Nelson Mandela, Mahatma Gandhi, Winston Churchill, Mother Teresa). This removes the need to use very generic words such as 'leader' in the search. Henry points to two other important ways of helping children narrow down the search process, namely activating prior knowledge and using key words effectively. *Students who possess prior knowledge of a topic before attempting to locate information in traditional texts have increased success* (2006, page 618). While the girls had been studying the topic of 'Founders and Leaders' they had no introduction to any of the actual leaders they were researching. Had they already encountered, say, Mother Teresa, the homework could have been to search for further information about her life and what made her special. Armed with some knowledge, the search would have been more informed and, therefore, quicker. This raises an interesting question of whether internet-based research projects should be the starting point of any topic or only used as consolidation or finding further information. You might consider that, until the skills of searching and analysing very large chunks of information are well embedded, the latter might be a sensible option. Teaching children to use key words when searching can, again, narrow the search considerably. So, while entering a search for 'Mother Teresa' brings up millions of hits, the addition of key words such as 'place of birth', 'date of death' not only reduces the number of entries remarkably but directs the children towards more relevant websites. The point is that this has to be taught to most children and is a separate skill that many will not pick up naturally; all of which brings into question the assumptions that able readers will necessarily be able to search the web efficiently and that internet research can be used effectively either as homework or as an independent activity.

The other major hurdle that Kirsty and Jessica encountered was making use of the information once they had found it (covering points 3 and 4 of the SEARCH model). Here, there are strong links to traditional literacy skills, namely skimming, scanning, inference, deduction and reading texts critically. On each page of results, the ability to run very quickly down the page to pick out the overall gist of each result, then to make a judgement about how useful it will be (are we the intended audience, is this just trying to sell something, is it too general, does the URL give us any clues as to its relevance to young people?) is even more important on the internet than it would be if searching through a shelf of books at the library since, as Henry points out, *When students read conventional text print, they can be fairly confident that the information is more accurate than what they find on the Web* (2006, page 620). Similar skills come into play when a website is accessed, though this is complicated by the navigational issues, and the plethora of sound and images mentioned earlier in this chapter, as well as pop-ups and advertisements that appear with increasing regularity. All of this makes the experience of searching the internet much more involved and complex, and potentially therefore more time-consuming, than using print-based texts. Also, it is worth pointing out that, while these skills mostly appear in the English National Curriculum, they are higher-order skills, many appearing in the Level 4 and 5 descriptors.

So, some of the skills are linked to those of traditional reading, some are either new or need to be adapted to meet the demands of online reading; many of them are higher-order skills and they all need to be taught explicitly. Simply assuming that 'good readers will be OK' will not work, as was shown in the case study. Nor will the assumption that, as children are generally very at home with computers and technology, their experience with the internet will make online reading a low-level activity in terms of teaching/ intervention. As Henry says, *Teaching students how to search and how to read on the Internet needs to be a focus of classroom pedagogy for the future* (2006, page 624).

Key idea: **Online writing: blogging, fan fiction, internet projects**

If we accept that online reading forms part and parcel of our daily lives and is here to stay, what about writing? Can the internet be used as a vehicle for writing and, if so, does this encourage and even improve writing skills? Below are three short case studies showing how the internet has been used to promote writing.

CASE STUDY

Quad blogging

Schools are organised into groups of four (it could be four schools in the same country, different countries, or even four classes in the same school) by signing up to a quad blogging website (such as www.quadblogging.net). Each week, one school is responsible for putting together a blog (the 'focus blog') that the other three schools then comment on. The responsibility for establishing the focus blog changes each week. Schools can sign up for a four-week period or longer, with new quads tending to appear at the start of a new school term. School bloggers can request to be linked to 'quaddies' from specific countries or take 'pot luck'. Countries as diverse as the UK, Saudi Arabia, Canada, New Zealand, Nigeria, Panama and the USA are represented on the site. The focus school can decide what goes into the blog to fit in with what is being studied and they are guaranteed an audience by dint of being part of a group of four.

CASE STUDY

Fan fiction

Fan fiction is a term given to a type of writing in which the author copies the style of writing of a book/author of which they are a fan, often including characters from the original book and then weaving new stories into the original or different setting. These stories (usually short stories) are then published to fan fiction websites, free of charge, where they can be shared by others. The biggest of these sites is www.fanfiction.net, which contains works from a variety of genres. There are examples of sites which are dedicated to one particular author/genre, such as www.fanfiction.mugglenet.com, which contains stories relating to the Harry Potter series of books and characters. Reviews can also be posted. The site contains many thousands of stories.

CASE STUDY

Internet projects

Similar in principle to quad blogging, yet on a potentially far wider scale, are internet projects. These are projects that take a central theme and use this as a vehicle to promote communication between children from different schools, cities and countries. Children can talk about, ask about and add information to, the project that is being undertaken. Projects can be temporary, focusing for instance on a one-off event, or they can be permanent, some of them running for several years. Two prominent internet projects are the Flat Stanley project (www.flatstanley.com) and the Journey North project (www.learner.org/jnorth). The Flat Stanley project began in 1994, encouraging children to send paper cut-outs of the character to different parts of the world and to use this as a way of informing others about your own lifestyle, culture, etc. This has grown into an online project, with a Facebook page and its own app, and now serves 6000 schools in 88 countries. Journey North tracks wildlife migration and seasonal change around the world and allows students to report sightings and keep a track of changes in various countries.

Critical thinking exercise 3

A Consider how quad blogging could help to develop writing skills in children. Are there any advantages to this over paper-based writing techniques? Can you think of any downsides or limitations?

B Discuss the possible role of fan fiction in motivating children to write. Is this a legitimate forum for children expressing their writing skills or could it be seen as an immoral (and even illegal?) 'rip-off' of existing work? Could you think of a way of incorporating it into the classroom?

C Analyse the possible impact that participating in an internet project could have. In what is already a very busy timetable in most schools, is there time for such projects? Are these luxuries that are best left for homework and the holidays? Do they get in the way of the 'real' teaching of writing?

Comment

Each of the above studies has at its heart three major factors: purpose, audience and motivation. For successful writing to take place, it can be considered that children first need to establish what the purpose of their writing is, i.e. why are they doing it. 'Because the teacher says so' is not an unusual response to this question and it is not altogether unreasonable in that the teacher sets up most of the routines and work schedules in any given classroom. In a similar vein, the question of audience, i.e. who this piece is intended for, is central to the writing process, according to The Primary National Strategy (DFES, 2006). Again, all too often the target audience for any piece of writing is the teacher, for similar reasons as before. Many studies have shown, however, that children and, in particular, boys, respond much more enthusiastically to any piece of writing if the reason for doing it makes sense to them and if the target audience is 'real'. So, if they were writing a letter of complaint, rather than writing it to an imaginary person (say, a local councillor) about a made-up issue (too much litter on the streets, for instance), they would be far more motivated if given the opportunity to write to the head teacher to campaign for longer playtimes, with the letter actually being delivered. As the National Strategy says *make sure that, wherever possible, the audience goes beyond the immediate classroom.* The beauty of quad blogging is that there is a very real audience, usually of the same age as the writer, and the purpose is clear. If you are the focus school, there is a need (and a deadline) to have something posted so that others can comment on it. The same goes for the 'commentators' who are responding to a real person. Because the blogs are often about what has been learned in the classroom, there is relevance to the age group, obvious links to other subjects, and the sheer interest of finding out what children of their age are doing in other countries. The motivation comes, not just from using technology, but from the cultural and real-life communication links that can be made. This case could be made for blogging in general of course and, indeed, many schools are now establishing a class

---

blog. The advantage of quad blogging, according to David Mitchell, the project's coordinator, is that *A Blog needs an audience to keep it alive for your learners. Too often blogs wither away leaving the learners frustrated and bored. Quad blogging gives your blog a truly authentic and global audience that will visit your blog, leave comments and return on a cycle* (2012). In other words, it should be a self-perpetuating model. Anyone visiting the site will immediately see the enthusiasm from the children and the range of subjects they tackle. Clearly little, if any, of this could be achieved through traditional print-based Literacy teaching, certainly not with the immediate feedback that online work can give a child.

Similar benefits in terms of motivation, audience and purpose apply to fan fiction and internet projects. While there are few examples of whole class or school topics relating to fan fiction, it is easy to see how children could get excited about writing about their favourite characters and settings. Again, the audience is very real, and the fact that reviews can be posted adds another purpose to the work. The Flat Stanley project has been described as a modern day 'pen pal' scheme but it is a much more instant one and, based as it is, around a well-known text, it promotes a love of reading and fictional writing (children often create new adventures in their own part of the world for Stanley) as well as the benefits of communicating with people overseas. Indeed, the project is credited with persuading Jeff Brown (author of the original book) to write a sequel, some 40 years after the original publication. The other advantage of the Flat Stanley project is that it appeals to younger children and could quite easily be undertaken at Key Stage 1.

There are, as well, benefits in terms of writing skills, to each of the above projects. Blogging and the Journey North project will often be encouraging children to engage in non-fiction writing, either explanations or instructions or recounts of events and perhaps even journalistic or persuasive writing, depending on the context. Fan fiction could be an excellent way to 'tune children into' a particular genre and could particularly relate to the development of plot, character and setting, as well as review writing. Flat Stanley could aid understanding of story structure for younger children and would be an excellent introduction to letter writing.

So, to use a phrase sometimes seen in blogs, what's not to like?! OFSTED are happy, the children are motivated and several writing skills are being enhanced. There are, however, some issues that need to be addressed, such as coverage, consistency, assessment and, somewhat strangely, given what we have just said, motivation. Any successful curriculum will be planned so that there is coverage of all the required elements in an even, consistent way across the year. The very nature of the quad blogging and internet projects would make it difficult to predict just what genre of writing would appear for the children to respond to. For instance, if Year 3 are in the middle of a unit of work on 'stories by the same author' (say Roald Dahl) and the school they are linked to in New Zealand posts a blog about the a study they have done of the national rugby union team, it is hard to see where this would fit in. As a one-off, it would matter very little but there is the potential for this to happen every (or most) weeks, either disrupting the work on Roald Dahl or reducing the blogs to a token gesture. Many schools, of course, might have their 'blog day' so that every Friday could be set aside for composing and sending their blogs; they might even set it as homework, so that there is little interference with the rest of the week's work; they may even calculate that the benefits of blogging outweigh any partial disruption. Nevertheless, the structure of the Primary National Strategy (and indeed any scheme of work) depends on a buildup of skills that are then applied in a given context, and it is hard to see how something as potentially sporadic as blogging could fit into that structure.

Embarking on a whole project such as Flat Stanley could be very powerful but teachers would have to consider how they could assess and what evidence they might keep. This would not be an impossible task by any means, but would not be as clear-cut as having work written in books.

And finally, the issue of motivation or rather, we might say, of maintaining motivation. The very nature of something being exciting and interesting can be about novelty and being different from the normal routine. If that novelty *becomes* the routine then part of the raison d'etre for having it disappears. Keeping the children interested in projects that might run over a long period of time could be a challenge. Fortunately, the ever-changing nature of the blogs should prevent this from happening and evidence from the websites does not seem to indicate any 'tailing off' in interest even from those who have been engaged for quite some time.

Undoubtedly, then, the benefits that each of the above case studies brings to children as writers outweigh any potential limitations. As with any resource, they are there to be used by the teacher and all good teachers will adapt them so that levels of motivation are maintained and so that their use fits in with the rest of the English curriculum.

Key idea: **Social media in the classroom – does it have a place in supporting Literacy?**

Can the use of Twitter or other social media ever have a place in the classroom? Is it a harmless pastime that should be confined to evenings and weekends or could it actually have benefits in the classroom in terms of enhancing children's reading and writing? Does it detract from traditional literacy skills and can it serve as a distraction from 'real' work? The case study below looks at its use with a Year 2 class.

CASE STUDY

Using Twitter with a Year 2 class

In 'Using Twitter in the classroom' (2010) Martin Waller describes how he uses Twitter to encourage and extend the writing of his Year 2 children. It is used as a free writing exercise, where the children are open to write what they want (subject to the 140 character limit per Tweet that applies to all Twitter users). The feed is displayed on the interactive whiteboard for all to see and the children tend to write about what they have been learning at school that day. They have also started to use the services of twitpic, so that photos of their work can be displayed and they are even beginning to get some followers that the children can engage with in a supervised way. There are just three rules governing its use: no real names of any of the children are to be used, to protect identities; they are not allowed to check any replies – an adult must do this in case of any inappropriate language and/or content; and they are only allowed to stay on the class Twitter page.

Martin reports that it has been a great success and quotes a Tweet from one of his (formerly reluctant) writers: 'I like writin'.

Critical thinking exercise 4

A Discuss how often you make use of social networking sites and how familiar you are with them. Could this familiarity be used to good effect in the classroom or should Twitter *et al.* 'know their place' – i.e. be kept for evenings and weekends?

B Analyse what learning could take place through a medium such as Twitter.

C Consider what benefits (other than familiarity and motivation) they could bring to the classroom.

Comment

Waller (2010) claims that *Extending the range of texts that children study can only be of benefit in helping them to understand the vast array of domains that literacy embodies in our society* (page 14). He also points out that it gives real purpose and audience to his pupils' writing and that, because their work is displayed (via the feed on the interactive whiteboard), it lends importance and a sense of pride to what they write. Because they are writing about what they have learned, it is allowing them to consolidate their work and gives the writing a truly cross-curricular feel. The opportunity to share it and engage with followers brings about what he terms *inter-generational literacy* (page 15) and, perhaps unsurprisingly, he praises the engaging qualities of it, especially to reluctant writers. The 'free choice' element takes away any threat and allows children to use the resource as and when they feel comfortable, and the school have dealt with the potential dangers by establishing their three simple rules. What is unclear from the study is the extent to which it has developed their writing skills (something Waller acknowledges).

In terms of other benefits, a study by Larson (2009) of 6th Grade American pupils using an online learning community in place of traditional methods of literacy learning, suggested the following. The asynchronous nature of the task (i.e. the fact that children could choose when to post comments) allowed for greater inclusion in that pupils could spend as much time as they wanted formulating their responses. Again, the fact that the posts were placed at a time and pace to suit the students meant that 'conversations' could take place without interruption so that the learning from these conversations was more in-depth. It also allowed less outgoing students to contribute as they could do so in their own time without the pressure of an immediate audience (although, interestingly, it was still the more socially outgoing students who posted the most). The language used was very 'chatty' and soon came to resemble that of chat rooms and social networking sites ('UR so right!', 'OMG!' etc.) At first, the teacher was concerned by this and attempted to get the students to use more formal language but then concluded that, for the pupils, this discussion board had the status of a conversation (as group work might in a classroom), that it did not detract from the quality of the comments they were making about the books they had read and, indeed, even *enhanced their conversations by adding voice and expression* (page 646). The pupils' comments consistently *brimmed with respect, kindness and support for one another's opinions and ideas* (page 648).

So what can we gather from these two studies about social media? Both point to motivation, ease of use and greater engagement on the part of the children. By giving the pupils space to contribute when they were ready, it took away some of the pressure of participation, especially for less confident or less able children. It did not seem to act as a distraction or lead to inappropriate conversations, and there is no evidence that the abbreviated language used in the second study went beyond that online discussion forum; it did not seem to 'leak' into the children's written work.

But did either of these studies actually benefit the pupils in terms of reading and/or writing skills? Interestingly, neither provides (nor purports to provide) convincing evidence that attainment increased because of the use of social media. Both seem to attest that the true value of it at the moment is its accessibility, ease of use, familiarity to the children, powers of motivation and the connections it allows pupils to make with others. So, is there a place for social media in the classroom? You might consider that there is but that maybe that place at the moment is alongside traditional methods of teaching and learning Literacy.

Conclusion

In this chapter you have considered the extent to which online reading takes place on a regular basis. You have analysed the skills involved when reading online, how these differ from traditional print-based reading skills and how we might help children to develop them. You have discussed the role online writing can play in increasing motivation for and complementing traditional writing skills. Finally, you have reflected on the role of social media and how it can add to the Literacy curriculum in the classroom.

Further Reading

Coiro, J. (2003) Exploring Literacy on the Internet. *The Reading Teacher,* 56 (5): 458–64.

Coiro, J. and Dobler E. (2007) Exploring the Online Reading Comprehension Strategies Used by Sixth Grade Skilled Readers to Search for and Locate Information on the Internet. *Reading Research Quarterly,* 42 (2): 214–57.

Larson, L. (2009) Reader Response Meets New Literacies: Empowering Readers in Online Learning Communities. *The Reading Teacher,* 62 (8): 638–48.

Mitchell, D. (2012) Quadblogging. Available at: http://quadblogging.net (Accessed 12 November 2012).

Waller, M. (2010) Using Twitter in the Classroom. Available at: http://changinghorizons.net (Accessed 12 November 2012).

www.fanfiction.net (no date) (Accessed 12 November 2012).

www.flatstanley.com (no date) (Accessed 12 November 2012).

www.learner.org/journeynorth (no date) (Accessed 12 November 2012).

4

Finding things out – information literacy
Mike Toyn

Chapter Focus

This chapter will consider what it means to be information literate and will draw connections between this and definitions of literacy that were discussed in Chapter 1. It will encourage you to reflect on your relationship with information and what kind of relationship you wish to foster within the children that you teach.

The critical thinking exercises in this chapter focus on:

⊙ what **information filters** exist that limit or control the information that is available to us;

⊙ how **definitions of information literacy** are analogous to definitions of literacy and the importance of an understanding of definitions which are more encompassing;

⊙ how **frames of information literacy** can be used to identify the way in which you teach information literacy within your classroom;

⊙ finally, the importance of **creating information** if we wish to be fully information literate.

The key ideas discussed are: **information filters, definitions of information literacy, frames of information literacy** and **creating information.**

This chapter is particularly relevant to the following Teachers' Standards (2012):

Part 1: Teaching

A teacher must:

1 **Set high expectations which inspire, motivate and challenge pupils**
   ⊙ set goals that stretch and challenge pupils of all backgrounds, abilities and dispositions
2 **Promote good progress and outcomes by pupils**
   ⊙ demonstrate knowledge and understanding of how pupils learn and how this impacts on teaching
   ⊙ encourage pupils to take a responsible and conscientious attitude to their own work and study

/continued

> **CHAPTER FOCUS** – continued
>
> **3 Demonstrate good subject and curriculum knowledge**
> - ◉ have a secure knowledge of the relevant subject(s) and curriculum areas, foster and maintain pupils' interest in the subject, and address misunderstandings
> - ◉ demonstrate a critical understanding of developments in the subject and curriculum areas, and promote the value of scholarship.

Introduction

Chapter 1 discussed how the term *literacy* can be defined and, perhaps unsurprisingly, a similar debate occurs when considering information literacy. This has implications for the way in which learners are taught and learn about information literacy and also for the place of information literacy in society.

This chapter will consider four key points that build together to develop an understanding of information literacy. First, is the idea of information filters, which will include a discussion of the organisational filters that exist that limit the range of information that we are exposed to. This will then lead into an exploration of different ways of viewing information literacy and the implications that this has for teaching and learning. Following on from this will be a more detailed discussion of elements or frames (Bruce *et al.*, 2006) of information literacy. A more detailed discussion of elements or frames (Bruce *et al.*, 2006) of information literacy will then follow. Finally, the chapter will conclude with an exploration of the role of the creation of information as a key element of information literacy.

There are any number of websites available via a quick internet search that quote staggering figures for the amount of information that is generated annually and how this increases year by year. We clearly live in an information rich age and you may have come across phrases such as 'Information Overload' or 'Information Abundance', which create images of us being overwhelmed by information or having more of it then we could possibly ever need. Thus, it would logically follow that it would be helpful to be information literate in order to effectively interact with this information.

It is worth taking time to consider what is meant by information and some of its characteristics. You might like to stop reading for a while and make a list of things that you would consider information. It would be easy to imagine that many lists would contain things like facts and figures, news, non-fiction books, etc. However, I wonder if you would have things such as famous art works or song lyrics in the list. Whitworth (2009) considers information to be the product that arises when humans interact with their environment, which is a very broad definition but I think it serves very well. For example, consider an explorer in an unexplored part of a rainforest; as they move about they see, hear, smell, feel and possibly taste the environment around them. They might

---

sketch, photograph, video, collect samples, or write descriptions of the environment and it is these interactions that would give rise to information about this new environment. In a similar way, an artist who experiences the world around them and then attempts to represent these experiences through the medium of their art is generating information. The purpose of this discussion has been to emphasise that information is more than simply facts and figures and needs to be thought of in broader terms to avoid constraining information literacy into something as limited as 'how to read an encyclopaedia'.

Whitworth (2009) uses the term 'Information Obesity' to describe the abundance of easily available and frequently low quality information that is available. Debates about public health and obesity often cite the need for people to make informed choices about their food consumption and criticise organisations that market foods low in nutrition but high in calories. Pursuing this analogy would suggest that consumers of information need to be informed in order to make the best use possible of available information – in other words they need to be information literate.

Key idea: **Information filters**

It would not be unreasonable of you to question the need for information literacy, particularly if you have access to an internet-enabled smart phone. You might be able to recall a recent occasion when you wanted to check a train time, find all the films an actor had starred in, or find a recipe, and you have gone to an internet search engine in order to quickly and easily find the information you needed in order to get a solution to your query. You might have simply clicked on the top search result to find this solution and not visited any other results to cross check. However, I wonder if you would buy clothes in the same way? Would you walk down the high street to the store with the biggest name and largest store front, walk in, ask for some clothes in your size and buy without trying them on or considering alternatives? This section addresses the notion of what information is available to you and why this might be different to the information that exists.

Before reading on, place a bookmark in this page, close the book, close your eyes and listen. Think about what you can hear and what it tells you about what is going on around you. Continue listening and try to focus on those sounds that you were not aware of before when you were reading. Perhaps you became aware of the sound of traffic, music or TV. It is highly probable that once you began to focus on sounds then you began to be aware of more than you originally thought. This is not because the sounds were not there before; it is because your brain was filtering them out. (An excellent example of this can be found here: www.youtube.com/watch?feature=player_embedded&v=vJG698U2Mvo). Hopefully, this brief activity will have emphasised the point that there is so much information available to us that we have to filter it in order to be able to carry out our daily lives. As well as this sort of filtering, which is done to reduce the cognitive load on our brains, we also make use of a cognitive bias known as the confirmation bias. This is where we seek information that fits with our existing thoughts and knowledge base; in other words we are predisposed to accept information that confirms what we already think and know. A classic example of this concerns gun control in the USA, where those in favour of one side of the argument will accept and believe information that supports their belief and will disregard information that does not. Basically, we are not really very good at listening to both sides of an argument if we have already formed an opinion. You might find that you read a particular newspaper as it favours your political viewpoint: this is an example of the confirmation bias in action. All of this is important as we need to be aware that as a species, humans have some flaws when it comes to dealing with the information that is available to them and recognising this is an important aspect of information literacy. However, as has already been explained, being able to filter information makes it possible for us to cope with day-to-day life. Indeed, Whitworth (2009) states *filtering is the fundamental basis for any relationship with information* (page 3). But there are other ways that information is filtered and an understanding of these will help with later discussions about information literacy.

In order to understand the way in which information is filtered, it is necessary to take a step back and think a little about the role of society and culture and how power is allocated within these. (If this is of interest to you then you would do well to start by reading Hall (1980) who was a pioneer in the area of cultural studies.) Livingstone (2003) makes a key point when she notes that for information in print or audio-visual form (as opposed to internet-based information) the means of producing these are not equally available to all. A second key point is that the maker of them is in control of their content. If we consider both of these points together, then it is apparent that whoever has the means to create information has the power to control its content and this power is not evenly distributed. This means that even though the amount of information that is contained in books and TV/film archives is beyond comprehension, the perspectives that this information contains does not equally represent the views of all within society.

Critical thinking exercise 1

Livingstone (2003) puts forward the dilemma about which information source would offer the 'best' account of environmental hazards: Greenpeace or the Department for Environment, Food and Rural Affairs.

A Select an education-related topic, perhaps one from the list below and conduct a search for information on it.

/continued

> **Critical thinking exercise 1** – continued
>
> - Assessment
> - Curriculum reform
> - Phonics
> - Homework
>
> B **Identify** three sources of information on your chosen topic. One should be an 'official' source such as the Department for Education; another should be a media report of the issue, perhaps the BBC Education website or the *Times Educational Supplement*; the final one should be a source of your own choosing, perhaps a blog written by a teacher.
>
> C **Reflect** on the similarities and differences between the way that the issue is presented and the reasons why there might be these differences.

Comment

The activity above should have emphasised the fact that the information provided about your chosen topic was different or had different emphases according to its source. This is because the creator of that information was in control of the message. In other words they were filtering what was made available to you. It is worth noting that I specifically mentioned print and audio-visual media and made a comment about internet-based information. Livingstone (2003) highlights that the internet grants the power-to-publish to a much wider audience, particularly to people who would not be able to publish information through print or audio-visual media; but it is not universally available and, as we will see later, how that information is made available via the internet is subject to filtering.

Kellner and Share (2005) discuss the idea of information being filtered according to where power resides in society and they note five 'core concepts'. Of these core concepts, two are relevant to this discussion. First, they argue that news (which we can interpret as information) is non-transparent (*ibid*, page 374), they also argue that media (again we can substitute information) are organised to gain profit or power (*ibid*, page 376). One example of this comes from an historical perspective, Connell (1979) writes about coverage of political events from the 1970s and provides an analysis of the way in which mainstream media (television and newspapers) reported these events. He points out that news programmes not only have to broadcast information about current events, but that they also have to make it viewable and have to sustain the viewers' interest. He also focuses on the use of language; for example, he quotes a presenter commenting on a meeting between striking workers and their employers: 'Well, at least you're sitting together here on a very cold night, and let's hope that kind of spirit moves on' (*ibid*, page 143). This leads to a discussion of who is doing the hoping that is mentioned. Is it the workers, is it the employers, is it the general public? The very use of the phrase *let's hope* implies that a positive outcome to the meeting will be generally welcomed. The key point here is that the message has been constructed, it is not a transparent portrayal of a story and an awareness of the way in which this information has been filtered is crucial to a critical, information literate person.

A second, more current example, is the debate highlighted by Goldacre (2012) who argues that pharmaceutical companies do not disclose full details of their medical trials if the findings would be detrimental to their profits, even if there is a risk of patient harm. This is an example of Kellner and Share's (2005) concept that media is organised to gain power or profit and for the purposes of this discussion it is another example of the way in which information is filtered and controlled by those that hold power within society. This tension is clarified by Catts and Lau (2008), whose UNESCO report titled 'Towards Information Literacy Indicators' is an attempt to describe what characterises information literacy. In it they note that in democracies, citizens must be able to free to engage in *active information seeking* (Catts and Lau, 2008, page 10); however, they stress that central governments and organisations often seek to control behaviour and that they can do this by controlling the information that is available. Awareness of this is key to a critical information literate person.

Finally in this section, is a discussion of the role of technology in filtering the information that we receive. Most notably is the way in which search engines operate. It is easy to perceive these as neutral and benign, simply trawling the web and doing a pretty good job of matching appropriate websites to our search terms. However, one should not forget that they all operate using different algorithms (or sets of rules/decision making instructions) to decide which pages are ranked top of the list. It must also be remembered that search engines require money to operate and thus are commercial organisations and they have to strike a balance between operating in a commercially successful way and providing responses to search terms that users find effective. Users would soon stop using a search engine that only directed them to sites that had pay-to-view content; likewise, search engines would soon go out of business if the search results that they produced did not earn them enough money to make a profit.

This section should have raised your understanding of the limitations that humans have in dealing with information as well as some of the embedded ways by which information is filtered. This means that it is impossible to be fully informed and have complete access to all information about any topic; an understanding that is vital for a critical information literate person.

Key idea: **Definitions of information literacy**

As you read in Chapter 1, there are different ways in which literacy can be defined ranging from a very functional perspective focused on the decoding of words, through to more holistic definitions, which equate literacy with being able to make

/continued

Key idea: **Definitions** – continued

sense of their world and make contributions to it. Likewise, there are similar debates that relate to information literacy. First, this section will consider a functional definition of information literacy, its benefits and its limitations. Then will come a consideration of a cultural definition followed by a discussion of critical information literacy.

Functional information literacy

This has its analogue in definitions of literacy, which refer to being able to decode words. It is characterised by sets of criteria that define what an information-literate person can do. In other words, functional information literacy is defined by a set of skills. Livingstone (2003) makes an interesting point in relation to this by using the example of driving a car: when someone can drive a car, you might say that they have the skills to do it, you are not likely to describe them as literate in car driving. This hints at some of the limitations of this definition, but before focusing on that, a greater discussion of functional information literacy is needed.

There are numerous examples of the functional definitions of information literacy. These range from primary school-based materials such as QCA (2000, page 179), which is a scheme of work for ICT based on a functional approach to information literacy. There are also commercial schemes, which adopt a similar approach such as Big 6 Skills (Eisenberg and Berkowitz: no date). At higher education level the Association of College and Research Libraries and American Library Association (2000) provides a widely adopted framework while Catts and Lau (2008) working for UNESCO offer a set of information literacy indicators with the intention that these can be applied globally. A quick perusal of any of these might leave a reader thinking that they are pretty comprehensive and that little more would be needed in order to support the development of information literacy. They can be typically described by the following structure:

- Work out what information you need.
- Work out where you might get this information.
- Gather the information.
- Evaluate it.
- Build it into your existing knowledge.
- Evaluate if it has met your needs.

In order to understand why this sort of functional approach might not be an adequate approach to understanding what information literacy is it will be helpful to think of literacy for a moment. There are undoubtedly a number of skills that underpin being literate such as being able to recognise letter shapes, being able to match graphemes to phonemes, being able to know the meaning of the words that these combinations

---

make. However, think for a moment of all the benefits that you gain from being literate. Imagine someone who is a keen cyclist: they might enjoy reading magazines and websites containing information about cycling, they might read the instructions that come with bike parts in order to be able to fit them correctly, they might read road signs so that they can navigate when out cycling, they might enjoy having discussions with friends about cycling, and so on. Think of something that is of interest to you and think about all the ways that being literate allows you to enjoy it.

The previous critical thinking exercise should have highlighted that being literate facilitates more than simply being able to decode words and understand their meaning. It is highly likely that some degree of communication would have been involved, perhaps discussions or conversations with others who share your interest. These might be verbal or text-based discussions. The purpose of considering this is to recognise that being literate facilitates a wide range of activities and that it is more than simply the act of decoding words, there is an interactive element to it. Likewise, we now need to consider how this interactive element relates to information literacy (Hull, 2003).

Interactive information literacy

This can be thought of as a way of addressing the limitations of a purely functional approach. A purely functional approach would define information literacy as the ability to identify, find, evaluate and use the required information without offering an explanation of *why* they need to do this. When you were thinking of the benefits that you got from being literate, you were, essentially thinking of the reasons why literacy was important to you. It also creates a scenario where someone who is information literate is simply a passive consumer of other people's information. As we have seen, information is something that arises from humans' interactions with their environment and thus it is something that we all generate. Therefore, any approach to information literacy which is solely based on the consumption of other people's information does not fulfil its purpose.

Interactive information literacy is one in which learners are more involved in deciding their information needs and will be better equipped to consider the context in which the information will be used. There are two aspects to this, first is the idea of being better informed about your information needs. This is an important point and has more depth to it than might be initially imagined. In order to know your information needs you need to know what you already know and you also need to know what you don't yet know. This cannot happen in a vacuum and it is through interaction with others that this awareness will develop. Being able to share and discuss information needs with others is a key aspect of this. The second important point is the context in which the information will be used because, as a rule, we don't generally require information for the sake of it, but for a purpose. Frequently, in a professional role like teaching, information has a value or purpose because it will be shared and communicated to others. This is the point where information stops becoming subjective, or related to the individual, and starts becoming *inter-subjective* (Whitworth, 2009, page 16) as it is the point where information can begin to have a transformative impact. However, it is easy to argue that there is yet another aspect of information literacy which moves it from simply describing a procedure to obtain information, into something which is a powerful tool. This aspect can be described as *critical information literacy* (Hull, 2003, page 4).

Critical information literacy

What distinguishes this from the forms of information literacy that have already been discussed is the understanding of the value of information and how it fits into culture and society. For example, someone visiting www.martinlutherking.org without an understanding of the struggle for black rights in the USA and the history of racism might not realise that this site is insidiously racist. Thus a person who has critical information literacy understands something of cultural studies, as discussed earlier, and is able to question information in relation to this wider issue. They are able to place the information that they locate and use it to aid their understanding of society and culture. They are also able to use it to influence the culture in which they live, they are not passive citizens but they are active actors who can use this information to transform their environment. An example of this might be a teacher who receives a resource pack from 'Kick it Out' (www.kickitout.org an organisation which seeks to eradicate racism from football). They might consider why they have received the pack and the extent to which racism is an issue in their school. They might decide to discuss with other teachers about the pack and then adopt a whole school approach using not only the resource pack but other materials as well. They might then seek to transform the school environment by using these educational materials. In this example, there is more to information literacy than simply following a procedure to locate and evaluate information; the social context of the information and the purpose of using the information is important as is the desire to transform.

It should be noted that this discussion has not been intended to be a critique of functional definitions of information literacy. These are important as they help users of information to develop important skills that will be needed to work with information effectively. However, by now I hope you realise that a skill set on its own does not constitute what could adequately be classed as a literacy. By adding to these functional definitions the elements of interactive and critical information literacy the wider role of information can be considered. The next section will look at a framework for considering different aspects of information literacy and, in particular, the way in which they can impact on pedagogy.

> **Critical thinking exercise 2**
>
> **Consider** a time when you needed to develop your pedagogical subject knowledge in relation to a particular area of the curriculum. Think in detail about the process that you went through in order to achieve this, the resources that you used, the way that you used them, the colleagues you worked with and whether you shared your new-found understanding with others.

Comment

Probably without realising it at the time, your approach to developing your pedagogical subject knowledge will have embodied your understanding of what information literacy is. The next section will provide a brief summary of how particular responses might demonstrate each of the three definitions of information literacy.

Functional information literacy would be summarised by a search technique based on strategies for finding information, using particular sources such as the internet or key books that were known to have been useful in the past. It might have involved evaluating the knowledge selected to confirm that the information was relevant to the topic and the year group that it was to be taught to. It might have ended up with a search for a lesson idea or activity that could be used with minimal adaptation.

Interactive information literacy would be characterised by a search strategy that recognised from the outset the information that was required, this would then be followed by a search strategy that aimed to find information that was adequately matched to the learners' pedagogical approach. Consideration of the effectiveness of the information would consider how well the information matched the needs and how well it suited their pedagogical approach. The outcomes of the search might have been shared with other professionals. The outcome would be that they are able to select and plan an activity which is integrated to the needs of their class and their preferred teaching style.

Critical information literacy would include an understanding of how the relevant information would be found, it would also be shared and discussed with other professionals. There would, importantly, be a consideration of why the information was presented in the way it was and some degree of reflection about the value and best way to use the information. There would be a transformative and collaborative element to it such as hosting a staff meeting to share views about the way in which a new aspect of good practice within that subject had been identified.

Key idea: **Frames of information literacy**

Bruce *et al.* (2006) propose a six-fold classification of ways of interpreting information literacy. Their classification arises from the idea that teaching and learning can be viewed differently by different people. For example, some might view learning as being given facts. While others might consider it from a more constructivist viewpoint where educational experiences are provided in order to present a stimulus to the learner that will encourage them to build the experience into their own knowledge frameworks. By adapting this idea from the broad spectrum of teaching and learning to the area of information literacy they have categorised six discrete ways of viewing this area. Some of these can be seen to be analogous to the *functional, interactive* and *critical* classification that was discussed in the previous section but the six frames of literacy is more useful when it comes to considering information literacy in relation to pedagogy.

It is worth considering the relationship between pedagogy and information literacy as some things that can easily be taken for granted can have some hidden implications. Take, for example, the range of information that is available via the internet; this is frequently viewed as a valuable resource by teachers who perceive it as a benefit to their pupils. However, Whitworth (2009) makes the point that if learning is simply reduced to the act of retrieving information that has been created by others then it is analogous to the behaviourist model that sees learners as empty vessels that need to be filled up with knowledge. Thus, educators need to think about the relationship between information literacy and pedagogy to ensure that their classroom practice is aligned as they would wish. For example, children may be presented with a problem such as finding suitable flowers to plant in the school's flower bed. They might then access information about flowers such as what time of year they flower, their colours, how much they spread, etc. They would then need to use this information to construct their understanding about a possible solution to their planting problem. It is also worth remembering the role that the teacher plays in helping pupils respond to the information they come across, as was highlighted by the www.martinlutherking.org example in the previous section.

The classification provided by Bruce *et al.* (2006) is as follows:

- Content frame
- Competency frame
- Learning to learn frame
- Personal relevance frame
- Social impact frame
- Relational frame.

These will each be taken in turn and related to the previous discussion in this chapter where relevant, and their impact on pedagogy will be considered.

First, the content frame. This views information literacy as content and in practice you might see it as a subject on a school timetable. You might even have experienced it yourself if you have had any sessions on how to access university library resources for example. It would tend to be focused on how learners use a set of tools for working with information and might have assessments associated with it that would test how well learners have mastered these tools. The limitation of this frame is that it simply focuses on the technical mastery of the tools and does not support learners in deciding what to do with the information.

The competency frame is rather similar, but rather than focusing on providing learners with information about the content they need to learn, as in the content frame, it has its focus on how competent learners are in finding and using information. The shift in emphasis is that this frame is concerned with how well users can perform, rather than simply giving them instruction. It should be obvious that this is somewhat analogous to the definition of *functional information literacy* that was discussed in the previous section. Indeed, the Association of College and Research Libraries & American Library Association (2000) has titled their work 'Information Literacy *Competency* Standards for Higher Education' (author's emphasis), which leaves little doubt as to which frame their guidance can be aligned to; this is an approach which has been adopted by many university libraries and hopefully the previous discussion will have emphasised the limitations of working only with this kind of approach.

If searching the internet for information to fill up a learner's mind can be equated with a behaviourist approach then the learning to learn frame has some similarities with constructivism. This frame sees information literacy as a tool to help with learning, where the learner is aware of their learning needs and can source appropriate information in order to combine it with their existing knowledge. Learning in this frame might be presented as a problem-based learning approach where a problem is presented and relevant information needs to be located in order to help resolve the problem. This means that the learner needs to be involved in the evaluation of the information in order to evaluate whether it meets their needs or not. However, there are two criticisms of this frame. First, the learner is not encouraged to adopt a critical stance and to question the information in relation to the power structures that exist within society. Second, and perhaps most important pedagogically, is the criticism of this approach presented by Egan (1990) who argues that it does not make sense to suggest that learning to learn means that it is possible to reap the benefits of learning without actually doing any learning. He goes on to point out that in order to recognise problems and solve them requires the learner to have internalised a body of knowledge, without this learners are not able to recognise what they need to know in order to solve the problem.

The personal relevance frame has some similarity with the definition of interactive information literacy that was discussed earlier. As its name suggests, this frame is concerned with the relevance of information in relation to the individual. Indeed, it goes a little beyond this as it also incorporates a consideration to the relevance of information literacy to the individual. This frame might be embedded in a pedagogical approach, which would be situated in the context of the learning and would be aware that information literacy might be different for different learners or groups of learners. If you have ever experienced Problem-based Learning then you would have come across a personal relevance approach to information literacy. You would have been presented with a problem that required you to access, assess, assimilate and use information in relation to a problem that would have been relevant to your learning. Importantly, you would probably have been expected to reflect on the experience and the quality and value of the information you had worked with.

The next two frames – social impact and relational frame – broaden the definitions of information literacy and begin to consider elements such as power relationships in society (Bruce et al., 2006) in the same way as the definition of critical information literacy. They embody the need for learners to question the status quo in society and to use information for transformative purposes. The distinction between the social impact and the relational frame is that the relational frame can be considered to be a culmination of all the previous frames. It is concerned with helping learners to see the world around them and the role that information plays in it in the same way Freire (2000) talked about reading the world.

It should be apparent that there is a noticeable hierarchy in these frames, for example, it would be hard to support learners to develop a personal relevance relationship with information if they didn't also have a relationship with information that could be summarised within the competency frame. However, it should be equally apparent that limiting learners to a competency frame will mean that their information literacy skills will be underdeveloped. A consequence of this is that learners should be encouraged to go beyond simply consuming information that others have created and to begin creating information themselves. This will form the final key idea of this chapter.

Critical thinking activity 3

You are reviewing some plans for a science lesson on life processes. Your plan from last year began with a brief introduction and then progressed on to setting the children the challenge of finding out, via the internet, the things that are required to sustain life. There was a quiz at the end of the lesson where children were tested on their knowledge. You have identified that this plan would benefit from some development as it is rooted securely in the *competency* frame as

/continued

> ### Critical thinking activity 3
>
> children's competency in finding the information is determined by their ability to answer the quiz questions correctly.
>
> You have also identified that this lesson has an implicit behaviourist approach to information as you are expecting that children will access the information online which will 'fill them up with knowledge' that can be regurgitated via a quiz.
>
> **Select** one of the other frames of information literacy and **consider** how you might embody a different approach to information in this science lesson on living things.

Comment

Which frame you selected (and assuming you didn't select the content frame) will impact on how your response will be structured. For the purposes of this section, it will be assumed that you selected the social impact frame.

You would have recognised that the relationship between information and society is important and you would have also wanted to ensure that the information could potentially be used for transformative purposes in relation to the way that power and information are distributed within society. Consequently, you would have realised that it would have been difficult to achieve this from within a lesson that did not have any cross curricular links. An example might be that you begin by asking the children to find out the essentials for sustaining life. This could then have progressed into an investigation into a group or groups of people for whom maintaining these essentials is not easy, e.g. fuel poverty among the elderly or other low income groups. This might have been followed by some action to try to address this issue, for example a fund raising activity, or awareness raising, such as a letter to the local press or MP.

Key idea: **Creating information**

> In Chapter 1, you will have learnt that literacy is simply more than decoding words on a page, it is about being able to take meaning from them and also being able to place that meaning in the wider context of the world in which we live. Indeed, it is even broader than this as a useful definition of literacy would also include an element of communication, in other words we would expect a literate person to be able to communicate effectively with others about the world in which they live.
>
> /continued

Key idea: **Creating information** – continued

As has already been mentioned, definitions of literacy have been discussed elsewhere in this book but I'd like to briefly revisit this as an introduction to this final key idea. In the same way, we might expect a person who is information literate to have a degree of functional information literacy combined with an element of critical information literacy in order to be able to place the information they find and use in a wider context, we might expect them to also be creators of information for others to use, rather than simply passive consumers of information.

The need for critically information literate learners to be involved with the construction of information which is relevant to their community is an idea discussed by Hess and Ostrom (2007, page 247); it is also the subject of an entire chapter by Whitworth (2009). It is important to note that both of these sources relate to the construction of information which is relevant to their community. The aspect of community is important as it is what gives the information value and makes the sharing of it useful and, more importantly, transformative.

You may already have seen examples of this from your experiences in primary schools. Schools might decide to become involved in working to create safe routes to school which might require them to gather data about the way in which children travel to school, the routes they take, the distance from school that they live, etc. They might then use this information to liaise with Local Authorities about potential developments that would support changes to the local environment such as altering speed limits, improving footpaths, providing cycle storage facilities and so on with the anticipation of a reduction in car use, improved health and well-being of pupils. This short case study shows how children and schools can be involved in deciding their information needs, considering the organisation elements that currently affect their community (such as poor footpaths) and using, creating and communicating information to make transformative changes.

Kist (2005) writes of a school in America that has taken this approach to heart: *Bernahl [the school 'librarian'] was intrigued with the notion that a school library could be a place for production as well as consumption of resources* (ibid: 79). He outlines several of the approaches that the school has put into place and how they all revolve around the idea that the pupils should be involved not just in using the library to gather and find information but that they should be actively involved in creating their own information. This might be in the form of an audio recording of a music production that has been inspired by a particular artist, composer or performer (Kist, 2005, page 81). Alternatively, it might be an interactive video showcasing learning that had resulted from an information search in a science class (Kist, 2005, page 85). The final part of this section will present a case study to give some insight into how these ideas might be embodied in a scheme of work about healthy eating in a Key Stage 2 class.

CASE STUDY

A Year 4 class are engaged in a topic of work on 'Healthy Eating'; so far they have tasted some different foods, some of which were new to them, they have watched adverts for different types of breakfast cereal, they have looked at publications about the 5-a-day campaign and they have begun to do some learning about the role that different food types play in growth, health and development.

The following day, one of the pupils comes into school with a printout from the BBC website (Roberts, 27 March 2012) and is telling everyone who will listen that chocolate is good for you. The teacher decides to use this as an excellent opportunity to draw together some of the ideas that the class has been learning about. Subsequently, they do activities:

- On why the story would have been on the BBC website and why it would have been one of the most popular stories.
- To help develop an understanding of how chocolate is produced and consequently raise awareness of fair trade.
- Where they discuss what a balanced diet might consist of and compare their own food consumption over a week to this.
- Where they compare the meals on offer at lunchtime and compare these to their understanding of their balanced diet.

As a result, they meet with the school catering staff and discuss the food choices that are available and reach an agreement where some changes are made to the weekly menu. They also prepare a poster to take home with the aim of encouraging a change to the content of lunch boxes that are brought to school.

The Head is impressed by the outcomes and contacts the local newspaper, which visits the school in order to run a feature on the initiative.

Comment

This is not an unusual scenario (although in reality, it is probably one that would be part of a whole school approach rather than through the actions of one class) and it embodies many aspects of information literacy.

First, by considering the feature from the BBC website, the pupils were encouraged to think about what filters exist and how they control the information we receive. They understood that the article appeared on the website because such a story would be popular as chocolate is well liked but widely regarded as a food that should be consumed in moderation. Thus they were developing their understanding that this story had been chosen by an editor because of its interest value, not necessarily for its news value. (In reality, its news value is quite low as the article only reports on a link between frequency of chocolate consumption and weight rather than offering any proof of a connection between the two.) This can be considered to be an example of critical information literacy.

Second, the children have made decisions about their information needs and how to meet these. They have done this through reviewing published materials, internet sources, advertising materials, personal diaries, interviews with catering staff, etc. By making these choices for themselves and evaluating their effectiveness they have been able to make critical choices about the value of this information.

Third, by producing a poster to take home they have been involved in creating their own information. This information did not exist in this format beforehand and the children had to decide on an appropriate manner to present this information and also to make crucial decisions about what to include and what to omit.

Finally, the activities led to a transformative use of information. It was not gathered to be learnt for a quiz or test nor was it gathered in order to 'fill the children up with knowledge'. Instead, it was used in a constructivist manner to bring about a change to their local environment.

Conclusion

In this chapter you have considered what is meant by information literacy and made comparisons to the definitions of literacy that were introduced in Chapter 1. A critical part of this understanding has been an appreciation that information literacy goes beyond a set of skills relating to information retrieval. Wider aspects of information literacy that you have been introduced to include critical information literacy where an understanding of the place of information in society is important; using information for transformative purposes via the relational frame of information literacy where information is used to transform an individual's understanding of their environment or to impact on the environment in which they live; also the importance of allowing children the opportunity to be creators of information.

Clearly, it is not always possible or appropriate to incorporate these wider aspects every time children are working with information, but it would be doing them a disservice to ignore them all the time.

Further Reading

For an extended discussion of our relationship with information: Whitworth, A. (2009) *Information Obesity*. Oxford: Chandos.

For further details about the six frames of information literacy: Bruce, C., Edwards, S. and Lupton, M. (2006) *Six Frames for Information Literacy Education: A conceptual framework for interpreting the relationships between theory and practice*, in Andretta, S. (Ed.) *Challenge and Change: Information literacy for the 21st century*. Adelaide: AUSLIB Press.

For some inspiring examples of the way information literacy can be embedded into school practice: Kist, W. (2005) *New Literacies in Action: Teaching and learning in multiple media*. New York: Teachers College Press.

Interesting reading that will promote a critical approach to information:

Goldacre, B. (2009) *Bad Science*. London: Fourth Estate.

Goldacre, B. (2012) *Bad Pharma: how drug companies mislead doctors and harm patients*. London: Fourth Estate.

Thompson, D. (2008). *Counterknowledge: how we surrendered to conspiracy theories, quack medicine, bogus science and fake history*. New York: W.W. Norton.

5 Aural and oral literacy

Jayne Metcalfe

Chapter Focus

This chapter contributes to children's developing understanding of the role of digital music and sound effects in everyday life. It focuses on how teachers can support children to develop their speaking and listening, reading and writing skills through creating and editing sound artifacts (music, podcasts, sound effects), and begin to understand how sound relates to communication through sharing their work with others.

The critical thinking exercises in this chapter focus on:

◎ **reflecting** on the role that music plays in your own and children's lives and how meaningful music experiences can be provided in the classroom that include the use of new technologies;
◎ **articulating** ways in which music can promote children's learning in literacy;
◎ **considering** the processes involved in music remix and how this can be introduced into the classroom and can help develop children's ICT capability with audio software;
◎ **discussing** podcasting, what is involved in creating a podcast and the benefits of podcasting in the classroom in terms of literacy development, and the wider curriculum.

The key ideas discussed are: **musical culture, digital music and literacy, music remix** and **podcasting.**

This chapter is particularly relevant to the following Teachers' Standards (2012):

Part 1: Teaching

A teacher must:

1 Set high expectations which inspire, motivate and challenge pupils
  ◎ establish a safe and stimulating environment for pupils, rooted in mutual respect
2 Promote good progress and outcomes by pupils
  ◎ demonstrate knowledge and understanding of how pupils learn and how this impacts on teaching

/continued

Chapter Focus – continued

3 **Demonstrate good subject and curriculum knowledge**
   - ☉ have a secure knowledge of the relevant subject(s) and curriculum areas, foster and maintain pupils' interest in the subject, and address misunderstandings
   - ☉ demonstrate a critical understanding of developments in the subject and curriculum areas, and promote the value of scholarship
   - ☉ demonstrate an understanding of and take responsibility for promoting high standards of literacy, articulacy and the correct use of standard English, whatever the teacher's specialist subject

4 **Plan and teach well-structured lessons**
   - ☉ impart knowledge and develop understanding through effective use of lesson time
   - ☉ promote a love of learning and children's intellectual curiosity
   - ☉ contribute to the design and provision of an engaging curriculum within the relevant subject area(s)

5 **Adapt teaching to respond to the strengths and needs of all pupils**
   - ☉ have a clear understanding of the needs of all pupils, including those with special educational needs; those of high ability; those with English as an additional language; those with disabilities; and be able to use and evaluate distinctive teaching approaches to engage and support them.

Key idea: **Meaningful music**

Music is the lifeblood of every culture in the world. Music transcends language and differences around the globe. … It has the power to communicate ideas, to show emotion, to express feelings with or without words. (Hummell 2011, page 18)

Critical thinking exercise 1

A **Reflect** on the role that music plays in your life. What do you like to do while listening to music? Where and how do you listen to music? How has this changed over time?

B **Compare** your experiences now and when you were a child.

C Now **consider** the role that music plays in children's everyday lives.

CASE STUDY

Children's everyday music experiences

Charlotte is six years old; she has long grown out of her toys that provided early musical experiences such as her singing nursery rhyme book, percussion mat, Disney princess keyboard and musical mobile phone. She gained great pleasure from pressing the keys or buttons to see what sounds or effects were produced, from sharing and joining in with nursery rhymes and mimicking the actions of her parents talking on their mobile phones.

Her karaoke machine is now her toy of choice. She pops in her favourite CDs and loves to listen and sing along to her favourite tunes using the microphone; she knows many of the words to the songs off by heart. 'Baby you're a firework', a chart hit for Katy Perry, and her 'Disney Princess' songs are her favourites. Sometimes she sings alone, sometimes with friends, sometimes in her bedroom, sometimes in the lounge. Occasionally, with encouragement and practice she will put on a show and perform for the family. The ease of use, portability of the CD player and fun factor all help make this possible. At her weekly ballet classes Charlotte also enjoys rehearsing her ballet moves to popular music such as Rihanna and Taio Cruz.

Jamie is 10 years old, he likes to listen to a range of popular music; Olly Murs, Michael Jackson, Jessie J and JLS are firm favourites, he likes music with a strong beat. He sometimes puts on CDs, but usually he can be seen confidently scrolling through his play list on his iPod to select his track of choice, from time to time he will watch the accompanying video on the small screen. Sometimes the music may just be playing in the background while he is doing his homework, playing computer games on his Nintendo DS or building with his Lego; he may or may not sing along, depending on his mood and what he is doing. At other times he just likes to curl up or stretch out on the sofa or his bed and listen with his earplugs and 'chill'. Jamie is learning to play the guitar at present and loves to imitate the pop stars on TV. At the moment, however, Jamie is most looking forward to his birthday treat, going to an Olly Murs concert with his best friend, accompanied by Mum of course!

Dad also has an iPod which he uses when he goes out running. He has spent a lot of time creating his playlist of the 'right' music to ensure it has the maximum effect when he is training. Mum enjoys listening to the radio in the morning while she is getting everyone organised for work and school and music also seems to help make activities like the household chores enjoyable, or at least more bearable!

/continued

CASE STUDY – continued

The family own a Nintendo Wii and the 'Just Dance' game has provided much fun and laughter. Different members carefully try to follow the choreography of the on-screen coach, who is performing different dance routines to music, ranging from chart hits to classic dance party tracks. The on-screen lyrics also provide an opportunity to sing along to the soundtracks too. All the family listen to music and sometimes sing along to songs they like while in the car. This has become an opportunity to share and talk about musical preferences and in turn socialise with family members.

Comment

It is clear that music is a key element in this family's life and plays multiple roles. Music is very much a part of daily routines and free time at home and also an important way of socialising with friends and other family members. The children, even young Charlotte, show awareness of different kinds of music and artists and are able to express musical preferences and justify their choices; contemporary popular music is their favourite. They like to listen and play on their own and in company; the portability of music helps make this possible. They learn quickly how to operate equipment independently and readily transfer these skills to new technologies as they arrive in the home.

It is highly likely that these children's everyday musical activities are different to that of your own childhood. Digital music players such as iPods and MP3 players, computer software and hardware, internet websites, and mobile phones are increasingly being used to access music over 'older' modes of listening to music such as CD players, television and radio and as such *create aural and musical environments that are significantly different from those of [their] 'pre-digital' parents and educators* (Young, 2007, page 330). Increasingly, new technologies provide anytime, anywhere access, but also enable children to listen and to 'view' music. Technological innovation is thus seen as a key factor in changing the nature of children's music experiences. Young (2007) highlights some of the key changes, these include:

- A change in musical cultures. Musical participation and production is now possible in the family home through the use of digital TV, screen-based entertainment, multi-media players, electronic games and toys and the internet. Mobile technologies and internet sites like YouTube also provide a global audience for home productions.
- The richness and depth that digital technologies bring to sound, for example in the form of music and film, and the multimodal experiences that result. *The aural experience alone may consist of several overlays, combining music with sound effects, with voiceovers and characters speaking* (page 335).
- Children are able to move easily between changing media and integrate different sources simultaneously.

- Music is generally not viewed as a single domain, but as one part of the mediascape that enriches children's lives.
- Children's musical worlds at home are connected to the cultural world at large; technology helps the two connect as music is easily accessed through the TV, radio and internet. Children begin to develop musical identities, which in turn play a part in defining their personal identities, for example, they imagine themselves in the role of their favourite pop artists, and enjoy imitating or aspiring to be them, music influences their dress code and friendship groups.

There have been some concerns over children's access to popular music and the associated commercialism, sexualisation and exposure to age inappropriate language, as well as the potential 'dumbing down' of children's music that these new technologies bring. However, in reality, social and family practices are positively transformed and children have shown that at home they are independent, tech savvy users that are ready to learn through music and associated media. As such, Young (2007) argues that these advances in technology offer *unimagined new possibilities* and *accessible resources for worthwhile and future-oriented learning* (page 333).

Critical thinking exercise 2

A **Discuss** the types of musical experiences that you have seen or have provided for children in the classroom and more widely in school.

B **Reflect** on the kinds of music children have opportunities to listen to and compose, the use of technology and children's levels of engagement. How do these in-school experiences compare with children's out-of-school music experiences? Is there any interplay between the two?

C **Articulate** how you can provide meaningful, relevant child-centred experiences in the classroom that include the use of new technologies.

Comment

Music sucks. Not music that I listen to, but music at school. We never get to do our music, the music we like (De Vries, 2010, page 3).

Despite children's enthusiasm and passion for music at home and in their everyday lives research shows children are often disengaged in music lessons at school. The lack of interplay between children's musical practices at home and school is cited as the key reason for children's negative attitudes (Young, 2007; De Vries, 2010; Griffin, 2011).

When interviewed by De Vries (2010), children were confident that music lessons and other music opportunities in school like choir practice and dance club could be improved, and would be more engaging, if they took account of their musical interests and reflected practice at home. This included children having more choice and a greater say in the songs they sing and the music they listen to, but also access to computers

---

and music composition software so they can create and perform their own music. Older children also said they would also like the opportunity to bring their digital music players (iPods, MP3 players) to school so could listen to or share music with friends at break and lunchtimes. In addition, Ofsted (2012) found the use of music technology was inadequate or non-existent in 60 per cent of primary schools; this under use was identified as a major barrier to children's musical progress.

Pedagogical interventions

The following list includes ideas for meaningful, relevant child-centred musical experiences in the classroom that include the use of new technologies:

- Take an interest in children's musical preferences. The CBBC music site www.bbc.co.uk/cbbc/music provides access to the latest chart hits, audio and video clips featuring popular artists so that you can update your own personal knowledge of what is current in the popular music world. Remember though that some children's preferences are highly influenced by the music that their parents listen to, and some enjoy listening to some of the 'oldies' as well as what is current.
- Introduce a wider range of styles of music into the classroom, including that from children's home cultures. The BBC website www.bbc.co.uk/music/genres has links to audio and video clips from a range of musical genres which could be shared with children in the classroom.
- Provide opportunities for children to talk about and share musical preferences. Children could compile their own top 10 favourite songs or bring in their iPods or other portable MP3 music players so they can listen to and discuss each other's musical tastes.
- Plan for and provide access to computers and other music technologies such as electronic keyboards and music mats. Online virtual keyboards are useful for demonstration purposes with the whole class and also provide greater access to more keyboards. A good example can be found at: www.bgfl.org/bgfl/custom/ resources_ftp/client_ftp/ks2/music/piano/organ.htm. Useful music software for the classroom includes:
  Compose World www.espmusic.co.uk/index.html,
  2Simple Music Toolkit www.2simple.com/music/,
  MusicBox2 from Topoligika software www.topologika.co.uk/ and
  Sibelius Groovy Music www.sibelius.com/products/groovy/index.html.
- Allow time for children to play online music games, a good source is: www.bbc.co.uk/cbbc/games/by/type/musicgames. This includes games where children can direct and even star in their own music videos www.bbc.co.uk/cbbc/ games/music-video-maker-the-4-o-clock-club-game as well as learn rap skills www.bbc.co.uk/cbbc/posters/the-4-o-clock-club-ultimate-rap-skills-flow-lyrics. Both these resources could act as stimulus for children writing their own songs, composing the music and then creatively producing a music video.
- Encourage children to compose and share their own music with wider audiences. For example, music files and videos that children have created could be uploaded

to the school website or, for more global audiences, to YouTube www.youtube.com/.
- Don't restrict music to the music lesson, plan for opportunities to use music to support a range of subjects as well as the wider curriculum.
- Provide opportunities for children to select and put on music CDs, for example at music or dance club and during wet playtimes. Children can learn funky dance routines based on traditional music from India, China, Jamaica and Portugal at The Culture Club Stage school www.bbc.co.uk/northernireland/schools/4_11/cultureclub/stageschool/.
- Plan a class talent show where children have the opportunity to share some kind of musical interest; this could involve them playing some of their favourite music, sharing a composition they have made, or playing a musical instrument.
- Do Karaoke! Children sing along to recorded music with the lyrics on screen, although it is important for you to check the lyrics for inappropriate content. There are some online karaoke sites which include access to free songs such as www.thekaraokechannel.com/online#, alternatively the words and music could easily be presented in a PowerPoint.
- Draw children's attention to the use of orchestral music in, for example, pop music, TV adverts, film and game soundtracks. Use these popular culture experiences to extend their knowledge and understanding of the orchestra. Try the 'spot the orchestra' in the soundtrack of Harry Potter at: www.bbc.co.uk/orchestras/learn/listen.shtml.

The importance of building on children's social and cultural practices by providing meaningful, musical experiences in the classroom, that includes the use of new technologies has been explored, now we look at how music can support children's literacy development.

Key idea: **Music and literacy**

The literature suggests that music has the potential to support and enhance learning in many areas of the curriculum, but particularly language and literacy. Consequently, the links between these two domains and the role of music in developing children's literacy skills is increasingly being recognised.

Literacy is naturally developed through music (McIntire, 2007, no page).

Language, both written and spoken, has a great deal in common with music (Dyer, 2011, page 4).

Virtually any component of literacy can be put into a musical format (Walinsky, 2011, no page).

/continued

Key idea: **Music and literacy** – continued

Music is a universal language associated with moods, feelings and memories (Salmon, 2010, page 943).

Critical thinking exercise 3: Links between music and literacy learning

A **Articulate** what you see as the links between music and literacy. Take each of the quotes above in turn and say why you think these conclusions have been drawn.

B **Discuss** how music can promote children's learning in literacy.

C **Examine** your own use of music and technology to support children's literacy development.

D **Consider** any additional pedagogical interventions that could enhance your classroom practice.

Comment

Links between music and literacy
Hansen and Bernstorf (2002, page 2) identify a number of similarities in the way we learn music and how we learn to read.

 Most basic skills used in text reading or decoding (i.e., the breaking of the visual code of symbols into sounds) find parallels in music reading. Instrumentalists and vocalists read music symbols. In choral music, one must additionally read text or lyrics as they correspond to the musical symbols.

Their ideas are confirmed by a number of research studies (cited by Bolduc and Fleuret, 2009; McIntire, 2007; Dyer, 2011), which indicate links between certain musical abilities and young children's early literacy development. For example, children who are able to discriminate one pitch from another and show awareness of differences in musical duration were found to be more phonologically aware. Musical activities were also found to have an impact on children's ability to identify rhymes and syllables and to recognise and decode words which all had a positive effect on children's reading and writing skills.

In contrast, Salmon (2010) identified the use of music and sound as a means of literacy engagement rather than on helping to develop children's phonemic awareness. Think about the following for a moment:

- The soundtracks of *Jaws* and *Chariots of Fire*
- The sound of bagpipes or the didgeridoo
- The National Anthem
- The song from the first dance at yours or a friend's wedding
- Sounds of children's voices (from a school or children's playground)
- Sounds of waves lapping on the shore and seagulls crying
- A scream
- Laughter.

No doubt you associated the soundtracks of *Jaws* and *Chariots of Fire* with the movies and made cultural connections as you linked the sounds of the bagpipes and didgeridoo with Scotland and Australia respectively. Did the National Anthem or music from the wedding trigger certain emotions? Did you connect the sounds of children's voices with, for example, a school or children's playground, the sound of waves lapping on the shore and seagulls crying with the beach, a scream with fear and laughter with happiness? It is also very possible that while you were thinking about these sounds in your mind, you could also 'see' the music. What kind of images did you create as you linked the sounds to personal or past experiences? Did you use any other senses to build your pictures? As can be seen here, music and sounds can be used to activate prior knowledge and help locate us in a time and place.

We are constantly surrounded by sound in our daily lives and young children can also be seen using music and sound to activate mental imagery as they connect their everyday experiences with the sounds they hear. You will probably have seen children in play situations 'driving' about using imaginary steering wheels making a brrrrrrrrrrr sound designed to imitate the noise of a running car engine, or rocking a doll while emulating a baby's cry. Mental imagery or 'visualisation' is proven to aid engagement, comprehension and meaningful response in relation to literacy (Massie *et al.*, 2008, cited by Salmon, 2010). According to Zimmermann and Hutchins (2008) good 'readers' create visual, auditory and other sensory images in their mind, which deepens their understanding of the text as they make emotional connections with what they read. They refer to this as the *movie in your head* or *making reading three-dimensional.* Similarly, music and soundscapes (an acoustic environment where a sound or collection of sounds creates a sense of place) can be used to promote thinking and stimulate creative writing as *music and soundscapes engage children in creative and imaginary tours in their minds* (Salmon, 2010, page 944).

Pedagogical interventions

The research clearly suggests that music has the potential to enhance literacy teaching in different ways, but what does this look like in the classroom, which skills does it help develop and how can technology support this process?

A number of popular strategies are explored below so that you have some practical ideas to try. First, suggestions for **musical activities** such as singing (which is seen as one of the most important activities for the acquisition of the language), writing new lyrics, using percussion, inventive musical notation and song-based texts are provided. These strategies help to develop children's understanding of pitch and musical duration, melody, rhythm and rhyme and phonological units of sound or syllables (Bolduc and Fleuret, 2009; Dyer, 2011). In turn this can help increase children's phonological and phonemic awareness and thus encoding and decoding skills used in the reading and writing process. In addition, singing and other musical activities can aid memory and recall. Second, **visualisation strategies** are suggested as a way to enrich and add interest and excitement to the text, as a way of scaffolding children's ability to think 'through' music, and as a starting point for creative writing (Salmon, 2010).

Musical activities

Singing

Create a collection of songs, which you can add to over time. Start with children's songs and singing games from your own childhood experiences and ones that you have heard the children singing, a couple that come to mind include, 'The farmer's in his dell' and 'The big ship sails through the alley alley O'. Inspiration may also come from books, CDs and websites. You can find a wealth of songs, with lyrics and sound files, on Sing Up www.singup.org/. LearnEnglish Kids is the British Council's website for children who are learning English as a second or foreign language; although all activities are equally of value to children whose first language is English. The British Council recognises the importance of songs in developing children's English skills and the site contains a wide variety of songs, audio files and supporting resources for children to enjoy. The songs can be accessed at http://learnenglishkids.britishcouncil.org/en/songs or a playlist of videos for the most popular songs at www.youtube.com/view_play_list?p= 089A3255E63E8D54. Each song is accompanied by an animation and the lyrics are presented on screen too. As well as helping children sing the song this encourages them to make links between the spoken and written word. Other sites worth exploring include http://musicbus.com/resources/song-words/, http://freekidsmusic.com/, and www.laurasmidiheaven.com/Kids.shtml.

Include some singing, little and often, 10 minutes a day would be ideal. Choosing songs that relate to work being covered in class can help promote cross-curricular links, and remembering to include opportunities to sing along to popular music from time to time can enhance children's engagement. Incorporating some rap and beat boxing (using the mouth and voice to imitate percussion instruments) may also encourage those children who are reluctant participants to join in with singing and music sessions, it might also give you a bit of 'street credibility'. Encourage children to create rap songs which link to current work in the classroom. Start with simple sentences and a steady beat such as one of the GarageBand loops www.macloops.com/, and see how the rap develops. Next, try adding some beatbox sounds, try some of the beginner techniques at: www.youtube.com/watch?annotation_id=annotation_216200&feature=iv&src_ vid=IVkYhBx-_2Y&v=ZjUcHBArKHY. Finally, add some dance movements, the performance could then be filmed and presented as the children's own music video.

Using percussion to emphasise syllables

Choose a word, this could be a child's name and 'play' it using body percussion or an instrument to emphasise the accented syllables. For example, a child would clap or tap out HO-lly. Words with the same number of syllables are then combined to create rhythmic sequences – HO-lly, JO-seph, LO-la. An electronic or online keyboard could also be used for this activity, for example www.bgfl.org/bgfl/custom/resources_ftp/client_ftp/ks2/music/piano/organ.htm.

Using inventive musical notation

Download an audio file of a song with which children are familiar and which has a simple melody, Sing Up www.singup.org/ is a good source. Use the play and pause button to play it in short phrases. Children in groups or individually should use their own inventive musical notation to represent the song and its associated sounds in writing.

Writing new lyrics

Select a traditional tune such as 'Twinkle Twinkle Little Star' or any song that the children know well. The choice of song will clearly vary according to children's experiences, age and culture, although it can be helpful to choose rhyming songs or those that contain patterned language or alliteration as they lend themselves to a wider variety of literacy activities.

Present the lyrics on the interactive whiteboard so that all children can see them clearly and they can easily be edited; for example, 'Three blind mice' may become 'Three blind fish see how they swim' or individual rhyming words could be substituted to develop children's phonological awareness, for example 'Humpty Dumpty sat on a ball' Alternatively, children could write completely new lyrics that fit with the tune, additional verses that fit with the theme of the original song or the current class topic, or they could even write lyrics to help them remember a key skill, for example a spelling rule or a particular word family. The website Songs for Teaching www.songsforteaching.com provides a wealth of lyrics and music aimed at teaching a variety of language skills such as phonemic awareness, grammar and spelling rules as well as supporting students with English as an additional language. They include songs such as the 'pronoun rap' and the 'compound word workout'.

Using music software to emphasise sound symbol correspondence

Provide opportunities for children to use software such as Compose World Play www.espmusic.co.uk/composeworld_play_desc.html where graphics are used to represent phrases of music. Children click and drag the images to build a tune. This process helps children to link sounds and visual symbols in the same way they will learn the letters of the alphabet and their associated sounds to develop their phonemic awareness.

Visualisation

Adding songs and sound effects to children's literature

Use percussion instruments, everyday objects and body sounds to create sound effects to accompany readings or retellings of stories such as *The Three Little Pigs* or *The Three Billy Goats Gruff.* Encourage children to vary the pitch and tempo (speed or pace) duration of sounds; for example, high sounds for the pigs and low sounds for the wolf, short knocks on the door, long 'huffs and puffs'. This can help define a character, create excitement or add to the mood of a story, it also promotes interaction and can help the story come alive for children. The sound effects can be recorded using free online software such as Audacity http://audacity.sourceforge.net/ which enables editing and playback. Create simple tunes to fit with parts of the text in a story. This would be easier with text that already has rhyme or rhythm and would work especially well with repetitive text such as *'I'll huff and I'll puff and I'll blow the house down'.*

Listening to film soundtracks

Music is an important part of film. Listen to soundtracks of popular movies or those that are less familiar to children and discuss the role the music plays and the 'pictures' it helps create.

Consider how the music:

- establishes the setting. Can you identify the time and place?
- adds to the mood and helps create atmosphere;
- portrays aspects of character;
- creates drama and impact;
- provides continuity or signals scene changes.

Creating and listening to soundscapes

A soundscape is an acoustic environment where a sound or collection of sounds creates a sense of place. Use voices, body percussion and musical instruments (traditional or electronic) to create soundscapes linked to a particular theme; for example, space, the city or countryside, the seaside, a storm, a spooky Halloween night or a tropical rainforest. Record and edit the soundscape in audio software such as Audacity or GarageBand so that it can be shared with a wider audience. Alternatively, compose a soundscape using audio files downloaded from the internet; Find Sounds www.findsounds.com/ and Sound Bible http://soundbible.com/ are both useful sites for finding a range of sound files and effects. Talk to children about what they 'see' as they listen to the soundscape. Encourage them to establish personal connections and share what they think, feel and can remember in different ways. Use the soundscape as a stimulus for storytelling or to write poetry.

Online soundscapes

Simulate the sounds of different natural environments and create soundscapes by combining different sounds using online resources such as:

www.bbc.co.uk/cbeebies/razzle-dazzle/games/razzle-dazzle-animalsoundscape/ for EYFS/ Key Stage 1, and for Key Stage 2 www.wildmusic.org/soundscapes/soundmixer http://www.wildmusic.org/soundscapes/buildsoundscape.

Key idea: **Remixing music**

Ferguson (no date) defines remix as combining or editing existing materials to produce something new. Although this 'concept' now includes images, art, film and video games, in fact any kind of media, its origins lie in music. Remixing music became most popular in the late 1980s and early 90s and while it was most prominent in hip hop music, remixes of other musical genres, such as pop and heavy metal music also became common. Today, music remixes of TV and film soundtracks, children's songs and nursery rhymes can also be found.

Critical thinking exercise 4

A **Listen** to the very first *Dr Who* theme tune at http://news.bbc.co.uk/1/hi/ entertainment/7512502.stm.

Now listen to one of the many remixes at http://music.dannystewart.com/album/ doctor-who-themes-and-remixes.

Discuss what you understand by the term 'music remix' and what is involved.

B **Identify** the general educational benefits of remixing music with children in the classroom and how it can contribute to children's literacy development.

C **Reflect** on different kinds of pedagogical interventions you could introduce into the classroom so that children have opportunities to engage with digital music remix.

Comment

What is music remix?
One of the key things you probably noticed is that elements of the original *Dr Who* theme tune are still recognisable in the remixes; this is one of the key features of a music remix. Remixing music entails taking an existing song or music track and reworking it in some way to create a new version, while retaining elements of the original. This process involves some or all of the following: reordering or taking away existing parts of the track; and adding samples or bits of pre-recorded music and sound, such as vocals and drum beats. Another form of remixing, known as a 'mash up', is where two or more songs are combined to make one song in which both parts of the original songs remain identifiable. Part of the fun for audiences can be trying to recognise the different samples when they are remixed with other songs.

Listen to the ABC song www.youtube.com/watch?v=kZQTT8VRL64. Can you identify the source song and other samples that have been added? 'ABC' by The Jackson 5 and the traditional ABC song were probably two you recognised.

The benefits of music remix in the classroom
As well as the obvious pleasure that people of all ages seem to gain from making music, remix provides opportunities to work and experiment creatively with digital technologies. So what are the educational benefits of music remix? Jacobson (2010) identifies at least three, these include:

1. development of 21st-century skills required for the digital age;

2. creative use of existing material to make meaning and express ideas;

3. analysis and interpretation of remix music.

Jacobson (2010) views digital remix music as a text to be crafted and created as a way of expressing meaning. Similarly, Lessig (2005, cited by Knobel and Lankshear, 2008) views music remix and other forms of digital remix as new tools for writing. The concept of writing most of us hold is that of writing with text; however, today's digital generation draw on their 'cultural reservoir' as they increasingly use images, video and sound to express their ideas. As such, these media, singly or combined, become their 'words', and provide more interesting and relevant ways to 'write'.

Lessig argues that the idea of remix and taking existing cultural resources and combining and manipulating them into something 'new', sharing them, remixing them, sharing them and so on, is how cultures have been made. There is, however, debate centring on whether remix is copying or stealing, or as Lessig would argue, a form of creativity which supports digital literacy practices. The issues of intellectual property rights and copyright are explored in greater detail in Chapter 9.

Although these more broad-ranging literacy practices are currently more common among teenagers and out of school than in school, they are already filtering into the classroom.

Experience shows that younger children soon pick up on the digital practices of their elders and so in turn these methods will become more common place for primary-aged children. Technological innovation and development has resulted in remixing becoming more accessible for all ages, the practice of creating simple digital remixes in the primary classroom is now explored.

Creating remixes

Children can be introduced to online activities such as Rowdy Remix from the CBBC to simulate the practice of creating a musical remix www.bbc.co.uk/cbbc/games/horrible-histories-adbc?game=remix or Incredibox www.incredibox.com/en/#/application, which involves becoming the conductor of a group of human beatbox. Incredibox can be used for remixing, and teaching and reinforcing other musical concepts; a wealth of ideas for using this online tool can be found at www.midnightmusic.com.au/2012/08/using-incredibox-to-introduce-remixing/.

Creating remixes with audio software is also a relatively straightforward process.

You will need: editing software, computer, suitable audio tracks.

1. **Select a track to remix** – Choose something that appeals personally.

2. **Import the track into the software** – Suitable software includes Audacity which can be downloaded free at http://audacity.sourceforge.net/ or GarageBand www.apple.com/support /garageband/, developed by Apple, and which allows users to create and edit music.

3. **Listen the track again** – Identify which parts of the track to keep intact, which parts to change or delete.

4. **Dissect the track** – This could involve deleting parts, cutting some loops or sections to repeat. When identifying sections to use as loops, check you have the section you want, i.e. it starts and finishes in the right place. Decide where you want the loop to start and paste this into the software.

5. **Add your own sounds** – This could involve adding parts or all of an entire track, or tracks. Remember that you need to retain some of the original so beware that additional tracks do not dominate.

6. **Experiment** – Try the various effects available in the software and apply as appropriate. This may include changing the pitch, speed and tempo of the track to adding echoes.

7. **Build the remix** – Repeat steps 3 to 6 until you are happy with your remix track.

8. **Export the remix** – Export as a WAV file.

This is what the process may look like in Audacity.

1. Track imported into Audacity. Chosen track is the *Batman* movie theme tune available at www.televisiontunes.com/.

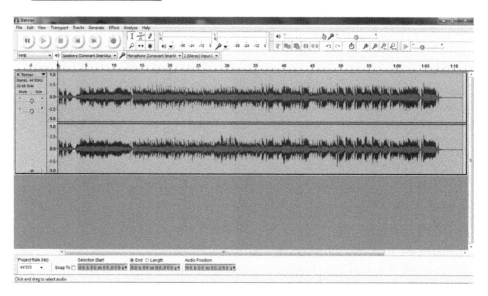

2. Loop identified and cut.

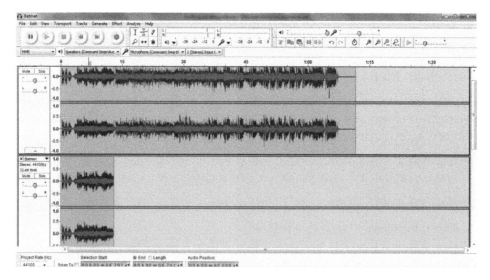

3. Loops pasted into the software.

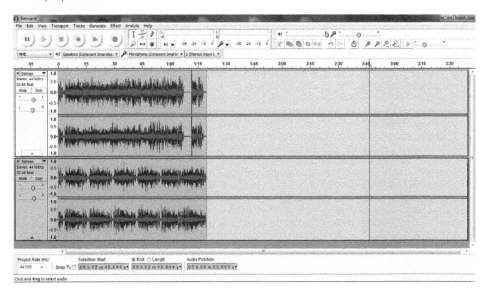

4. Additional track added, this was the Super Mario game music, also available at www.televisiontunes.com/. Tried several tracks, but many overpowered the original *Batman* track.

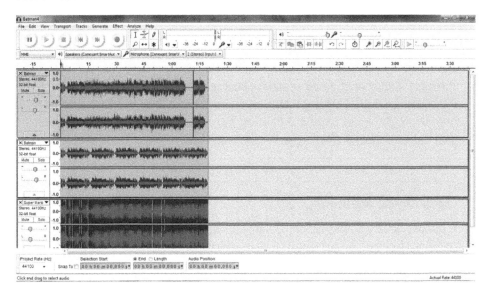

5. Experimented with various effects, chose the 'wah wah' effect.

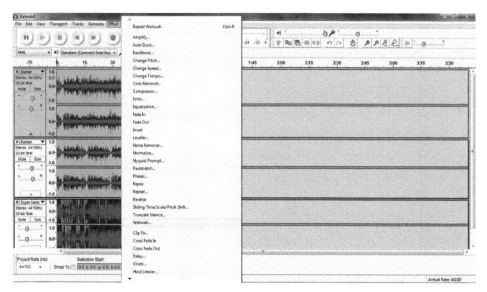

6. Exported the remix as a WAV file.

Version 2.0.0 of Audacity(R) recording and editing software was used for this work. [1]

[1] "Audacity(R) software is copyright (c) 1999-2013 Audacity Team. The name Audacity(R) is a registered trademark of Dominic Mazzoni."

Key idea: **Demystifying podcasting**

> There are a number of misconceptions about podcasting and concern that creating or even downloading a podcast requires a vast array of technical know-how. Demystifying this process is thus key if children and teachers are going to reap the benefits of podcasting in the classroom.

Critical thinking exercise 5

A **Discuss** what you understand by the term 'podcasting'.

What is podcasting?
The term podcast is sometimes used to refer to an audio file, which is published on the internet where it can be listened to by others. Technically speaking, the term podcast actually refers to a series of audio files or episodes, usually with a common theme,

which are published at intervals on the internet, rather than 'one-off recordings'. Posting audio on the web, however, is not new; it is how the files are distributed that distinguishes them from other multimedia files on the internet. The addition of a file, called a 'feed', to each episode enables users to subscribe to the series and receive new episodes automatically as they become available. A tool known as an aggregator or 'podcatcher' such as iTunes, Zune, Google or My Yahoo detects when new content has been added to a podcast and downloads it ready for listening at a time and place convenient to the user.

Activity: Downloading a podcast

1. Go to the BBC site www.bbc.co.uk/podcasts/genre/childrens where you can find a selection of podcasts designed to be used with children.

2. Select a podcast series of interest, for example CBeebies Radio podcasts.

3. Click on one of the 'podcatcher' applications such as Google Reader to subscribe to the podcast, the software will do the rest. Alternatively, click on RSS feed where you can subscribe to the podcast. There are usually instructions to follow on the screen, if not look for buttons or links named 'Add feed' or 'Subscribe'.

4. Wait for the next episode – easy as 1 ,2, 3!

The term podcast is derived from combining the words iPod and broadcast and although the term has become synonymous with Apple's iPod, you can listen to a podcast on any portable media player or computer that is capable of downloading and playing MP3 files. Creating a podcast doesn't require an iPod or Apple computer either; a microphone, PC or laptop and an internet connection is all that is required. Audio recording software such as Audacity http://audacity.sourceforge.net/, can be a useful addition and allows sounds to be recorded, edited, saved and exported as MP3 files which can then be uploaded to the web. If this still sounds a bit technical, software packages such as Podium from Lightbox Education, aimed at teachers and children, have been designed to make the creation and publication and management of podcasts even easier.

Critical thinking exercise 6

A **Discuss** what you understand is involved in creating a 'podcast'.

B **Consider** the benefits of podcasting in the classroom in terms of literacy and the wider curriculum.

Comment

How do I create a podcast?

Let your children listen to a selection of podcasts before they start. This is a great way of finding out what podcasts are all about, and discovering what it is possible to do. You may discover some great ideas which you could also try yourself.

Try to remember the 5 Ps:

1. Plan

2. Perform

3. Produce

4. Publish

5. Promote

1. Plan

Pre-production planning and preparation are essential. Careful consideration should be given to the organisation and management of the process as well as the content.

Organisation:
*   Establish groupings and the different roles members of the group will take at different stages of the process.
*   Ensure children are clear about their roles and the importance of teamwork and good communication.

Content:
*   Identify the purpose of the podcast and the target audience.
*   Decide on a suitable format that will engage the audience throughout.
*   Script the content, or at the very least produce a detailed outline.
*   Think about the beginning and the ending and how different parts will be linked together, for example through the use of music or sound effects.

2. Perform

It is important that children get the opportunity to perform and record their podcasts in the best possible conditions in order to produce a quality recording. The following tips should help:

*   Find a time and a place that is quiet and distraction free as possible.
*   Set up and test the equipment and software. Consider positioning of the equipment and the children and whether an internal or external microphone will be used. Microphone headsets can help achieve clearer recordings.
*   Rehearse the podcast and receive feedback.
*   Click on the 'Record' button to record the podcast. Speak clearly into the microphone and at a normal volume. Take short breaks by pausing the recording if

necessary or create a series of shorter recordings and link them together to form one episode.

3. Produce

Children need to be happy with their podcast. Playback of the recording is useful for confirming whether re-recording or editing is needed. The latter may involve deleting unwanted sounds or adding additional music or sound effects to further enhance the podcast. The editing process is easily carried out using the audio software. The following should be carried out as required:

Playback
- Playback the recording, this can usually be done from the beginning or from a selected point in the audio track or a section of the recording can be played back.
- Identify if and where editing is needed.

Editing
- Re-record the audio if necessary.
- Delete any unnecessary pauses or unwanted sounds like coughs.
- Even out different volume levels using a free program called Levelator www.conversationsnetwork.org/levelator.

Adding effects
- Select parts of the audio recording and add effects, for example, fade in and out or add some echo.

Adding sound or music
- Import sound files or music children have created.
- Import sound files that have already been downloaded.
- Download and import some of the many sound files available online.

It is important that any that copyright is not infringed when adding music and sound effects. The following sites contain Podsafe audio which is freely distributed online and so can be legally used in a podcast:

Free Music archive http://freemusicarchive.org/about/

Royalty Free music http://incompetech.com/m/c/royalty-free/.

Once the children are happy the podcast can be saved as an MP3 file and it is ready to be published. Saving the podcast as a project means you can come back and additional episodes can be added at a later date. This means everything will also be in one place.

4. Publishing

Publishing your podcast simply means uploading it to a server so that it can be accessed by other people. This can either be locally, i.e. to your own school network (website or blog) or globally using a 'hosting service'. The latter allows you to upload your podcasts to their website through a web browser; a website to host your podcast and the 'feed' is also created as part of the service. Some hosting services are free, although most require a subscription. Examples include:

Podium /www.podiumpodcasting.com/

Radiowaves www.makewav.es/

PodOmatic www.podomatic.com/ (unfortunately, the free version includes advertisements).

5. Promote

Once one or more episodes of a podcast are published, you will want to tell your audience where they are and encourage them to subscribe so that they receive automatic updates as they become available.

Why podcasting?

The benefits of podcasting in the classroom and beyond are increasingly being identified and consequently its use by both teachers and children, to support teaching and learning, is growing. Podcasting:

- is inexpensive and does not require high levels of technological knowledge;
- is fun and highly motivating;
- creates purposeful opportunities to communicate with authentic audiences, both within and beyond school. Children also learn the importance of tailoring their podcasts for different audiences. Collaboration can also be encouraged if audiences are invited to give feedback such as making comments to the children about their work;
- provides opportunities for children to showcase their work and celebrate their achievements with authentic audiences, both within and in the wider school community;
- supports inclusion and promotes personalised learning and can be a powerful tool for those with special needs. This includes using podcasts as an alternative means of expression, especially for those who have language or communication difficulties or who lack confidence writing. Children are able to record their ideas orally and replay the audio recordings to check they make sense. Podcasts can also be replayed to aid understanding, this can be particularly helpful, for example, for EAL children. Resources and activities are also easily tailored according to individual needs;
- promotes children's knowledge and understanding in a number of key curriculum areas, most notably ICT, English, PHSE, Citizenship and Modern Foreign Languages (MFL);

- encourages creativity and establishes meaningful cross-curricular links between subjects. Consider for a moment a project where children are asked to create a podcast guide to their school or local area. Children would be working creatively with a real purpose and audience across several areas of learning such as English, ICT, History, Geography and Citizenship;
- develops a wide range of transferable skills such as team working, creative thought, story boarding, drafting and editing, rehearsing, presenting, and receiving and responding to feedback from others;
- uses the kinds of new technologies that are increasingly becoming part of children's everyday lives. Podcasting therefore not only extends children's ICT skills and capabilities, but helps connect children's home experiences with school;
- facilitates and strengthens home-school links. Podcasts can be an effective tool for communicating with parents and the wider community. For example, podcasts containing school news and homework requirements could be posted on the school website. This could be particularly useful for those with literacy problems or communities where English is a second language. Lesson content could also be made available to children who miss lessons, for example, because they are ill or snowbound.

Podcasting across the curriculum

Podcasting can be used in a variety of ways to support learning and teaching across the curriculum and both in and outside the classroom. Portable sound recorders such as Easi-Speak Microphones www.tts-group.co.uk/shops/tts/Range/Search?search=easi+speak make podcasting 'out in the field' possible. A range of ideas for making podcasts and sources of some ready-made podcasts are presented below:

Ideas for creating podcasts

English: **advertisements** to support a variety of topics, school, national or global **news stories**, sets of **instructions**, book **reviews**, **storytelling**, telling jokes, **debates**.

Maths: monthly **maths problem** that children need to listen to and try to solve.

Science: **scientific findings**, this could involve the results of investigations, seasonal changes, plant and animal life.

History: **interviews** with parents and grandparents as well as members of the community and local historical figures.

Geography: **observations** while on field trips, **sharing information** with partner schools to enhance community links and highlight, for example, geographical and cultural similarities and differences.

PE: **sports commentaries** or **sports report**, of for example a football match between the school and another local school team.

Art: **commentaries** on pieces of art/artwork.

Music: **songs, musical compositions**.

Ready-made educational podcasts
The BBC produces a number of ready-made educational podcasts which are available to download at intervals; they cover a number of curriculum areas and can be accessed at: www.bbc.co.uk/podcasts/genre/learning.

Listen and Play and *Playtime*: Songs, traditional rhymes, stories and movement activities for children from three to five years.

Something to Think About and *Together*: Collective worship/assembly resources for Key Stage 1 children and Key Stage 2 children respectively.

Time To Move and *Let's Move*: Dance resources for children aged five to eight covering popular cross-curricular topics.

The Song Tree and *Music Workshop*: Music resources for children aged five to seven and nine to eleven respectively.

www.bbc.co.uk/podcasts/genre/childrens

CBeebies Radio: Stories for young children.

Aesop's Fables: Forty of Aesop's best-loved fables.

A Christmas Carol: Charles Dickens' classic tale of Ebenezer Scrooge abridged in nine episodes.

Conclusion

In this chapter you have reflected on the role that music plays in your own and children's lives and how meaningful music experiences can be provided in the classroom that include the use of new technologies. You have articulated ways in which a range musical activities and visualisation strategies can promote children's learning in literacy. The processes involved in music remix and how this can be introduced into the classroom have been considered and how this process can help develop children's ICT capability with audio software. Finally, you have found out about what is involved in creating a podcast and the benefits of podcasting in the classroom in terms of literacy development and the wider curriculum.

Further Reading

Ferguson, K. (no date) www.everythingisaremix.info/ (Last accessed 22.3.13)
Knobel, M. and Lankshear, C. (eds) (2010) *DIY Media: Creating, sharing and learning with new technologies*. Oxford: Peter Lang.
Salmon, A. (2010) Using Music to Promote Children's Thinking and Enhance Their Literacy Development. *Early Child Development and Care*, Vol. 180, No. 7, August 2010, 937–45.

Young, S. (2007) Digital Technologies, Young Children, and Music Education
    Practice, in K. Smithrim and R. Upitis, *Listen to Their Voices* (pp. 330–43).
    Waterloo, Ontario: Canadian Music Educators Association. Available at:
    www.academia.edu/352647/Digital_Technologies_Young_Children_and_
    Educational_Practice.

6 Visual literacy
Ian Todd

Chapter Focus

This chapter focuses on visual literacy, defining what it is, assessing its importance in a world dominated by visual media. We invite you to consider whether visual literacy *could* be incorporated into classroom practice, whether it *should be* and, if so, what might be some practical ways of using it to enhance the traditional teaching of literacy.

The critical thinking exercises in this chapter focus on:

- ⊙ **analysing** the skills that can be developed by using visual literacy materials and approaches;
- ⊙ **discussing** the value of using still and moving pictures in the classroom;
- ⊙ **comparing** the ideas described in the case studies with what you have already seen of classroom practice;
- ⊙ **considering** how the use of visual literacy fits in with the current government agenda concerning the teaching of reading.

The key ideas discussed are: **what is visual literacy, why does it matter, visual literacy and reading, visual literacy and writing, visual literacy and speaking and listening.**

This chapter is particularly relevant to the following Teachers' Standards (2012):

Part 1: Teaching

A teacher must:

2 **Promote good progress and outcomes by pupils**
- ⊙ demonstrate knowledge and understanding of how pupils learn and how this impacts on teaching
- ⊙ have a secure knowledge of the relevant subject(s) and curriculum areas, foster and maintain pupils' interest in the subject, and address misunderstandings

/continued

Chapter Focus – continued

3 **Demonstrate good subject and curriculum knowledge**
   ⊙ demonstrate an understanding of and take responsibility for promoting high standards of literacy, articulacy and the correct use of standard English, whatever the teacher's specialist subject
4 **Plan and teach well-structured lessons**
   ⊙ impart knowledge and develop understanding through effective use of lesson time
   ⊙ promote a love of learning and children's intellectual curiosity
   ⊙ contribute to the design and provision of an engaging curriculum within the relevant subject area(s)
5 **Adapt teaching to respond to the strengths and needs of all pupils**
   ⊙ have a clear understanding of the needs of all pupils, including those with special educational needs; those of high ability.

Introduction

This chapter begins with a case study showing the prevalence of images in today's society and how we (and our children) interact with them. It then goes on to discuss ways in which the use of images in the classroom can support the teaching of reading, writing and speaking and listening. The critical thinking exercises explore the value of using pictures and film when teaching Literacy and discuss the possible tensions between the use of visual literacy and more traditional methods of teaching children to read and write.

Key idea: **What is visual literacy and why does it matter?**

We live in a world in which we are surrounded, some might say bombarded, by both still and moving pictures. The visual image dominates our daily lives, reaching into our working days and our children's school routines. Film, photographs, advertisements, television programmes have all become part of our diet of entertainment and information. Stafford (2011: page 1) describes *visual literacy* as the *active process of reading, interpreting and understanding visual media*, i.e. not just allowing that information to 'wash over' us but actively understanding and interacting with it. Why we should want to do this and what relevance it might have to the classroom will be explored further.

CASE STUDY

7.30 a.m. on an overcast July morning. The 'Darth Vader' alarm clocks in the bedrooms of my two children beep loudly. As they crawl out of bed to switch them off (or 'bash them on the head') they glance at the time, which tells them they need to get dressed. They stumble through the lounge and catch the weather forecast on TV – lots of grey cloud symbols and graphics of rain. Although they only see it in passing as they move through to the kitchen, already the conversations about Sports Day and the likelihood of it being cancelled (again) have begun.

As Matt tucks into his breakfast cereal, he looks at the picture of the female Olympic swimmer on the back of the packet. 'Can't wait till we go to the Olympics!' he announces, for the third time that week. 'Yeh, and I can't wait till my swimming day on Friday – it's the last of the year and we're getting the floats out!' says Sam between mouthfuls.

After breakfast, Matt is ready first and snatches some precious time on his Nintendo DS, as everybody else finishes preparing for school/work. As we eventually climb into the car and back off the driveway (in a rush, as ever) the seat belt warning sign flashes and beeps to remind me to 'belt up', accompanied by a chorus of exclamations from both boys on how I am 'breaking the law'. The radio plays the latest song from Adele, a singer popular with virtually everyone except Sam who expresses his usual disappointment with the choice of music ('It's well rubbish'). In an attempt to walk some of the way, we park about half a mile from school and proceed on foot, waiting for the 'Green man' at the pedestrian crossing and playing the 'yellow car' game – a simplistic yet highly addictive exercise which consists of being the first to spot as many cars of that colour as possible. Just before I kiss them goodbye, we notice a picture from the latest *Batman* film on the side of a bus, which leads to the inevitable pleas for a trip to the cinema and the habitual response of 'We'll see'. We all realise, as the boys cross the road that 'We'll see' really means 'Keep plugging away enough and I'll probably give in'.

As I turn to leave them, Sam shouts from across the road, 'Dad, I forgot to do my reading!'

Critical thinking exercise 1

A **Consider** the case study above. **Think** about a typical morning in your life. Make a list of the signs, symbols, still pictures and moving pictures you encounter that
/continued

Critical thinking exercise 1 – continued

contain little or no written text. Does the length of the list surprise you? What does that tell you about how images are used in our daily lives?

B **Analyse** the skills you think my children are using in order to be able to interpret the visual images around them. Are these skills that could be used in the classroom?

C **Discuss** the use of pictures and imagery in the classroom. Do you think they can enhance our traditional print-based approaches to teaching literacy or could they be a hindrance?

Comment

The start of a typical day in my household and not dissimilar, I suspect, from that of thousands of other families with primary school aged children. Before even arriving at school, the children encountered several images and sounds, all of which gave them information, stimulated thought and conversation and provoked emotions in them. But more than this, they were *interacting* with these images, interpreting them, questioning them and using the information for a variety of purposes. The sounds from the alarm clock told them they needed to get up and the time signalled the need to get dressed before breakfast. Although not listening to the weather forecast, the symbols on the weather map immediately informed them of the possibility of rain. This provoked not just an understanding of what the weather would be like that day but led to a grasp of its implications (the traditional cancelling of Sports Day) and this in turn led to feelings of disappointment and frustration. The photograph of the swimmer invoked excitement for both boys, as they made links between an image and future events, while the 'belt up' symbol allowed them to speculate on the various punishments that would befall me for 'breaking the law'. And so the story goes on. The formal school day has not begun and yet the skills of inferring, predicting, persuading, discussing, expressing viewpoints and speculating have all been used.

All of this without a single line of traditional print-based text having been read. It is ironic then that as a parting shot Sam informed that he had not done his reading when, in fact, both he and his brother had been engaging in many higher-order reading skills already, albeit using alternatives to the printed word to elicit these skills.

So, what is visual literacy, why does it matter and how does this link to the morning habits of my family? The term has been variously described as the *ability to construct meanings from visual images* (Giorgis et al., 1999, page 146), the *ability to find meaning in imagery* (Yenawine, 1997, page 1) and the *active process of reading, interpreting and understanding visual media* (Stafford, 2011, page 1). Most authors agree that it is about understanding that which we see and hear and then using that understanding to some benefit. Many talk about actively engaging with sounds and images and, as we shall see later in the chapter, many of the skills that are traditionally associated with reading and writing can, it is claimed, be achieved by using still and moving images as well as print-based media.

But why should any of this matter? It is the recognition that images form an integral part of our lives and the opportunity for using that to our advantage in the classroom that makes it so relevant. Not that images and imagery are at all new. Although the term 'visual literacy' was first used in the 1960s, history is peppered with pictures and symbols that carry meaning. Consider the use of cave paintings and totem poles of the past, all of which signified more than just marks on a wall or carvings in wood or stone. They passed on information, elicited emotional responses, symbolised power and so on. The difference now is the sheer abundance of images and their place in our popular culture and everyday lives. Stafford (2011) does not exaggerate when he talks of being bombarded by images and Goularte (2010) points to the *proliferation of images in our culture making visual literacy a vital skill* (page 2). My own children's experience bears this out. In a little over an hour (and with only a passing glance at the television) they encountered a substantial number of pictures and symbols, all carrying meaning, all producing a response, all requiring interpretation. So it can be argued that there are two distinct reasons for incorporating visual literacy into our teaching.

First, because we *can*. We can take advantage of an abundant resource and use it to develop many of the skills we would hope to see in sophisticated readers. We will see in this chapter how it can complement traditional print-based reading skills but also how it can help to develop the areas of speaking and listening and writing, how it can be taught alongside more formal approaches such as phonics and print-based learning and should not be seen as a threat to that or as damaging in any way. As Hobbs says, media and technology can be allies not enemies (2001, page 3).

Second, because we *must*. The profusion of images in society is not just about art or decoration. They carry messages with them, some obvious, many subtle and hidden, and in preparing our children to be informed, sophisticated, responsible members of a future society, we need to teach them to interpret those messages and make informed decisions based on this; to distinguish between *what is seen with the eye and what is 'seen' with the eye* (Bamford, no date, page 1).

Key idea: **Visual literacy and the teaching of reading**

Many models of teaching reading have been proposed over a number of years but most have the same or similar goals: namely to produce fluent, confident readers who can understand texts at both a literal and 'deeper' level (for instance being able to 'read between the lines' or infer meaning) and who gain pleasure from what they read.

The Independent review of the Teaching of Early Reading carried out by Jim Rose (2006) splits the teaching of reading into two separate processes: language comprehension and word recognition, and this report has been largely credited with the 'push' by successive governments on the teaching of systematic synthetic phonics (SSP) as a way of decoding sounds to read words and encoding them to be able to spell successfully. SSP teaches children what could be described as the 'mechanics' of reading but it is worth noting the role that Rose attaches to the teaching of reading comprehension, describing it as having *equal, and eventually greater, importance* (2006, page 39). He suggests strategies such as *discussing characters, story content and interesting events* (page 39) as ways of improving understanding. Hobbs (2001, page 46) discusses the need to *be able to visualise, making the leap to transform printed symbols to actions, events and ideas* when reading for meaning. This idea of picturing what you read is one which many children find extremely difficult. The programme of study from the National Curriculum for English (2001) says children should be taught to *reflect on the meaning of texts, analysing and discussing them with others* and should be taught to *use inference and deduction, look for meaning beyond the literal and distinguish between fact and opinion and consider an argument critically*. It is hard then to deny the importance of comprehension in reading nor to dispute the level of sophistication expected from a typical reader at the end of their primary years. Put simply, if they haven't understood it they haven't really read it.

So where does visual literacy come into this? Can watching films or looking at pictures possibly help a child's reading? If we focus on the areas of comprehension, analysis and response to a 'text', we will see that it can. One reason for this is that images are so accessible (irrespective of whether children have mastered decoding) and that children from an early age already have significant experience of them. As the British Film Institute points out in their 'Look Again' project, *television and video are among the first cultural experiences of most children in the UK* (2003, page 3). Roberts notes that, *Children are already visually literate before they start school* (2000, no page). So, if children are already 'switched on' to the world of images, then by examining and interpreting what they see, we can begin to explore comprehension at increasingly sophisticated levels without their being encumbered by the printed word. This is not in any way to devalue the role of phonics or book-based literacy, merely to suggest that the use of images and the interrogation of those images alongside more traditional teaching methods can enhance comprehension skills.

CASE STUDY

A Year 4 class are doing a unit of work on persuasive writing and, as part of it, they are exploring the language used in television advertisements. The teacher selects four children's advertisements, all designed to persuade pupils to buy toys. After each advertisement has been watched the children work with a talk

/continued

CASE STUDY – continued

partner and discuss one thing they have remembered about the ad, then report their findings to the whole group. This soon elicits features such as the product itself (which is featured throughout and is usually in a prominent position), the tune or song used (invariably catchy – indeed many children joined in spontaneously while watching), the people involved (always happy, attractive, stylishly dressed, etc.), and the slogan (short, sharp, often rhyming). Occasional features of language (words such as wow, love, only (referring to price)) are also acknowledged. They now watch each a second time and the teacher asks the question 'Why are those features in the ad?' This time when the children do their paired work they have to use the word 'because'. So, 'They use a catchy tune because it sticks in my mind and makes me remember the advert', etc. As they feed back to the whole group the teacher scribes key words (such as 'slogan') and brief reasons why they are used, guiding and extending the children's understanding and challenging some of their thoughts.

Throughout the week, one day is spent on each element of the advertisement that was identified (slogans, use of powerful verbs and adjectives, writing 'stage directions' for the characters in the ads). This in turn leads to a shared writing activity where the class plan a TV ad together and, towards the end of the unit, each group is given the task of trying to sell an item, in the style of a TV advertisement, with the Head teacher judging the most convincing one.

Critical thinking exercise 2

A **Discuss** the benefits of using television advertisements when teaching children about persuasive language. Are there any limitations? Can you suggest any alternative media that could have been used?

B **Analyse** the specific reading skills that are being developed in the above case study.

C Given that Her Majesty's Chief Inspector, Sir Michael Wilshaw has been recently quoted as saying that children should be 'reading novels and poems' to improve their reading skills and comprehension, **discuss** whether the use of television to teach reading is simply frivolous and time wasted.

Comment

The choice of a medium that makes use of song, moving pictures and sometimes cartoons may seem like a strange choice to boost children's reading skills but, when trying to teach pupils to find hidden meanings and subtle, unspoken, unwritten messages, advertising is a great area to explore. Adverts of all descriptions abound with inference, deduction, persuasive language, opinion dressed up as fact, word play and some of the most succinct, clever use of language to be found anywhere. It also has the cultural familiarity described above and the short, snappy nature of the ads makes for a very pacy, fast-moving lesson.

In the example above, the teacher is getting the children to question what they encounter, not to take messages at face value and to actually articulate why something is happening. In pairs, the pupils are deconstructing the meaning of what they have seen at quite a sophisticated level for Year 4. This would have been harder to do with a story or a poem because the level of written language, the maturity of the text and the cultural references may have been too difficult for many of the children to understand. In a sense, the words would have got in the way!

Alternatives might have been the use of posters or advertisements taken out in newspapers or magazines. These would have had the advantage of having to rely more on language, since moving pictures and sounds would obviously not have been an option and it could be argued that greater use of powerful verbs and strong adjectives would have aided future writing exercises for the children. However, although this unit of work does culminate in writing (indeed it includes writing throughout), the benefits of this particular session are in those higher-order reading skills. Think of it as a 'training exercise' for looking for hidden meanings in harder written texts, since the skills required would be the same. Here they can be practised in a more accessible way.

So, is it frivolous? It is certainly fun and none of the children involved really thought they were doing 'proper work'. Too much of it at the expense of print-based texts would certainly be a mistake and could be counter-productive, in that what they gained in comprehension skills they might be losing in terms of word recognition and experience of literature but as an alternative to books, with very clear learning objectives in mind and careful planning by the class teacher, it works very well.

Key idea: **Visual literacy and writing**

> The teaching and learning of writing can be seen as having two distinct, separate yet linked, elements, namely composition and transcription.

The importance of the composition stage of writing has been reflected in the structure of the Primary National Strategy for English (2006) which divides the teaching of Literacy into units of work, each lasting a few weeks, depending on the genre and the age of the children. The units have an increased focus on composing ideas within a given genre, building throughout the unit to the final transcription stage.

So how then can visual literacy aid in the teaching of writing? Well, first there is the motivational factor. It is fun! as Stafford says (2011, page 3). For many children, especially boys, writing is a daunting, off-putting process, which appears to have neither relevance nor interest. It is no secret that the gap between girls' and boys' writing attainment is wide and has not really narrowed in a decade. Could it be that many children, boys most especially, are put off by traditional, print-based approaches to teaching writing? Successive studies (by the Primary National Strategy, British Film Institute and a great many local education authorities among others) have pointed to the huge motivational benefits of using film, pictures or other visual prompts when teaching writing. Combined with the familiarity and perceived relevance to children's daily lives of visual imagery (as discussed earlier in this chapter) this could be seen as a good starting point to developing children as writers. As Hobbs (2001) points out, using technology helps to connect the classroom to the living room.

But is this enough? Does simply making things more fun actually help with the writing process? Just because children are enjoying themselves, are they actually learning anything? Stafford warns against using visual imagery as *simply a trendy attempt to make the curriculum entertaining* (2011, page 2). If motivation and enjoyment are not in themselves enough to produce confident, expressive writers, it is perhaps worth considering them as a key that opens a door to young writers that was previously locked. Once that door is open, and children choose to enter a world of writing, what specific benefits can visual literacy bring?

Focusing primarily on the tricky area of composition, the gathering, organising and processing of ideas, the British Film Institute in their 'Look Again' project (2003), asserts that film can extend vocabulary, help in re-telling stories, sequencing and the identification of characters for younger children. This can be developed for older children by aiding them to identify and improve narrative structure, openings, settings of stories and character profiles, areas also highlighted by Roberts (2000). Stafford (2011) points to the use of comic books to aid sequencing skills and even as an aid to teaching direct and indirect speech when considering transcription. Indeed, several authors and studies point to the power of visual literacy to help in the development of plot structure, characterisation and setting.

CASE STUDY

A Year 1 teacher does a shared 'reading' session with her class. The difference is that, having shown them the title and front cover, all the words inside are covered up so that only the pictures are showing. As she proceeds through the book she invites the children to say what is happening, what they think will happen next, what the characters are saying, thinking and feeling and where it is set. She encourages them to use clues from the pictures, such as facial expression and constantly asks them questions such as 'How do you know?' and 'Why do you say that?' Sometimes the children answer by putting up their hands, sometimes they discuss as a pair, using talk partners and sometimes they write key words on their whiteboards. The teacher's focus is on using the

/continued

CASE STUDY – continued

pictures to get the children to discuss, generate ideas and understand the basics of plot and characterisation.

The above activity leads on to group work where the higher ability are given copies of the pictures from the book and they write their own words to the story. This is an independent activity. The middle ability group (working with a teaching assistant) are given the pictures but they have been shuffled out of order. They re-order them as a group and then do a guided writing activity with the class teacher, composing sentences to accompany the pictures. The lower ability group also have the pictures shuffled but have a series of sentence starters such as 'First of all', 'Next', 'Then', 'Finally'. They work with the teaching assistant to re-order the pictures and begin to compose possible sentences to describe what is happening. The plenary brings together the children's efforts then compares them with the original.

A Year 4 class are working on settings. The class teacher shows them a picture of Rivendell, from *The Lord of the Rings*, and leads the discussion, asking questions such as 'What can you see?', 'What can you hear?', 'What might you smell?', 'How might you feel if you were there?' The children use a combination of talk partners and small groups to respond and to brainstorm key adjectives and descriptive phrases to describe what they see. This leads to a shared writing activity where the teacher models the language and phrasing that could be used to write a setting.

In groups, the children are then given a different picture. The higher ability group write their own setting independently. The middle ability work in pairs, using the key words and phrases brainstormed earlier as prompts, to produce a setting as a joint piece. The lowest ability do a guided writing activity with the class teacher, creating a setting between them.

Critical thinking exercise 3

A **Consider** the use of pictures in the above case studies. Does the absence of words help or hinder the children in the development of their writing skills?

B **Analyse** the value of talk/discussion in the above examples. What could be its value in teaching writing?

C **Compare** the above examples with any teaching of writing you have seen in school. What are the main differences?

Comment

The use of the 'picture book' for Key Stage 1 and the pictures for Key Stage 2 both served as motivating forces. While sharing a 'big book' with a Year 1 class was by no means unusual, the lack of words provided something of a 'twist' on the normal routine, gaining everybody's attention immediately. The Year 4 class were convinced that they were not 'doing Literacy' and again motivation was high. It was noticeable just how much more animated, confident and involved the least able children were. Clearly, they were completely at home with the visual media and, as there were no words, there was no barrier to their involvement. And yet, how can a book without words possibly lead to children producing words of their own? Key to this (aside from the enthusiasm and motivation) was the skill of the teacher in directing the discussion around the areas of characterisation and plot structure. The lack of words here actually forced the children to come up with answers of their own regarding what had happened and might happen next and also around what the characters were saying and feeling. Undoubtedly, reaching their own conclusions (albeit skilfully guided towards this by the class teacher) gave them ownership of the story and will have allowed them to internalise the key features rather better than if it had just been presented to them. By following this up with either writing, or pre-writing, activities the teacher is making the link between pictures, the spoken word and the written word. In this sense, the lack of words, if guided and manipulated by a skilled adult, can actively help the writing process.

Similarly, with the Year 4 activity, the discussion was open-ended enough for children of all abilities to contribute at their level and yet structured enough to direct them towards the vocabulary and stylistic conventions of writing a story setting. It also gave those children (many of them boys) with limited reading experience ready-made ideas of what a setting could look like. For many children, 'imagining what it could look like' is a major struggle, both because they have not read widely enough (or been read to) to have a built-in store of different settings, but also because they have not yet mastered what Hobbs calls the link between *printed symbols…and ideas that are clearly written in the mind's eye* (2001, no page). By using the picture as a starting point, then carefully organising the discussion and follow-up activities, the link between pictures, ideas and words is made more explicit.

Central to both activities in the case study is the use of talk. Virtually all of the major studies on improving writing in the last decade focus on the central role of discussion, both child-child and child-teacher. The government document *Talk for Writing* (DfE, 2008) *refers to the developmental exploration, through talk, of the thinking and creative processes involved in being a writer.* It also points to the value of *creating new 'stories' orally as a preparation and rehearsal for writing.* This concept of 'oral rehearsal', giving children the opportunity to articulate their ideas and language verbally before committing anything to paper is said to be especially valuable for those children (again, often boys) who are reluctant to write ideas down for fear of 'looking silly' or 'getting it wrong'.

The use of imagery (whether still or moving) lends itself very well to discussion. Partly this is because of its accessibility to all (even very young children), partly due to the motivational factors described above (children will want to discuss something that grabs their attention!) and partly because not having words already there does not constrain or limit any ideas the children may already have. As stated already, of course, simply showing children a film or a picture and letting them have a chat about it, will not turn them into sophisticated writers. The skill of the teacher in selecting the appropriate image, directing the discussion and then creating activities that will lead to actually 'putting pen to paper' cannot be under-estimated.

Key idea: **Visual literacy and speaking and listening**

> The role of speaking and listening in teaching and learning can perhaps be considered in two ways: its value in allowing other parts of the curriculum to be learned more effectively and its value per se, i.e. the goal of producing children who are articulate speakers and careful listeners.

OFSTED, in their report on *Excellence in English* (2011), attested that good quality oral work benefited reading and writing, a sentiment echoed by Rose in his Independent Review of the Primary Curriculum (2009). Indeed, the work of Vygotsky (1978) on the Zone of Proximal Development highlighted how children gradually become more independent learners as teacher input decreases and their confidence and knowledge grow. Many authors have pointed to the role of talk, including paired discussion, in not only affording this greater independence but in allowing children to formulate their own ideas to achieve it.

So, speaking and listening (and talk in particular) can benefit reading, writing and the ability of children to learn independently. But is it just a means to an end or does it have value in its own right? The DFES, in its *Improving Speaking and Listening Skills* document (2007) talks of spoken language being *at the heart of... human interaction, at home, at work and in society* (page 2) and goes on to outline its benefits in terms of employability and sociability. Consider, on a daily basis, the number of spoken interactions you have with friends, family and colleagues. Even in the world of email, Twitter, text and Facebook, conversation still occupies a significant amount of time. Within the classroom, however, talk between pupils can be seen as wasted time, distracting children from the 'serious' task of writing and teacher-pupil talk can often be a one-way process, with the teacher dominating the dialogue and asking a series of closed questions, eliciting brief, even one-word, answers.

If, then, speaking and listening skills are central to our everyday lives and crucial to future employability, can visual literacy help to increase the opportunities for its inclusion and improve the quality of how it is taught?

CASE STUDY

A Year 6 class are studying a unit of work on journalism and are focusing on the language used in broadcast journalism, specifically news programmes. Their teacher splits them into groups and each group watches a series of short clips from news broadcasts varying in style, language, content and delivery. One group focuses on BBC bulletins, another on the children's *Newsround* programme, another watches footage from CNN, one concentrates on Channel 4 news and the final group look at the '90 second' broadcasts from Channel 5. As well as looking for the so-called '5 ws' of journalism – 'who, what, where, why and when' and how they are represented, the groups are also noting down examples of vocabulary used, length of reports, subjects reported on, tone of voice used, in addition to some technical issues such as close-ups, wide shots, etc. As the groups watch the clips, each member has something different to watch for. After watching the clips, the groups meet and share their ideas. Each group member reports back on what they have been watching. The groups then prepare a short verbal presentation for the other groups, summarising their findings.

Following on from the above, each group writes their own news report in the style of footage they have been watching and then films it using Windows Movie Maker. The films are edited and shown to the rest of the class at the end of the unit.

Critical thinking exercise 4

A **Analyse** the type of talk that takes place in the classroom. How much of it is teacher-pupil, pupil-teacher, pupil-pupil? Do all children have the opportunity to contribute? How many have the chance to say more than a few words?

B From the case study above, **discuss** what opportunities for speaking and listening have been created using visual literacy.

C **Consider** your own views on speaking and listening. Should it be central to the learning process and valuable as an educational goal in its own right? If so, can visual literacy really help this when we constantly hear and read that television is killing the art of conversation?

Comment

The above case study not only involves children being shown examples of visual literacy but has them actually producing an example of this (i.e. a film) themselves. The opportunities for discussion afforded by watching the news clips can be categorised as **exploratory** (Barnes, 1992), **reflective** and **evaluative**. They are thinking aloud, gathering and sharing ideas and reflecting on the types of language, expression and news stories used. They are evaluating the types of message being presented and explaining their decisions to others. Because the discussions that follow the news clips are child-led, there are no teacher-dominated, closed questions and the observation of this part of the lesson showed a much increased level of participation for all. This was no doubt helped by the fact that every child had a specific role and that they were working in small groups, giving more opportunities for each to contribute. Listening skills were vital and central to the exercise. The children had first of all to listen to the broadcasts as they had to report to others on specific elements of it. Compare this purposeful, active listening to some of the passive listening (or no listening at all) that may take place during a traditional shared reading session. Listening also formed part of the preparation of the verbal presentation to the other groups, though this was perhaps the most challenging time, given the inevitability of some children being more dominant than others. While the activities were child-led, they were however teacher-facilitated. The role of the adults was to ensure that nobody dominated and everybody had a chance to contribute.

In terms of the verbal presentation to other groups and then making and showing the final film, the focus was on so-called **presentational talk** (Barnes, 1992). The children identified the differences in language between how they would talk to each other in a group, or on the playground, and how they would present to an audience. Changes in speed, diction and formality of language were all identified and used. The fact of being presented to by their peers had a major effect on listening skills, with greater concentration noted than for an 'ordinary' plenary.

Not only, then, did the use of visual literacy help children to gather ideas for their news broadcasts and give them the opportunity to discuss, plan and orally rehearse the scripts they would use for the finished product, it also gave numerous opportunities to develop speaking and listening skills in their own right. So how does this sit with the notion that 'Television is destroying the art of conversation'? The answer to this is possibly that it depends how it is used and how much it is used. Short clips mean that children were not staring at the screen for long periods and the fact that they had specific features to look for made the whole experience far more active and engaging than just watching a film at home. The follow-up activities were also crucial, in that a great many opportunities for discussion were identified and planned for. So yes, TV is compatible with conversation but yet again the skill of the teacher in finding the 'right TV' and using it as a vehicle for further discussion rather than as an end in its own right made the difference between a worthwhile learning opportunity and just a pleasant viewing experience.

Conclusion

In this chapter you have explored the powerful place that images hold in society and how children are exposed to them on a daily basis. You have considered how we can harness the power of films and pictures both to motivate and excite children but also to make learning more relevant and meaningful to them. You have discussed the role that visual literacy can have in developing higher-order reading skills and in helping pupils compose and develop ideas for writing. You have analysed the strong link between imagery and speaking and listening and the profound effect that talk can have on many aspects of learning. Finally, you have evaluated the place of visual literacy in the current educational climate, alongside more traditional methods of teaching Literacy.

Further Reading

Barnes, D. (1992) The Role of Talk in Learning, in K. Norman, *Thinking Voices: The Work of the National Oracy Project.* London: Hodder and Stoughton.

BFI (2010) *Using Film in Schools – A Practical Guide.* Available at: http://industry.bfi.org.uk/media/pdf/g/h/Using_Film_in_Schools_-_A_Practical_Guide-Dec2010.pdf. (Accessed 15 August 2012).

DFE (2008) *Talk for Writing.* Available at: http://education.gov.uk/publications. (Accessed 15 August 2012).

Goularte, R. (2010) *Visual Literacy and Descriptive Writing.* Available at: http://share2learn.com/cabe2010workshop.pdf. (Accessed 1 August 2012).

Hobbs, R. (2001) *Improving Reading Comprehension by Using Media Literacy Activities.* Available at: http://teachwithvisionml.files.wordpress.com/2009/04/medialit.readl.pdf. (Accessed 3 August 2012).

Stafford, T. (2011) *Teaching Visual Literacy in the Primary Classroom* (1st edition). Oxon: David Fulton.

Yenawine, P. (1997) *Thoughts on Visual Literacy.* Available at: http://vtshome.org/system/resources/0000/0005/Thoughts_Visual_Literacy.pdf. (Accessed 1 August 2012).

7

Lost in cyberspace? Children and social media

Jayne Metcalfe and Debbie Simpson

Chapter Focus

This chapter takes as its starting point the enthusiasm of many children outside of school hours for online social networking and online social gaming. The theoretical background to children's development of language, literacy and communicative practices through engagement in social media is considered, and it is suggested that this is wider and richer than is generally acknowledged in school.

The critical thinking exercises in this chapter focus on:

- ⊙ **exploring** the attitudes of yourself and others to technology;
- ⊙ **analysing** your experiences of technology in schools;
- ⊙ **considering** issues of social networking for the perspectives of teachers and schools;
- ⊙ **reflecting** on online identities; exploring the educational potential of online games.

The key ideas discussed in this chapter are:
social networking, gaming, identity, embedded values, e-safety, managing disclosure and **privacy**.

This chapter is particularly relevant to the following Teachers' Standards (2012):

Part 1: Teaching

A teacher must:

1 **Set high expectations which inspire, motivate and challenge pupils**
   - ⊙ establish a safe and stimulating environment for pupils, rooted in mutual respect
   - ⊙ demonstrate consistently the positive attitudes, values and behaviour which are expected of pupils
2 **Promote good progress and outcomes by pupils**
   - ⊙ encourage pupils to take a responsible and conscientious attitude to their own work and study

/continued

Chapter Focus – continued

4 **Plan and teach well-structured lessons**
- ◉ promote a love of learning and children's intellectual curiosity
- ◉ set homework and plan other out-of-class activities to consolidate and extend the knowledge and understanding pupils have acquired

Part 2: Personal and Professional Conduct

1 **Teachers uphold public trust in the profession and maintain high standards of ethics and behaviour, within and outside school by**
- ◉ having regard for the need to safeguard pupils' well-being, in accordance with statutory provisions.

Introduction

As you have seen throughout this book a guiding principle of new literacies theorists is to examine the widening gap between the literacy practices valued in schools and those that are engaged with by children in their everyday lives. The chapter seeks to raise your awareness of the educational potential of the new literacy practices of social media, gaming and virtual worlds, while acknowledging that teachers have a responsibility to guide children in making safe choices in their use of technology. Teachers are sometimes disappointed when they introduce a new technology that they believe will be popular with children, such as computer gaming or blogging; only to find that children are unenthusiastic about the approach. The chapter therefore looks at what social practices underpin the appeal of particular online tools and suggests that simply grafting technology on to an existing lesson is almost always going to lead to a disappointing experience for both teachers and pupils.

CASE STUDY

NeverSeconds blog

In April 2012 nine-year-old Martha was helped by her father to set up a writing project on her blog. Martha's blog 'NeverSeconds' was an illustrated commentary documenting the lunches on offer at her primary school. With permission from her school, Martha photographed or drew a picture of each meal and rated it against various criteria: taste; the number of mouthfuls it took to complete; the type of course offered; a health rating; price; and, jokingly, the number of hairs in each meal.

/continued

CASE STUDY – continued

In May 2012 Martha's father used Twitter to publicise his daughter's blog:

> My primary school daughter is blogging her £2 school lunch experiences.
> I'm speechless http://neverseconds.blogspot.co.uk Please comment.

Celebrity chef Jamie Oliver re-tweeted the link, drawing the attention of his thousands of followers to Martha's blog, and the resulting publicity reopened the debate about the price and quality of school meals.

In June 2012 Martha invited her readers to support *Mary's Meals*, a charity dedicated to help provide meals in underprivileged schools in Malawi, Liberia, Kenya and Haiti. Martha explained:

> There was a comment on my blog that I am lucky to have any lunch as
> some children get none so I started to raise money for Mary's Meals.

By mid-June Martha had raised more than £45,000, far in excess of her £7000 target, but not everyone was happy with her blog. On the morning of 14 June 2012, following a newspaper story about the blog entitled 'Time to Fire the Dinner Ladies', Martha was told that her local council had decided she would not be permitted to take any more photos of her lunches. In response to the ban, Twitter users began sharing photos of their own lunches with the hashtags #neverseconds and #MyLunchForMartha to show their solidarity. Following extensive media coverage, the blog registered three hits per second and almost 1500 supportive comments were left by its visitors. The council retracted the photo ban on Martha the following day. They also announced a School Meals Summit bringing together catering staff, students and council officials to revaluate school meals.

During her school vacation in summer 2012, Martha headed to Malawi to see one of the new school kitchens paid for by Mary's Meals from the more than £100,000 of donations by readers of Martha's blog. The blog has had almost nine million hits and children from all over the world now use it to share images and comments about their own lunches.

Educationalist Ewan McIntosh showcased *NeverSeconds* on his own blog edu.blogs.com and commented,

> *Martha shows every facet of great learning: real world change,
> making the environment around her better, sharing her thinking
> with the world, having a conscious for the world beyond her
> immediate horizons, and robustness in the face of incredible
> media and social media pressure…She'll go far.*

Comment

This case study illustrates that primary-aged children can and increasingly do engage with social media, which in this chapter is defined as any web-based technology that allows shared activities and dialogue among a network of individuals. Sometimes, children's online activities can have a significant impact on their lives and the lives of others. The technical barriers to engaging with social media are falling, just as children's opportunities for unsupervised access to the internet are increasing. Evidence suggests that the use of social media is firmly embedded in children's everyday lives. Just over a third (38 per cent) of British children aged 9 to 12 have a profile on a social networking site, and 44 per cent of boys and 29 per cent of girls have played games with other people on the internet. Indeed 57 per cent of 9–12 year olds who access the internet do so using a games console (EU Kids Online, 2011).

For Martha, her blog readers and the children who have benefitted from the Mary's Meals charity the impact seems to have been overwhelmingly positive; and this has been reported widely in the mass media. However, newspaper and TV stories more commonly focus on the threats and dangers to children posed by social media; scary headlines such as 'Facebook puts vulnerable children at risk of depression, warn doctors'; or 'Children, some aged five, commit thousands of child sex offences' [following internet use] are a regular feature of newspapers.

Before considering the benefits and threats of social media, however, it is worthwhile recapping the types of technology that we are discussing in this chapter.

Children and social media

Types of social media fall into several different categories, although the boundaries between some of them can be blurred. The examples below regularly top the polls of most popular online destinations for children; although if you talk to the children in your class you may discover new favourites.

Blogs, like Martha's are arguably the most 'personal' spaces as they tend to have one authorial voice and bloggers typically post fairly substantial texts, sometimes accompanied by media and hyperlinks to other websites of interest. Blog readers are free to comment on and post feedback publicly to the blog author. Schools have adopted blogs with more enthusiasm than most other forms of social network, and many individual teachers host blogs for their pupils to share their work with a wide audience. One lively example, from a Blackpool school, can be found at http://stainingprimary.net/

Social Networks such as Facebook, Bebo and MySpace also provide personal pages, but their function is more overtly social than blogging. Users post messages and share media and web links with a chosen social circle of friends. Facebook is the best-known of the social networking sites and despite its minimum signup age of 13 there is evidence to show that increasing numbers of primary-aged children have a Facebook account.

Virtual Worlds such as Club Penguin, Habbo Hotel and MiniMonos are online spaces where children can explore, play games and socialise with other children. The best examples allow children to have an impact on the virtual environment through interaction: expressing their creativity and individuality by customising personal areas of their world. The companies hosting the sites seek to reassure parents by offering a range of safety features such as protection of children's personal data, moderation of user chat, and parental control of settings. Although such sites are initially free to use, payment is usually required for access to special features. Neopets, Moshi Monsters and Stardolls operate a similar model, although on these sites children focus on 'adopting' and nurturing virtual pets or dolls, decorating and showing these off to online friends. Again this is free to begin with, but special items need to be purchased.

Massive Multi-player Online Role Playing Game (MMORPG) communities such as Runescape, Free Realms and Chamber of Chat are similar to Virtual Worlds in that they have a recognisable environment and characters; however, the element of game play is emphasised. This is usually of the fantasy/adventure/role-playing genre. Players create a character and explore the game landscape. There is generally no set path for the game or specific ending, and the player is free go to any location in the game and engage in a variety of activities. Players can chat together and choose whether to cooperate or compete with each other.

Social media are, whether we like it or not, an established part of the landscape in the lives of many primary-aged children. As we will see, some experts believe that skills and competencies developed through engagement with social media can contribute to children's repertoire of literacy, and that these skills and competencies should be recognised as part of the 'tool kit' that children bring with them into school. This chapter considers the argument that too frequently children are required to leave these literacies at the school gate. It suggests instead that teachers should acknowledge that many children are beginning to develop online identities and rise to the challenge of preparing them for a lifelong engagement with technology.

In the next section of this chapter you will examine society's attitudes to children's use of social media and begin to analyse and articulate your own point of view. The following sections go on to look in more detail at three specific areas of social media: Social Networking, Virtual Worlds and Gaming Communities, and consider the educational potential of these tools in the context of New Literacy studies.

> At intervals e-safety guidance will be featured in safety boxes like this one, to help you design safe clasroom activities. They will also highlight opportunities for you to raise children's awareness of risky online behaviour and teach them strategies to deal with threats.

Key idea: **Inhabiting social spaces**

> **Is there a 'digital divide' between adult's and children's use of social media?**
>
> One perception frequently expressed by teachers struggling to embed the use of technology in their classrooms, is that their pupils know more than they do about computers and the internet. Some teachers fear losing control of a class if pupils are (at least superficially) more confident and digitally literate than they themselves, and they speak of feeling 'deskilled'.

The American writer and speaker on technology and education, Marc Prensky, suggested in 2001 that a gap was opening up between so-called *digital natives and digital immigrants*. He claimed that most teachers were 'digital immigrants': having encountered digital technology for the first time during adulthood they could never become really fluent in its use. Digital immigrants, like adult learners of a new language, always retain an 'accent' and are rarely mistaken for a native speaker. They are never fully comfortable or fluent with technology. 'Digital natives', on the other hand, have grown up around digital technology and are comfortable with using it in all aspects of their lives. Prensky's belief is that most teachers are digital immigrants and most pupils are digital natives, and consequently, *digital Immigrant instructors, who speak an outdated language (that of the pre-digital age), are struggling to teach a population that speaks an entirely new language* (Prensky, 2001, page 2).

According to Prensky, digital natives converse 24/7 with their contacts via text messaging and social networks, and thrive on instant gratification and frequent rewards. They prefer games to 'serious' work and find information presented graphically easier to understand than text. For them hypertext feels more natural than linear 'book' text. They multi-task easily: listening to music, chatting to friends or watching TV as they study. This behaviour is incomprehensible to the so-called *'digital immigrants'* who still make up the majority of the teaching workforce.

 Digital Immigrant [teachers] don't believe their students can learn successfully while watching TV or listening to music, because they (the Immigrants) can't. Of course not – they didn't practise this skill constantly for all of their formative years. Digital Immigrants think learning can't (or shouldn't) be fun. Why should they – they didn't spend their formative years learning with Sesame Street.

Prensky, 2001, page 3

Critical thinking exercise 1: exploring attitudes to technology

Think about four people whom you know well. If possible choose two born before and two born after 1982 (this year is considered to be a significant dividing date between digital natives and immigrants).

A **Consider** *which side of the chart below best describes each individual's attitudes to digital technology. If possible show them the chart to find out whether they agree with your assumptions about them. Are their responses as you predicted?*

Digital Natives	Digital Immigrants
Prefer receiving information quickly from multiple media sources	Prefer slow and controlled release of information from reliable sources
Prefer parallel processing (e.g. studying while listening to music) and multi-tasking	Prefer single processing and concentrating on one task at a time
Prefer processing images, video and pictures to reading text	Prefer to read or provide text information before pictures video or sounds
Prefer exploring multimedia information randomly, following hyperlinks	Prefer to tackle information linearly, logically and in sequence
Prefer to interact and network with others, often several people simultaneously	Prefer to work independently rather than network
Prefer 'just in time' learning – finding information when they need it from the most convenient source	Prefer to learn skills and accumulate knowledge ahead of time 'just in case'
Prefer instant gratification and rewards	Are comfortable with deferred gratification and deferred rewards
Prefer learning that is relevant, instantly useful and fun	Prefer learning according to a set programme for defined goals and assessments

Adapted from a table compiled by Jukes and Dosaj (2003): Source http://edorigami.wikispaces.com/

B **Analyse** your own experience of digital technology in schools. To what extent do you think that Prensky's classification is a true reflection of the attitudes of teachers and pupils you know?

C **List** the points you would make if you were arguing *against* Prensky's classification.

Comment

Critics of Prensky's classification consider it overly simplistic; ignoring the broader knowledge, experience and understanding that so-called digital immigrants may have about digital technologies and their potential value to society. While young people may be superficially confident and competent with technology they lack the maturity to use it effectively and efficiently. A division based entirely on age ignores the role of culture, personal interests and socio-economic factors that influence people's access to technology and the ways they use it.

Connaway *et al.* (2011) put forward an alternative vision of the online world as a place where people can live, or just visit for a while. People who create and maintain a persistent online presence, such as a Facebook profile or a blog, or belong to multiple communities online might be described as 'residents'. Those who call in with a specific object in mind, and are cautious about leaving too many online traces, are described as 'visitors'. Run through the critical thinking exercises above once more, this time using the Visitors and Residents table below.

Visitors	Residents
See technology as a tool to achieve defined goals or tasks	See the Web as a social place to meet friends and share information about their life and work
Prefer to be anonymous. Avoid having a persistent profile online and projecting their identity online	Many aspects of their persona persist online: status updates, shared media, blog posts and blog comments
Worry about privacy and fear identity theft	Consider that they 'belong' to a community which is located in the virtual. Happy to share opinions and data online
Consider that online social networking activities are banal and egotistical	Happy to go online to 'hang out' and form and extend relationships
Happy to use email or Skype to maintain relationships but share only minimal information on their Facebook profile	Maintain and develop a digital identity, i.e. through profiles in social networking platforms such as Facebook or Twitter
Dislike 'non-referenced' or non-expert opinion. Avoid 'crowd sourced' material such as Wikipedia	Collective authorship is not a concern, what matters is how relevant the information is to their particular needs
Do their thinking off-line	Distinction between online and off-line is increasingly blurred
Users, not members, of the Web placing little value in belonging online	Value online is seen in terms of relationships as well as knowledge. The Web is a network of individuals or clusters of individuals who generate content

Table derived from Connaway *et al.* (2011), *Visitors and residents: What motivates engagement with the digital information environment?*

The ideas of both Prensky and Connaway *et al.* may strike a chord with you, even if you don't accept all of their arguments, because of a widely held sense that there are two kinds of people: those who feel at home online and turn to digital technologies naturally as a source of ideas, information, social contact, services and entertainment, and those who are more comfortable seeking resources and human contact in the offline world. We may see this divide as generational, or we may feel that there are more complex factors in play. For teachers, however, the key question is whether there is a 'digital divide' between themselves and their pupils and, if so, whether this has a negative impact on children's learning. Many commentators assume that teachers fall into the visitors/immigrants camp and children are natives/residents. Your own experience might confirm or contradict this. What it is important to recognise is that networked technology has fundamentally changed the way that most people in the West lead their lives. Schools and teachers have a responsibility to think through the implications of these changes for their pupils.

Teachers need to talk, and listen, to children about how they use digital technologies in their everyday lives. Even if the generation gap between you and your pupils is still relatively small you may be surprised at the difference in culture. And, in the natural way of things, the age gap between you and your pupils will inevitably increase, so staying in touch with how children see the world is a good habit to nourish. Crucially also, you will bring a depth of maturity and experience to your conversations with children about their online experiences. Teachers have a responsibility for safeguarding and guiding children in online as well as offline worlds. Closing our eyes to the reality of children's experience because it doesn't fit with our preconceptions of what childhood or education is or should be, is always unhelpful.

The next section explores children's use of social networking and considers how it can help to shape their ideas about identify and interaction with others.

Key idea: **Social networking**

A key feature of social networking sites is the opportunity for users to project their personas online through creating profiles using text, image and video. Creating a social networking profile has been compared to creating a 'digital body' where children and teenagers can *write themselves into being* (Boyd, 2007).

While creating a profile can provide opportunities for children to express different aspects of their personality and experiment with different styles of presentation, there is often pressure on them to conform to stereotypes in order to belong to a social group. A child's social network usually consists largely of peers who they also know offline so their profile needs to remain rooted in reality: it cannot be entirely imaginary or based on fantasy. However, the aim of social networking is usually to gain and maintain attention from as many 'friends' as possible, so profile creation demands a level of 'publicity management' skills. Children may present the side of themselves that they believe will be well received by their peers or at least provoke a response. They may also try to provoke a response from you. By looking at their friends' profiles, children also get a sense of what types of presentations are socially appropriate and gain critical cues about what to present on their own profile. Additionally, children who are less confident in face-to-face situations have the time and space online to manage encounters. Children interviewed in one survey commented that they enjoyed social networking because it allows them time to think about what they want to say and how they want to represent themselves (Valentine and Holloway, 2002).

Considering some of the aspects of creating a profile outlined in the paragraph above it becomes evident that children are engaging in a quite complex set of literacy practices. Through trial and error and observation they learn how to present themselves in the online domain and discover what kinds of comments are appropriate. Experience of social networking has been shown to have a positive link with children's enjoyment of writing. A survey of 3001 pupils aged 8–16 from the UK (Clark and Dugdale, 2009) found that children who blogged or had a profile on a social networking site displayed greater overall confidence when writing. They were more prolific writers than their non-blogging or networking peers, held more positive attitudes towards writing and computer use, and viewed writers as role models.

Thinking through how we can divert some of the literacy benefits of social networking into classrooms, while safeguarding and educating children to manage risk appropriately, is a challenging task. Additionally, because some teachers asssume that children will not engage with social networking until they are beyond primary age, their safe use is typically not covered in e-safety lessons. However, children *are* using networking sites before they reach secondary school age, and research conducted by Passey (2011) shows that many of these children either feel unsafe or feel they are giving too much information when they do so. Added to this, Facebook has recently announced that it will be rolling out a site for the under-13s in the near future so children's engagement seems set to grow.

One approach teachers might take to open up the topic of social networking in their classroom is through setting up a 'profiling consultancy' where children can advise a selection of 'clients' on their network profiles. The clients might be book or film characters, sporting or TV stars or anyone the children suggest. It can be more challenging (and interesting) to create a striking online profile for someone who is not entirely good and lovable: for Draco Malfoy rather than for Harry Potter for example, or whatever baddies are popular with your class. This activity can link with work on characterisation and point of view in fiction.

E-safety guidance

The above activity provides opportunities to discuss e-safety aspects of profiles such as privacy and appropriate disclosure.

Critical thinking exercise 2: How much disclosure is too much in social networking?

Read the following extracts from a study of Australian children's use of MySpace social network.

Extract 1

It is of concern that a number of children are disclosing very personal information, such as physical address and telephone number, on their MySpace websites. It is important to remember that many of these children may have their sites set to 'friends only' and that the percentages are not high (12%), but given the very high number of users…it may mean that a significant number could be considered 'at risk'. There is some evidence in this study (and a lot [of] anecdotal evidence) of instances of bullying and misbehaviour having occurred using MySpace where schools have already been forced to take action. Children are accessing the websites not only outside school hours but also during classroom time, despite efforts to restrict website access and activities. The authors believe that children see the medium as transcending physical boundaries, meaning that teachers and parents will need to work together to ensure appropriate behaviour.

Extract 2

[T]he vast majority of children using social networking sites are acting responsibly and behaving in a similar way to how they would conduct themselves when meeting or making new friends at school, on public transport or in their local shopping centre. Those who value privacy in their personal lives are less likely (than those that don't) to give out personal details to strangers or to befriend people with whom they have little or no connection…there is a small percentage of children who might be considered at risk – and given the large numbers of users involved, could represent a serious problem for society. It seems the answer will not be in banning or forbidding use of the technology but for parents (and teachers?) to take an active interest in what the children are doing and to familiarise themselves with this new communications medium. Given the relationship between (1) age and information disclosure and (2) the value attributed to privacy and information disclosure it would appear that as children develop and become more aware of the risks involved and how important privacy is the more they exhibit more responsible behaviour. Therefore, the quicker they reach this level of awareness, the more able they are to embrace the technology with less risk. Proactive education is key.

From De Souza, Z. and Dick, G. (2008, pages 155–6)

/continued

Critical thinking exercise 2 – continued

The authors find that roughly one child in eight is disclosing personal information online that may put them at risk; however, this disclosure decreases as children learn to value their privacy. Given these findings, consider your responses to the following questions:

- What should the role of primary schools be in helping children to develop and protect their online identities?
- If you were tasked with writing a set of guidelines for children about using social networking, what would you include?
- What do you consider to be the implications for a teacher of maintaining a social networking profile?
- What measures have you taken to actively manage your own online identity?

Comment

In our day-to-day lives we feel entitled to privacy. For example, if a newspaper published pictures of you without your consent, you might feel that your privacy had been violated. While there is no specific Law of Privacy in the United Kingdom (UK), you may be able to sue the newspaper for damages under European Union (EU) privacy law. However, unless you are a celebrity, or royalty, you are much more likely to find unauthorised photographs of yourself online than on the front of a newspaper. Images of you can be uploaded with or without your consent to social networking sites, and 'tagged' with your name. They can be copied and potentially be made available to anyone who types your name into a search engine, for example a prospective employer, a pupil or the parent of a pupil. The phenomenon of online information 'going viral' will be very familiar to you if you have heard of 'cat bin lady' or 'Fenton the dog'. If you haven't, then an internet search for these terms will demonstrate just how quickly and how far digital information can spread without the permission of the people involved.

Recently there have been proposals for the law to be strengthened and clarified in light of the new challenges posed by technology, and in particular social networking. The EU Justice Commissioner has drafted new privacy legislation to protect personal data and an individual's right to privacy and the details of this law are still being worked out. Briefly the proposed law is based on four entitlements:

1. *The right to be forgotten* – it should be made much easier than it is at present to delete your own social network account.

2. *The right to transparency* – social networking sites should make users aware, in a way that is easy to find and understand, of the possible consequences of posting and sharing personal data.

3. *The right to privacy by default* – privacy settings should automatically be at the very highest setting when an account is created.

4. *The right to protection regardless of data location* – any online product (including social networking sites) that is accessible in Europe must comply with European Law, no matter where the company is based.

Even if these new regulations are applied, there may still be problems. As Facebook's Mark Zuckerberg points out, data and images that social networkers publish to their own profiles can be easily copied by others and published elsewhere. 'We can offer deletion in our own environment (Facebook) but we can't offer the same in other environments.'

It is clear then that we cannot rely on the law alone to protect our privacy; we need to address this also as a moral and ethical issue. The ethical challenge is for children to learn how much personal information it is reasonable to share online, and what the short- and long-term offline consequences of breaches of privacy might be. Children need to be helped to develop the proper distance in social networking – close, but not too close; distant, but not too distant.

As a teacher you can model respect for privacy through checking before sharing data about your pupils online to ensure that children cannot be identified individually. This is normally stipulated in school's Internet or E-safety policies.

Resources designed to help children learn about personal information and privacy

All the sites below include advice, activities and resources for children, teachers and parents.

Kidsmart: www.kidsmart.org.uk

www.kidsmart.org.uk/teachers/ks1/digiduck.aspx Digiduck's Big Decision, is an electronic story book aimed at children aged 3–7 years. The story explores the possible consequences of Digiduck posting a silly photograph of one of his friends online.

www.kidsmart.org.uk/ KidsSMART includes guidance for children age 8–11 about being a SMART surfer. The Social Networking, Digital Footprints, Mobiles and Chat areas all offer advice and top tips about sharing personal information and protection of privacy.

/continued

Resources designed to help children learn about personal information and privacy – continued

Childnet: www.childnet.com
www.childnet.com/kia/primary/smartadventure/default.aspx Kara, Winston and the SMART crew aim to teach Key Stage 2 children the 5 SMART rules so that children can make smart decisions online. In Chapter 3 of their cartoon adventures they learn about keeping their personal details safe when chatting or posting online. http://childnet.com/downloads/blog_safety.pdf A useful guide on social networking and young people for parents and teachers.

Thinkuknow: www.thinkuknow.co.uk/ Resources from CEOP (Child Exploitation and Online Protection centre)

www.thinkuknow.co.uk/5_7/hectorsworld/ Key Stage 1 children can join Hector Protector and his friends on their cartoon adventures which all focus on sharing personal information in a range of different scenarios.

www.thinkuknow.co.uk/8_10/cybercafe/Cyber-Cafe-Base/ 8–10-year-olds can visit the ThinkUKnow Cyber Café and help Griff and his friends keep their personal information safe when emailing, chatting or using other online technologies.

Chat danger: www.chatdanger.com/ Features true stories highlighting the potential dangers of sharing personal information using online services such as chat, Instant Messenger email and mobiles.

Caught in the web: www.bbc.co.uk/newsround/13908828 CBBC video that tells the story of a girl called Lonely Princess, who gets into danger after meeting someone in a chatroom. It highlights a range of online safety issues including the possible consequences of posting and sharing personal information.

Safemoods: http://safemoods.com/ The 3 Little Red Riding Mood animated videos address issues of privacy and safety on social network sites.

BBC Learning Zone: CLIP 9455: www.bbc.co.uk/learningzone/clips/cyberbullying-photos-and-videos-online/9455.html Janie finds out the hard way what happens when she uploads a video of herself singing to a website.

While we have children's best interests at heart when we monitor their online activities in school and question them about their online habits outside the classroom, we do need to remember that they too have an entitlement to some privacy in conducting their social relationships. This means thinking carefully in advance about how you will manage discussions about e-safety sensitively. School leaders and teachers are increasingly aware of internet safety issues and most schools now incorporate e-safety lessons into their curriculum. A recent survey of schools in England by Passey (2011) found that while the vast majority of teachers and school leaders believed that social networking safety should be taught in school, only about half of school practitioners felt confident to undertake this currently and more than 80 per cent of teachers considered that they needed further professional development. While most of their pupils questioned indicated that they would tell 'someone' if they felt unsafe or unhappy when using the internet it is less clear that the adult concerned would be confident in knowing what action to take. Passey notes that, *if parents, teachers or 'someone' is not clear about what to do, then it is possible that inappropriate action could result* (page 12).

If you are uncertain about your approach to e-safety, work through your planning with more experienced colleagues or seek advice from a trained professional in e-safety matters. You should also consider signing up for professional development with an accredited provider such as CEOP www.thinkuknow.co.uk/teachers/training/.

Key idea: **Virtual identities**

Childhood and adolescence is time a of identity formation, as we try out new ways of representing ourselves. Young children's role play is an important way in which they imagine what it might be like to be a princess or a pop star, a space traveller or a truck driver. At an early age children create idealised or imaginary characters though 'dressing up' clothes, toys and simple tools, and in so doing explore aspects of their personalities and gauge the effects of their behaviour on others. For example, Wohlwend (2009) found that even five- and six-year-old children were culturally sophisticated enough to distinguish between the implied characters of their Disney Princess dolls (passive and over-feminised) and contrast this with their own rather more active personalities. Through role play they explored multiple ways of seeing themselves, later developing some of their ideas into play scripts.

> She's really a princess, but I'm pretending she's a super-hero. Her powers make her fly. She can make tornadoes. She can use power from her hands to make fire. Sometimes she makes the bad guy dead with her fire (page 75).

Technology, however, provides new tools for role play and children's formation of personal identity.

Children can add the resources offered by multiplayer games, virtual worlds and cyber-pet shops to the media of text and screen enjoyed by previous generations in order to construct imaginary worlds and confirm their sense of self. Online, children can choose different names, styles and personas to adorn their digital presence, and perform their identities on a large and public stage. Cyberspace can be liberating because gender, race, age and appearance, are potentially absent or can be concealed, modified or exaggerated. Online, children can be whoever they choose to be and can slip in and out of various identities. It can also, of course, be risky as children may be confused by the feedback they receive, and may become the victims of sexual predators or cyber bullies.

Identity development through avatars

An avatar is generally used to conceal a user's real identity as they participate in an online community such as a multiplayer computer game or an internet chat room. 'Avatar' is derived from a Sanskrit word meaning 'the human form of a god or mythical being', and online avatars can be images of anything from symbols to animals. *The ability to create fantastic creatures or even pose as the opposite gender allow for ample opportunity to explore different roles and identities, which can influence the user's self-image and offline identity* (Whitaker and Bushman, 2009, page 1059).

The interrelationship between young people's online and offline identities was explored in the BBC television show *Noah and Saskia* (BBC, 2007–8) where two teenagers met in an internet chat-room using personas very different from their true selves. They became friends, but each feared the other would discover their true identity. Although the characters deceived each other with their 'false personas', their relationship was depicted as positive. They could express aspects of their personalities through their avatars with which they were uncomfortable or lacked the confidence to express in real life. For example, Saskia's alter ego 'Indy' projected the confidence and independence that nervous and shy Saskia found hard to express offline. Throughout the series, playing at being Indy helped Saskia to become more assertive.

Experimenting with avatars in school

Avatars are, as noted above, a projection of individual identity aimed at an audience of other people. They may be a truthful representation of the offline personality, or they may not. In this aspect they can be seen as related to the branding of commercial products. In our social networking profiles and through avatars we aim to present an image that will appeal to our 'customers': people whose attention we seek to capture and hold. This suggests a number of ways that both avatars and profiles can be explored in the literacy classroom, perhaps linked to an analysis of advertising and celebrity press releases. Children can be encouraged to experiment with projecting different images both in images and in text and these can be published safely on the school Learning Platform/VLE. Avatar and profile creation raises children's awareness of how easy it is for people to project a misleading image of themselves, which may offer an opportunity to raise e-safety issues. The difference between benign and malicious purposes for using false identities can be hard for children to grasp. E-safety involves not revealing too much personal information, while at the same time being cautious about taking other people online at face value.

Some Learning Platforms include avatar creators; however, a list of avatar creation tools that may be useful for teaching can be found at http://primaryschoolict.com/avatars/.

> **Critical thinking exercise 3**
>
> Parents and teachers often have very real fears about the dangers of social media use by children. To balance this view, identify some arguments you might make to support the view that social media can play a *positive* role in a child's development.

Comment

Our identities are formed through self-expression, feedback from others, and reflection on that feedback which may then lead us to modify our behaviour. This process for a child, traditionally takes place in a circumscribed world of home, school and local community. Children observe and are observed by a relatively small and stable population of well-known others, which places limitations on the identities they can explore; they cannot dramatically alter the size and shape of their bodies, their gender or the colour of their skin, for example. Children's opportunity for self-expression is also restricted by social and cultural norms or financial constraints. For every 'Billy Elliot' who overcomes stereotypes to achieve self-fulfilment there are many thousands of children who don't.

Online, however, different rules apply. 'On the Internet, nobody knows you're a dog' is a frequently cited cartoon first published in *The New Yorker* (1993), which makes the point that in the anonymity of cyberspace nobody knows who you are. The potential for 'invisibility' or creating an 'other' self can feel like a superpower to individuals who have yet to develop a confidence in their identity. This 'invisibility' can be liberating because gender, race, age and appearance are potentially absent or can be creatively exaggerated. Young people, who feel marginalised or 'different' in their immediate circumstances, may find acceptance in the diverse communities online. Even children who socialise exclusively online with people known to them in their offline world have reported feeling less lonely and less inhibited about expressing themselves online. (James *et al.*, 2009 page 28) suggests that *social validation, which is increasingly attained online, may prevent social alienation and disaffection and social harms such as bullying, hate speech, and violence.*

Key idea: **Computer games and education**

> Computer games in the 'edutainment' category, i.e. games designed specifically for the education market, have been used in schools to support teaching and learning for almost 20 years. You have probably seen examples of programmes where a series of literacy or arithmetic tasks are presented sequentially, often dressed up with a space or adventure theme, to be followed by a brief shooting
>
> /continued

Key idea: **Computer games and education** – education

or colouring activity as a reward. Amy Bruckman (1999, page 75) describes this style of game as *chocolate-dipped broccoli*: the learning content has a game tagged on to it in order to make seem more palatable. She argues that these games are based on an outdated model of learning and send a powerful message to children that learning is unpleasant; but if you do it then you can then have a go at something more fun. According to Groff *et al.* (2010) the key failing of the edutainment game is that the learner is fully aware of the learning objective, but it has little meaning for them. This can be contrasted with the kinds of computer games already popular with young people in mainstream culture where multiple learning opportunities are available as children engage in interactive, meaningful game play.

There are number of beliefs about computer gaming that are sometimes fuelled by the popular press: that computer games are addictive; that they can contribute to aggressive and antisocial behaviour; that they encourage sedentary lifestyles with a consequent increase in obesity in young people. While these concerns cannot be dismissed and it is acknowledged that playing computer games can have a negative impact on some users, many games do not follow these stereotypical views and it is well recognised that positive learning experiences can and do take place when playing games. In Scotland, teachers have been exploring the educational potential of computer gaming since 2006. You can read about the games-based learning project and some of its outcomes online at: www.educationscotland.gov.uk/usingglowandict/gamesbased learning/index.asp or download the *Gaming Handbook* by Ulicsak and Williamson (2010) from: http://futurelab.org.uk/resources/computer-games-and-learning-handbook.

Critical thinking exercise 4

A **Reflect** on either your own experiences of gaming or choose, and then explore, a game or game environment from the selection below. You may need to register for some of these but all are free to play at the basic level. Produce a thematic mind map to identify the learning opportunities from your chosen game environment.

Math Blaster www.mathblaster.com/
Muddle Earth www.muddleearthworld.co.uk/
Tiny Planets www.tinyplanets.com/
Mini Monos www.minimonos.com

/continued

Critical thinking exercise 4 – continued

Space Heroes Universe www.spaceheroes.com/
Moshi Monsters www.moshimonsters.com/
Bin Weevils www.binweevils.com/
Club Penguin www.clubpenguin.com/

B **Consider** how you might use one of the games above, or another you are familiar with, in the classroom to support learning.

C **Identify** how the game ensures a safe online experience for users.

Comment

Games as rich environments for learning
Games create learning spaces, where children use their imagination and natural inclination to play, to explore new ideas and identities and experience their world. They are safe places where children can engage with challenging, but achievable tasks or puzzles, where they can try things out and see 'what happens if…' According to Malone (1981) it is these elements of fantasy, challenge and curiosity that make computer games fun, and highly motivational.

Gee (2003) believes that games provide powerful learning environments because they create 'semiotic domains', which are *any set of practices that recruits one or more modalities (e.g., oral or written language, images, equations, symbols, sounds, gestures, graphs, artefacts, etc. to communicate distinctive types of meanings* (page 18). Interpreting these different modes and the interplay between them is thus required if players are to make sense of the game. Gee sees this as a four-step cycle, very similar to the scientific method, where players observe, question, hypothesise and test their ideas to make meaning. Players thus tend to learn to play computer games through interaction and practice with the game, rather than through instruction. Mastering the game is not about pushing buttons faster, but is about identifying, exploring and solving a range of problems of increasing complexity, in order to decipher the underlying system of rules. With this purpose in mind, users try out alternative courses of action and experience the consequences of their decisions and as such are seen to control and determine the gaming experience, rather than the designers. In addition, players take on different identities in order to become more familiar with the discourses associated with particular contexts and characters. For example, in 'LEGO City: Undercover' players take on the identity of Chase McCain and become involved in various covert operations under different guises in a bid to stop Rex Fury and his crime wave in LEGO city.

Games are also seen as key in promoting social and collaborative practices; they are an important part of children's culture and day-to-day conversations, but perhaps more importantly they, to quote the Scottish education Games Based Learning website, *create an implicit and explicit understanding that as a learner on our own we can be good, but as a learner in a connected team we can be much better.*

Consequently, gaming promotes collaboration and communication and the growth of active and supportive gaming communities means players' knowledge, skills, experiences and resources are easily shared. Massively Multi-player Online Games (also known as MMOs or MMOGs) such as Runescape www.runescape.com/, where large numbers of players, hundreds or even many thousands, play the same game simultaneously, usually require players to cooperate and communicate in order to be successful, and tools are usually built into the game to facilitate this process .

Although there is still some debate over the precise skills that games help to develop, evidence from research, presented by Groff *et al.* (2010), noted the development of the following:

- Personal skills (such as initiative and persistence).
- Spatial and motor skills (such as coordination and speed of reflexes).
- Social (such as teamwork and communication).
- Intellectual (such as problem-solving and logical thinking).

While some of these skills can clearly be developed by individuals simply engaging with a game, others are more likely to develop where games are played collaboratively, and communication and negotiation become essential.

Using games in the classroom

While many teachers believe that computer games may be motivating and can help support children's cognitive development and higher-order thinking skills, as well as their ICT development, Ulicsak and Williamson (2010) identified two main barriers to their use in the classroom. First, practical issues, such as cost, licensing, identifying suitable games, access to computers and resources as well as problems fitting gaming into the school timetable. Second, understanding how games can be used to support learning, as educational potential and links to the curriculum are not always obvious, especially as teachers often lack knowledge and experience in this area.

From a new literacies perspective these difficulties arise from attempts to integrate literacy practices that value social interaction, discovery-based learning and personal meaning-making into the existing school structure of curriculum, timetable and statutory assessments. A project studying the outcomes of the use of a virtual world to raise literacy achievement among Upper Key Stage 2 children (Merchant, 2010) found that the resource was relatively easily assimilated into the classroom in the guise of a stimulus for traditional literacy practices. The teachers in the project created a range of 'SATs type' assessments around the resource, and devised literacy activities that focused on print-based literacy genres (such as persuasive writing and story openings). Some of the pupils were unconvinced by the approach; as one teacher commented:

Some boys who were really into computer games and the virtual world loved the ICT aspect. But when it came to writing they still *couldn't be fooled to write and still moaned.*

(page 146)

Merchant notes that there was less teacher attention paid to wider literacy practices engaged in by the children such as constructing shared and imagined narratives, playfully experimenting with text/chat genres and representing dialect speech in text.

The role of the teacher is clearly critical if learning is to be effective (Sandford and Williamson, 2005; Groff *et al.*, 2010; Ulicsak and Williamson, 2010). Teachers need to be clear about how games can be effectively integrated into the curriculum if they are going to be used successfully as a tool to support teaching and learning. They also need to be able to identify suitable games. According to Ulicsak and Williamson (2010) knowing which games or parts of games have relevant content to support learning can however be a major barrier to their use. The Consolarium in Scotland www.education scotland.gov.uk/usingglowandict/gamesbasedlearning/consolarium.asp provides support for teachers in the selection of games and their use in the classroom. As yet there is no similar initiative in England and no single resource which identifies games and maps them to the curriculum, or suggests how they might be used to support learning.

Sandford and Williamson (2005) suggest considering a number of characteristics when selecting games. These include whether the game offers authentic challenges, opportunities for children to explore 'what happens if…', and whether they are ethically and culturally appropriate.

Following research designed to investigate how children 'inhabit' and engage with online game environments. Jackson et al. (2008, page 35) identified 13 principles required for a successful virtual world for children.

1. Sociable – meeting and chatting
2. Creative – making avatar, making things
3. Control – owning and changing the space
4. A big 'outdoors' world to explore
5. Visible status – how am I doing?
6. Clear location – where am I? + easy transport
7. Mission and motivation – what's the purpose?
8. Some humour
9. Help when you need it
10. Chance to see professional video, their own work, and other children's
11. Somewhere to live – a home or town
12. Shops – buying stuff
13. A space away from adult rules

It is not always necessary for teachers to understand all the intricacies of a game, but if learning is to be effective teachers need a real purpose for using games and need to actively facilitate their use for learning rather than being seen as recreation at computer clubs and wet break times, or as a reward for good behaviour. Teachers also need to be aware of the risks associated with online gaming to ensure a safe experience for users.

The literature on computer gaming in education offers a number of practical suggestions for teachers when using games in the classroom.

- Consider children's age, prior knowledge and experience in the subject to be taught as well as children's gaming experience.
- Identify the key learning outcomes to be achieved and ensure a commercial computer game is the best tool for the job.
- Select an appropriate game. Check that the game:
  - supports key learning outcomes, identify the precise role of the game in achieving these. This may mean using some, but not all of the game elements;
  - is culturally appropriate and avoids negative stereotypes;
  - is age appropriate, games should have a PEGI (Pan-European Game Information) age rating;
  - is easily accessed by all children, for example those with a physical disability;
  - has progressive levels of difficulty which can be matched to ability levels;
  - has save and exit points so it can be used in lesson-sized blocks of time;
  - is reasonably realistic/has an appropriate degree of realism for learning;
  - runs on the school network and there are sufficient resources.
- Find time to become familiar with the content and basic principles of the game by playing it.
- Identify how the game links to curriculum plans.
- Consider how children who are experts in the game, rules and content, or the game genre, can be used to support their peers.
- Determine how learning will be assessed and evaluated, and applied outside of the game context.
- Plan lesson/s which identify:
  - time for the children to familiarise themselves with the game;
  - how the game will be used e.g. individually, in pairs, small groups, whole class;
  - how to get to particular parts of the game (if required) and how to save progress;
  - the teacher's role and how learning will be facilitated;
  - opportunities for reflection, discussion and assessment;
  - a 'plan B' in case of technical problems.

Derived from Sandford et al. (2006) in Groff et al. (2010) and Ulicsak and Williamson (2010).

Gaming safety

Today, gamers are no longer confined to playing games with friends and family, online gaming means that games can be played with people all over the world; it also means that they can be played 24/7. Many games also include chat facilities either through the game itself or via the game website. Children need to remember that when playing games online they need to be careful about whom they trust, and should not reveal personal information. They should also realise that if another player is behaving badly there are often facilities to report or block the player. Teachers need to help children develop awareness of these risks.

Websites and resources that offer children, teachers and parents advice about keeping safe when gaming online

Resources for teachers, parents and carers:

Childnet: www.saferinternet.org.uk/downloads/resources/publications/Online-gaming.pdf

Ask about games: www.askaboutgames.com/?c=/pages/genres.jsp

Microsoft: www.microsoft.com/en-gb/security/family-safety/gaming-about.aspx

Get Safe Online: www.getsafeonline.org/protecting-yourself/online-gaming/

Daily Telegraph: www.telegraph.co.uk/news/uknews/1582862/Internet-and-video-game-safety-Ten-practical-tips-to-help-protect-your-children.html

Resources for children:

Kidsmart: www.kidsmart.org.uk/games/

Chat danger: www.chatdanger.com/games/safetyadvice.aspx

Although the use of commercial computer games in the classroom may initially seem daunting and there are still concerns over their use in the classroom, Gee (2003) identifies the many benefits which include:

- motivating learners to succeed and to continually improve;
- fostering self-esteem, self-determination and enhancing self-image;
- facilitating collaborative learning;
- implicitly developing learners' ability to observe, question, hypothesise and test;
- facilitating metacognitive reflection;
- developing complex problem-solving skills;
- making school an exciting place to be;
- offering inroads into other curricular areas;
- sharing practice features that show how games have enhanced learning in the classroom.

Conclusion

For some adult commentators, children's engagement with social media is a cause for concern. Fears focus on social isolation, addiction, moral corruption, psychological damage or physical abuse resulting from online contact. These fears are compounded by the limited ability of parents and teachers – particularly those who would consider themselves to be digital visitors/immigrants, to control children's internet use, (Valentine and Holloway, 2001). These attitudes take a very deterministic view of technology: that is a belief that technology itself is invested with the power to transform lives purely by being in existence. This view downplays the role of human agents to take control and responsibility for their own lives and actions. It also allows adults who are uncomfortable with the challenges posed by unfamiliar technologies to absolve themselves of responsibility for any damage caused to themselves or others through its irresponsible or inappropriate use.

New literacies advocates take a much more positive and optimistic view of social media and networked technology for helping children to develop the competencies they will need to thrive in a future society that we can barely imagine. Children need the adults in their lives to engage with them, and the technologies they enjoy, seriously and thoughtfully. They need us to guide them and teach them how to use technology in ways that keep them safe but help them to learn, work, socialise and play. Grafting social media, gaming and virtual world activities on to the existing curriculum and integrating them as best we can is a good beginning. However, Merchant (2010) argues that longer term, schools and teachers need to go much further: *rather than thinking that new technologies can activate changes in practice, we should begin to think about how changes in practice could create possibilities for using new technologies in innovative ways* (page 148).

Further Reading

Ulicsak, M. and Williamson, B. (2010) *Computer Games and Learning.* Bristol: FutureLab. Retrieved from **http://futurelab.org.uk/resources/computer-games-and-learning-handbook**

http://flockpost.com/2010/03/40-best-social-networking-websites-for-kids/

Teachers are well aware of how powerful a sense of an authentic audience can be in developing children's literacy skills, for example David Mitchell of Heathfield School has used blogging to encourage boys' writing, for examples and further details see: http://mrmitchell.heathfieldcps.net/2011/02/14/the-day-the-nation-took-notice-of-primary-blogging/.

New literacies and inclusion

Debbie Simpson and Mike Toyn

Chapter Focus

This chapter will consider how new literacies and inclusion interrelate. You will discover how traditional literacy, historically, maintained exclusion of particular groups and how the social aspects of new literacies can help to overcome this. You will also be encouraged to consider how to support the inclusion of selected groups in their engagement with new literacy texts.

The critical thinking exercises in this chapter focus on:

⊙ **identifying** learning activities that might not have been fully inclusive;
⊙ **accessing** meaning from texts in other languages;
⊙ **analysing** evidence related to gendered achievement in literacy;
⊙ **identifying** examples of literacy texts that you have been excluded from;
⊙ **considering** what dyslexic learners should be expected to achieve in terms of literacy.

The key ideas discussed are: **inclusion, English as an additional language, gender issues in literacy, special education needs** and **literacy**.

This chapter is particularly relevant to the following Teachers' Standards (2012):

Part 1: Teaching

A teacher must:

1 **Set high expectations which inspire, motivate and challenge pupils**
   ⊙ set goals that stretch and challenge pupils of all backgrounds, abilities and dispositions
2 **Promote good progress and outcomes by pupils**
   ⊙ be aware of pupils' capabilities and their prior knowledge, and plan teaching to build on these
3 **Demonstrate good subject and curriculum knowledge**
   ⊙ demonstrate an understanding of and take responsibility for promoting high standards of literacy, articulacy and the correct use of standard English, whatever the teacher's specialist subject

/continued

> ## Chapter Focus – continued
>
> 4 **Plan and teach well-structured lessons**
>   - ◉ contribute to the design and provision of an engaging curriculum within the relevant subject areas
>
> 5 **Adapt teaching to respond to the strengths and needs of all pupils**
>   - ◉ know when and how to differentiate appropriately, using approaches which enable pupils to be taught effectively
>   - ◉ have a secure understanding of how a range of factors can inhibit pupils' ability to learn, and how best to overcome these
>   - ◉ demonstrate an awareness of the physical, social and intellectual development of children, and know how to adapt teaching to support pupils' education at different stages of development
>   - ◉ have a clear understanding of the needs of all pupils, including those with special educational needs; those of high ability; those with English as an additional language; those with disabilities; and be able to use and evaluate distinctive teaching approaches to engage and support them.

Introduction

If you are reading this book then it is likely that you enjoy a high degree of literacy skills and many of your friends, colleagues and acquaintances are likely to be in a similar position. You may well be aware of the statistics regarding levels of illiteracy and also of numerous government initiatives aimed at increasing levels of literacy. You may well take you literacy for granted. However, historically, this has not always been the case. For many years in medieval Europe, the Church maintained control over literacy levels by ensuring the education in reading and writing was confined to the clergy and that the only texts available to them were religious texts. They employed a system of copying and reproducing texts that ensured that they were able to maintain a power base across a wide geographical area that lasted for a very long time (Leu et al., 2004). Another example which is relevant to this introduction is the profound change made by the invention of the printing press around 1450; this was such a significant event because it meant that printed texts could be made available to a much wider proportion of the population and this was something that worried the ruling classes.

The purpose of these two historical examples was to illustrate that literacy does not have a history of being an inclusive activity, rather it was an exclusive activity: one that was used to maintain power and order for long periods of time. As literacy levels have risen in the developed world, so has the opportunity for citizens to actively participate in society. The purpose of this chapter is to explore the relationship between new literacies and inclusion and to think about how the needs of some specific groups should be considered when working with new literacies.

Key idea: **Literacy and inclusion**

> As has already been considered in the introduction, literacy has historically been used as a tool of exclusion in order to maintain power and status. Thankfully, we live in much more enlightened times and access to literacy skills is a goal that is encouraged by the majority of states in the world. However, it is still not yet a fully inclusive area as the numbers of adults with limited literacy would show. This section will consider the importance of working to ensure inclusion when dealing with new literacies in order to facilitate full participation by all children in learning activities.

A way of summing up the key theme of this section is provided by Rief (1992) who notes *I need to remember to give my students the opportunities to say things in ways they have 'no words for'* – in other words, it is an exploration of the way that incorporating new literacies into classroom practice can support inclusion as it can accommodate a wider range of forms of expression, technologies and modes of representation than traditional print-based literacy. An effective example of this is provided by Begoray (2001), who did a two-year study into the impact of incorporating visual literacy teaching into a school in Canada. One episode that is recounted tells of a class teacher who had been reading a novel aloud only to find that many pupils were losing attention or even falling asleep. The teacher then restarted the novel and told the children that they were to picture what was happening and to make a movie of the events in their head and to sketch some of the scenes from the movie as the story was being read. The result of the change in approach was that the majority of the class were actively engaged in listening to the story and were better able to participate in subsequent learning activities. An analysis of this episode would suggest that it was successful as it allowed children to participate in an activity that they were otherwise being excluded from because of the mode of teaching being employed and the limited scope of literacy that it embodied. In contrast, the modified approach to the lesson made use of multiple modes of representation and drew on forms of media with which the children were familiar. In other words, their understanding of films allowed them to begin to gain a deeper understanding of the written text that was being read to them. The connections between the traditional written literacy and the new literacy of film and visual representation formed a pathway to learning.

The episode above raises a question: if such approaches and integration of new literacy approaches are so successful, then why are they not more widely used? This is a topic that Begoray (2001) goes on to discuss and she suggests that there are two factors that come to play. First, such approaches take time to prepare. It could be argued that in the example which has been discussed that the teacher was simply reflecting 'in-action' (Schön, 1987). However, to fully integrate approaches which embed new literacies takes time and effort and not all teachers will be willing or able to make this investment. The second factor is that new literacies can be undervalued and misunderstood. This is perhaps a more worrying factor as it suggests that new literacies have not reached a status which is equivalent to print literacies in the minds of many teachers and schools and consequently they are underused. An illustration of this would be the prevalence of printed texts in primary schools compared to the use of film and video. It is common practice in some schools for video to be most widely used at the end of term, as a way to entertain children while other tasks are undertaken by teachers, which is hardly a powerful education use of such a valuable resource.

The importance of a shift in pedagogy to accommodate new literacies is highlighted by Manfra and Lee (2011) in their study of the role of blogs in supporting low attaining learners. One of the key points that they make is that effective integration of a new literacy format is best supported by a change from didactic teacher-led learning where the teacher is the font of all knowledge to, what they term, 'equity pedagogy' (Manfra and Lee, 2011), which can be thought of as a constructivist pedagogy where the teacher acts as a facilitator or enabler for the children's learning. In their study, they make use of blogs as an example of a Web 2.0 technology, citing its value in enabling users to both construct and publish in a multimedia format that is accessible through a variety of social networks. This allowed the children in the study to easily create multimodal texts and to share them with audiences ranging from the local (within school) to worldwide (via the internet). In their study, based in the United States, they found that in classes where there was a high proportion of low attaining students, many of the lessons would be characterised by 'drill and practice' lessons where the aim was to support memorisation of key information. Their study aimed to evaluate the effects of an intervention that would move away from this approach and would incorporate:

- increased participation;
- higher order thinking; and
- utilisation of prior knowledge.

The approach that they took to achieving these was to encourage teachers to make use of technologies associated with new literacies in their teaching of history, specifically the use of blogs for pupils to record their personal responses to historical events and periods. The study found that this switch did increase participation and engagement and they cite a number of responses from pupils that emphasise the depth of engagement. What is of interest in this example is the way that the new literacy approach allowed the pupils to *exercise their voice in the classroom* (Manfra and Lee, 2011, page 99); in other words, it enabled the pupils to express themselves and to make a contribution.

Perhaps the most salient message from this study is not the transformative effect that a new literacy approach through the use of blogs had on pupil performance and inclusion but the need for a change to the teacher's pedagogy in order to facilitate this. In other words, simply paying lip service to new literacies is not adequate if they are to play a significant role in supporting inclusion, this must be backed up by a participatory pedagogy that is aligned with social constructivism

---

Critical thinking exercise 1: identifying inclusive literacy in your own practice

Consider a lesson that you have taught where the children were required to write down their ideas or responses. Were there any pupils who were not fully included in the activity? You might be able to think of some children who struggled to engage because they were weak writers or perhaps there were others for whom the activity was not very inspiring or motivating.

Now **think** if the activity could have included an opportunity for the learners to express themselves through a new literacy format or technology. Perhaps there might have been an opportunity for children to have represented their ideas in a visual or oral way or alternatively perhaps a Web 2.0 tool such as a blog, video hosting site or wiki would have allowed them to express their ideas.

Finally, **consider** what changes to your pedagogy and teaching approach would have been required if you were to adopt this alternative form of expression.

Key idea: **Learners with English as an additional language**

In order to understand the role that new literacies and technology can play in supporting learners with English as an additional language (EAL), it is necessary to have a good understanding of their learning needs.

Imagine that you travel to an unfamiliar country and as you look around you there is text on signs, shops, newspapers but you are unable to decode any of the words. If the country is not a Western-style democracy then there are likely to be very few contextual clues that might help you make sense of the text you can see. However, if you have ever travelled to other parts of the world you will know that it is not impossible to make sense of the world around you as you can use visual literacy skills in order to draw on graphical cues to make sense of your surroundings. This is not fool proof though as some cultural references may not translate such as the symbols that relate to male and female toilets. You may be able to draw on audio literacy in some situations, for example a fire alarm is likely to be universally recognised or if you are crossing the street and forget to look both ways then a yell or a car horn would alert you to the danger. Again, this might not be fool proof as car horns can be used for a number of different

/continued

Key idea: **Learners with English as an additional language** – continued

purposes around the world. The purpose of this thought exercise it to help give you a context for this section by helping you recognise the challenges that EAL learners can face and the enhanced difficulties that arise when there are few cultural conventions against which to compare the literacy information you receive.

Milton Keynes Ethnic Minority Achievement Support Service (2004) provides an excellent overview of this and highlights that there are two aspects to the learning of EAL children. First, they need to learn English and they also need to learn the curriculum. A further distinction can be made between the acquisition of a level of English that is required in order to sustain a conversation and the level of English that is required in order to engage in academic activity that is cognitively demanding. Consequently, a quadrant can be created with the degree of challenge on one axis and the degree of abstraction on the other as in Figure 8.1.

Figure 8.1 (Milton Keynes Ethnic Minority Achievement Support Service, 2004, page 7)

Work in sector B will develop the ability to undertake cognitively demanding activities, these will be activities that present challenge but also provide a context for them to relate the experience to. This is because constructivist learning posits that learners build their own knowledge and relate it to prior experiences and schemas, thus concrete experiences provide a context for their learning to take place. At the same time it must be recognised that children will need support in order to engage with activities in sector C as these activities will not have an obvious relationship to prior knowledge or familiar contexts.

In addition to these general needs, it is suggested by Milton Keynes Ethnic Minority Achievement Support Service (2004) that there are various practical steps that can be taken to support the inclusion of EAL learners which includes providing visual cues such as pictorial timetables, cards with images and words showing common, useful words and phrases needed in the classroom and physical demonstrations of instructions. In order to consider the role of technology in this, BECTA (2004) provided guidance on the range of roles that ICT can play in supporting EAL learners and they include:

- promoting inclusion and reflecting diversity;
- easy rectification of errors;
- visual timetables;

- collaborative activities;
- multilingual word processors; and
- bilingual stories.

The use of technology to create support tools such as visual timetables is easy and flexible and allows the learner to make use of visual literacy skills in order to place events in context. But the use of ICT to allow for easy rectification of errors is quite a different role for the technology; here it is being used to encourage learners to make attempts to use English with a reduced fear of getting things wrong. The use of a word processor also provides fluent communicators in English with a range of other tools such as underlining for spelling errors in one colour, grammar errors in a different colour as well as access to dictionaries and a thesaurus. However, Davies (2004) notes that while such tools can support learner independence, they rely on a degree of English learning to have been previously internalised for these to make any sense to the learner.

An area of education which is related to the acquisition of English language by EAL children is that of language learning and there is a significant history of computer assisted language learning (CALL) where the role of technology has been through an evolutionary process. Bax (2003) writes about the early use of technology in CALL being based on behaviourist learning paradigms where technology was regularly used to support 'drill and practice' learning of vocabulary and language. In this role, technology was acting as a tutor, this is in comparison to its next phase where technology was being used to support a communicative approach and was in a role of stimulus for the learner. Finally, Bax argues that technology is currently being used in CALL in an integrative way where it is valued as a tool to support language learning and draws on aspects such as multimedia and the internet to achieve this. The relevance of this is that multimedia and the internet can be seen as some of the new literacies that have been discussed throughout this book and thus how they are enabling EAL learners to acquire English speaking skills. In order to illustrate this, some examples of the use of multimedia will be considered.

Davies (2004) argues that multimedia can present many enhanced opportunities to activate prior knowledge as it allows the user a multisensory experience. She also makes the point that, contrary to some schools of thought, multimedia is more than simply books come alive as it allows the user to control the content. This is particularly important for EAL learners who need to have opportunities to learn at their own pace and to revisit materials often. Also, they may not need to progress through in a linear order and may need to spend more time on some elements than others; all of which are affordances that multimedia texts can offer because of the new literacies that they embody. Another role of multimedia texts is that when they are combined with presentation technology they can act as powerful stimuli for learning, which would be in the second stage of the evolution presented by Bax (see previous paragraph). In this role it is frequently used as a transmission tool but Davies (2004) suggests that in smaller groups it can allow many opportunities to support and develop discussion-based activities that allow EAL learners to develop their language skills.

Another use of technology to support the inclusion of EAL learners and to allow them to access literacy skills is through the use of computer mediated communication (CMC) – this can encompass both synchronous tools such as instant messaging services and asynchronous tools such as email and discussion boards. There is particular value to asynchronous tools as they do not require an immediate response and can allow a learner to develop their ideas about their response in their own time. If the topic of discussion is carefully selected by the teacher then it can provide a real and relevant context for the learner on which they can build their new knowledge.

Pagett (2006) writes about a study of EAL learners and their preferences for using their first language and English at school. Interestingly, she found that even when children were given the opportunity to speak in their first language or when their English skills were not sufficient to allow them to communicate effectively, they would frequently avoid using their first language because of a fear that it would show them as being different to the norm of the classroom. In this social context, technology has a twin role in supporting inclusion. First, the use of multimedia and display technology can provide a mechanism through which EAL learners can share ideas and information about their own culture, which would promote an inclusive and diverse classroom. Second, as technology can allow users to progress at their own pace with a reduced fear of making mistakes as they can be easily corrected it will allow learners to share their thoughts and ideas in English but without the pressure to speak fluently in front of a class or group.

Critical thinking exercise 2: visual messages and the context of language

Consider watching television for an evening and make a mental note of the different types of programme that might be screened. This might include news, weather, cartoons, documentaries, films, reality TV or music programmes. No doubt you will have other favourite programmes that you like to watch that you would add to the list.

Now imagine watching television for a night in a country elsewhere in the world where English is not spoken. Think about ranking the programmes on your list in relation to how easy they would be to extract meaning from. What do you **consider** to help you make this decision?

Comment

It is likely that part of your decision was based on the visual clues that the programme was likely to contain. For example, a weather forecast might be possible to understand based on the symbols presented on the map; however, you would need to remember that just like alphabets there is no globally agreed set of symbols that are used and you may not understand the symbols that are used for each weather condition. Another example could be a drama, you might be able to get the gist of a plot by watching what the actors do, their expressions and the responses of other characters, providing the context was a setting that had cultural relevance to you. You might even be able to replay some scenes over and over and begin to make guesses about the meaning of some words. In this example, it is the power of technology to allow you control the multimedia that enables you to extract meaning.

Key idea: **Literacy is not gender neutral**

Globally, nearly two-thirds (497 million) of illiterate adults in 2010 (775 million) were women.[1]

You will not find it difficult to suggest a number of factors that might contribute to low rates of literacy in women. In societies where there is strong stereotyping of male and female roles, inequality based on gender difference restricts educational opportunities for girls and women. As you have seen already in this chapter, education has been used over time by the dominant group in a society as a tool to maintain their superior position. In societies where the dominant group is male, resources are concentrated on boys' education and opportunities for girls are either limited or absent altogether.

In the UK where both sexes have equal access to education the difference between the proportion of women and men regarded as 'functionally illiterate' is less marked. Functional illiteracy is defined as having literacy levels (as an adult) that are at or below those expected of an 11 year old. This means being able to understand short straightforward texts on familiar topics and to be able to obtain information from everyday sources, such as popular newspapers. It means being able to express information and opinions in writing, with some adaption to the intended audience, (e.g. a short formal letter, note or form). These skills are regarded as the minimum for coping with the demands of everyday life. Around 16 per cent of men and 14 per cent of women in the UK today are not able to carry out these literacy tasks; and they are defined as functionally illiterate. This percentage is remarkably consistent between different age groups of adults, see Figure 8:2 (*The 2011 Skills for Life Survey: A Survey of Literacy, Numeracy and ICT Levels in England*, 2012, page 87).

1 Source: UNESCO Institute for Statistics, Data Centre, April 2012

	MEN						WOMEN					
	All	16-24	25-34	35-44	45-54	55-65	All	16-24	25-34	35-44	45-54	55-65
	%	%	%	%	%	%	%	%	%	%	%	%
Entry Level 3 or below	16	15	14	19	16	17	14	13	13	11	16	16
Level 1	29	31	28	24	34	30	28	27	27	25	28	31
Level 2 or above	54	54	58	57	50	52	59	60	60	64	56	54
Unweighted	2520	347	433	562	558	618	3304	385	683	745	720	770

Base: SfL2011 All aged 16-65 with literacy scores

Figure 8:2 Literacy Levels by age and gender in the UK 2011. Entry level 3 is the standard of literacy expected of an 11 year old. Level 1 corresponds to GCSE grades D–G. Level 2 corresponds to GCSE grades A–C.

While the proportion of the population with very low levels of literacy seems to be roughly consistent between the sexes, women's attainment overall is higher: a greater proportion of women achieve levels equivalent to GCSE grades A–C.

Turning to the picture in primary schools, you will be familiar with concerns reported widely in the media about the gap in attainment between boys' and girls' reading and writing skills by the end of Key Stage 2. According to a recent report (Jama and Dugdale, 2012) typically around 7 per cent fewer boys than girls reach expected levels in reading and around 14 per cent fewer achieve expected levels in writing (see Figure 8.3). These differences have been roughly consistent since 1999, and there is some evidence to show that girls are pulling even further ahead in secondary education and outperforming boys in nearly every GCSE subject (The report of the All-Party Parliamentary Literacy Group Commission, 2012).

	% achieving expected level		
	2009	2010	2011
Reading (boys/girls)	86 (82/89)	84 (81/87)	84 (80/87)
Writing (boys/girls)	67 (61/75)	71 (64/79)	75 (68/81)

Figure 8:3 Comparative percentages of boys and girls reaching expected levels in reading and writing at the end of Key Stage 2, age 11.

Critical thinking exercise 3: analysing gender-related data on literacy levels

Consider the data presented in Figures 8.3 and 8.4, in the context of claims that you may have seen in the media about girls 'outperforming' boys, leaving boys behind, 'beating boys' and so on.

Identify and write down as many reasons as you can think of to explain why boys are performing less well than girls in Standardised Literacy Tests, such as SATs. Now rank your ideas in terms most to least significant. If you have the opportunity, discuss your ideas with a friend or colleague. You may then like to compare your ideas with those discussed in section 3 of the Equal Opportunities Commission Report: *Breaking down the stereotypes: gender and achievement in schools*, available online **http://open.tean.ac.uk/handle/123456789/630**.

Comment

There is evidence to suggest that boys have more difficulty overall in attaining full literacy than do girls, and it is likely that your list will include a wide range of suggestions for why this might be so. Discussions around boys' literacy, especially in some parts of the media tend to use the language of crisis and seek to assign blame. Unduly 'feminised' primary schools, lack of male 'reading' role models, differences in learning styles and even in brain function between boys and girls have all been suggested. It must be remembered, however, that the perceived failure of boys and success of girls is measured by how they perform in relation to very particular and narrow understandings of what counts as literacy i.e. standardised testing. It is also over-simplifies: some groups of boys succeed in literacy and some groups of girls fail. New literacies theorists would also point to the possibility that forms of literacy which many boys enjoy, and in which some excel, are ignored or discouraged in school. This includes the material boys report engaging with outside school such as video game dialogue, fantasy, action and science fiction genre, fan fiction (fanzines), online chat and comics.

Rowan *et al.* (2002) warns teachers against rushing into interventions by *the air of urgency that characterizes claims that boys are now in crisis* (Rowan *et al.*, 2002, page 16). Simply grafting a sample of texts and activities thought likely to 'appeal to boys' on to an existing literacy scheme will have limited success; for an example of this see the research carried out by (Merchant, 2010) into the responses of boys to a video game resource in the literacy classroom (cited in Chapter 7 of this book): while the boys enjoyed the game elements they couldn't be 'fooled' into writing. Skelton *et al.* (2007) argue that teaching practices that aim to play to boys' and girls' perceived strengths and weaknesses actually exacerbate the problem.

> *The recent policy demands and targets around raising boys' achievement, and some of the short term strategies recommended to address these, have been found to have had an unfortunately strong impact on some teachers' understandings of gender difference. Some teachers now see such differences as inevitable and to be built on as a method for raising achievement. For example, they consider that girls and boys as groups have different learning styles, or that as groups they have different preferences for learning materials and content, and play to these differences in teaching practice.*

Skelton and Read, 2006, cited in Skelton *et al.*, 2007, page 47.

These findings beg the question of what teachers **can** do to tackle a perceived or actual crisis in boys' literacy, and new literacies theorists (and feminist theorists) suggest that we begin by encouraging both boys and girls to recognise and challenge the stereotypes of gender that limit their opportunities. Children are surrounded by cultural expectations of the roles of male and female and they usually adjust their behaviour to fit with the norms of their culture, although some children react by rejecting their designated gender role. More often than not, however, children from a very young age perform in gender typical ways and even tend to remember information better if it is consistent with gender expectations. Davies (1991) cited in Frawley (2008) describes a research experiment that you could try out in your own classroom. Young children (in this case aged three to four years) were read stories that overturned gender stereotypes, for example the daring princess slew the dragon and rescued the terrified prince. The children were then asked to draw pictures of the story and they were generally found to 'misremember' and reverse the roles to conform to more familiar gender stereotypes. The 'gender norming' impulse is powerful and it has been shown that at all ages in compulsory education children demonstrate a tendency to 'police' each other's behaviour and punish failure to conform to traditional gender norms (Skelton *et al.*, 2007, page vi).

The problem with stereotypical views is that they can lead to false dichotomies: where people of different genders are presented as opposites rather than individuals on a continuum of behaviours and preferences. This is a process that can lead to children of both sexes needlessly self-limiting their educational opportunities and, ultimately, their career choices. Of all the reasons that you, or I, or politicians or journalists, might arrive at to explain the perceived difference between the achievement of girls and boys in important areas such as literacy, none have been shown to be inevitable. Schools and individual teachers can have a significant impact on children's self-image and willingness to overcome self-imposed or socially imposed limitations. This impact is achieved through challenging rather than pandering to gender stereotypes. Skelton *et al.* (2007) suggest that one effective way to challenge stereotypical gender roles in schools is through practitioner reflection. Teachers are not always aware of their gender-differentiated classroom practices and it is therefore recommended that they self-audit the following:

- The expectations held of girls and boys.
- The language and style of interaction adopted in relation to girls and boys.
- The amount of classroom time dedicated to particular groups of pupils – boys/girls.
- The content of these interactions.
- The valuing of different types of behaviour (and achievement) according to gender.
- Teaching resources provided; in terms of whether these perpetuate gender stereotypes.

The authors recommend that teachers then work in groups to critically evaluate their existing practices and assumptions. This may be an activity you can carry out informally with a colleague or as a whole school during staff development time when next the subject of 'raising boys' achievement in literacy' is broached.

Key idea: **Multi-literacies and special educational needs**

Multi-literacies and technology can have an important role to play in supporting specific groups of learners with specific educational needs.

Before embarking on a discussion of the role of technology and multi-literacies in supporting learning, it is necessary to spend some time considering what is meant by special educational needs. (This is an extensive area and some suggestions for further reading are included at the end of the chapter.) In the same way that an understanding of what is meant by literacy has varied over time and location, so has the understanding of special educational needs. Riddick (2011) gives a good summary of the transition from a medical-based definition to a more commonly used social model. In the former, the need is defined in terms of medical descriptions such as what 'symptoms' the person displays. This definition very much places the disability on to the individual. However, in contrast to this, a social model recognises that there are impairments associated with certain conditions but these only become disabilities when looked at in terms of society and what the structures within society prevent the person from doing. In other words, it concerns the social restriction placed on people by the society in which they live (Riddick, 2011, page 225). An example of this might be that a wheelchair user becomes disabled in a society where there are no access ramps to allow entry to buildings.

A significant milestone in this debate and how it relates to education was the Warnock Report of 1978 (DES, 1978), which sought to embody a social definition of special education needs within the education system. It is not without its critics who argue that it still leads to individuals being labelled and that individual education plans are often focused on remediation for the child rather than changes to the school setting to support their accommodation. However, it has played an important role in the landscape of special education needs in the UK. This becomes particularly important when it is considered in relation to literacy and definitions of literacy. As has been discussed elsewhere in this book, historically, there have been a number of standards of literacy that have been proposed, which are frequently fixed. Consequently, they take no account of the needs of particular learners, which can make it hard to reconcile the need to consider disability from a social context. While there are many conditions that can give rise to special education needs, the one that is probably most significant is dyslexia. Thus dyslexia becomes a disability in relation to cultural norms of literacy (Riddick, 2011, page 224).

> **Critical thinking exercise 4**: what should we expect of dyslexic learners?
>
> **Consider** what you would expect a dyslexic learner to be able to achieve in relation to literacy. Do you expect them to be perfect spellers? To have legible handwriting? What about reading aloud?

Comment

This thinking exercise gets to the heart of the dilemma between making reasonable adjustments to support learners and the need to comply with national standards relating to literacy. Schools are expected to meet targets relating to the number of pupils that achieve level 4 in literacy but they are also expected to accommodate the learning environment in order to make it inclusive for dyslexic learners. Evidently this cannot always be achieved and thus it raises the question about how much teachers should expect of such pupils. Your response to the questions above might well have involved responses such as 'it depends on the child' and this is at the heart of matter: it is not something that can be determined by a national standard of literacy.

Faux (2007) outlines a specific interaction involving multi-literacies and technology that was undertaken with three learners with specific learning needs including dyslexia. While multiple literacies place more and new demands on learners they can have the advantage that they can make literacy more accessible. The focus of the intervention was to look at the way that *person-plus* (i.e. the learner in addition to ICT) can support and enhance the learners in engaging with new literacies. What is of interest is the way in which the study is related to theories of learning, in particular Vygotsky's zone of proximal development and the role that scaffolding plays in relation to this. The school where the setting took place had a strong focus on accurate spelling (it is worth considering this in terms of the definition of literacy that the school is employing) and the learners had become reliant on adult support for their spellings. This meant that they had very little freedom to go beyond the expected parameters of literacy and consequently they were working within a very narrow definition of what it means to be literate.

In Faux's (2007) study, the learners were introduced to a combination of technology and multi-literacies. They were expected to make use of text, sounds, voice and video in order to support sequencing and the appearance of the ideas that they wanted to communicate. This led to some creative expression once the learners were free from the restriction of writing. This might prompt you to think about definitions of literacy that have been discussed that relate to the ability to read and *write* in order to participate in society. Thus the technology was genuinely being used in alignment with a social model of special educational need. Previously, the learners were being expected to receive support in order to help them fit in with the convention in the school that was focused on spelling. Following the intervention, adaptations were put into place in order to allow the learners to participate in literacy activities.

The significance of this is that technologies and engagement with new literacies, although they can place new burdens on learners, provide opportunities to support inclusion and engagement with literacy. In the example that has been discussed, the tool used was TextEase 2000; this also provided a scaffold for the learners which reduced their need to seek adult support with spellings as they began to make use of the spell checker and text-to-speech engine in order to self-correct their spellings. Thus it not only promoted creative expression and literacy through new literacy tools, it also supported the learners' ability to spell in line with the school's narrow focus on accurate spelling.

While this section has focused on dyslexia and one specific intervention, it can be seen that new literacies and technology can form an important bridge between the social model of special education needs and the frequently narrow definitions of literacy that are used in schools.

Conclusion

This chapter has looked at a number of issues that relate to the new literacies and how they can be employed to make literacy more accessible for all. It has done this by focusing on some specific groups including those who have English as an additional language, females and those with special education needs (specifically dyslexia). However, the key points from this chapter should not be limited to these groups. The message is that the combination of a broad and deep understanding of literacy, an awareness of the role that technology can play, as well as familiarity with the scope of new literacies should be applied widely to support the general message of inclusion which formed the introduction to this chapter.

Further Reading

The most current version of TextEase is available here: www.textease.com/.

For more reading about special education needs either of the following texts would be good:

Peer, L and Reid, G. (2012) *Special Educational Needs: A guide for inclusive practice*. London: Sage.

Armstrong, D. and Squires, G. (2012) *Contemporary Issues in Special Educational Needs: Considering the whole child*. Maidenhead: Open University Press.

Considering pedagogy, ethics and the law in the 'remix' culture

Debbie Simpson

Chapter Focus

This chapter invites you to explore cultural, pedagogical, legal and ethical perspectives of digitised and networked information. In particular you will consider the practice of 'remix' as a literacy activity, and consider how you can harness some aspects of digital remix in order to enhance children's learning and social development. You will consider how to ensure that you understand and comply with copyright and intellectual property laws as they affect teachers and pupils in school. Beyond this you will consider the role of teachers in developing your own and your pupils' awareness of ethical behaviour when engaging with digital technologies.

The critical thinking exercises in this chapter focus on:

⊙ **considering** the potential benefits for children's literacy of the sharing and modification 'remix' culture associated with digital technologies;
⊙ **identifying** the legal and ethical issues associated with digital technologies that affect teachers, pupils and schools with regard to reuse and publishing of information;
⊙ **exploring** strategies for handling information legally and ethically;
⊙ **articulating** ways in which you as a teacher can play a part in modelling high standards of ethical behaviour and encouraging children to develop principles that take account of the sensitivities, needs and feelings of others.
⊙ The key ideas discussed are: **remix culture and new literacies, ownership of information, copyright and intellectual property law, creative commons** and **responsibilities of teachers and schools to promote ethical behaviour.**

This chapter is particularly relevant to the following Teachers' Standards (2012):

Part 1: Teaching

A teacher must:

1 Set high expectations which inspire, motivate and challenge pupils
   ⊙ establish a safe and stimulating environment for pupils, rooted in mutual respect

/continued

Chapter Focus – continued

- demonstrate consistently the positive attitudes, values and behaviour which are expected of pupils

2 Promote good progress and outcomes by pupils
- encourage pupils to take a responsible and conscientious attitude to their own work and study

4 Plan and teach well-structured lessons
- promote a love of learning and children's intellectual curiosity
- set homework and plan other out-of-class activities to consolidate and extend the knowledge and understanding pupils have acquired.

Introduction

'Babies with superpowers'

This chapter begins with a case study that introduces some of the benefits and challenges encountered by one Newly Qualified Teacher using digital technologies in her cross-curricular History unit. We examine the emerging 'remix' culture that digital technology makes possible and consider its affordances for children's learning. In Chapter 7 we discussed the implications for children's mental and physical health associated with issues of identity, safeguarding privacy and managing interaction with others online. In this chapter we take a closer look at the legal and ethical implications of using digital technologies. Children, teachers and schools can all be vulnerable to actual or reputational damage by falling foul of the law or by behaving unethically.

In a report on digital media and learning, Carrie James (James et al., 2009) describes young people engaging with digital technologies as *babies with superpowers* because their technical competence frequently outstrips their ability to understand and manage the possible consequences of their actions. It is easy for children using technology to get into situations that are potentially risky, possibly illegal and ethically questionable. It is the responsibility of adults to provide guidance to help children to use their 'superpowers' responsibly and safely so that they can make the most of the opportunities offered by technology for them to learn and have fun. This chapter includes practical suggestions for how teachers can use digital technology to inspire and develop children's learning while complying with current laws and modelling values of respect, honesty, trust and integrity.

CASE STUDY

Tudor presentations

Heather is a newly qualified teacher working with a Year 6 class. She asks her pupils to work in pairs to create multimedia presentations during the final phase of a unit of study on Tudor England. The activity takes place over several lessons.

Heather structured the lessons carefully, first introducing the children to examples of presentations and discussing with them the potential for using multimedia to develop and share their ideas. She identified appropriate websites and ensured that the children knew how to copy and paste text and pictures into their presentations. Heather was really encouraged by how quickly the children became independent in selection and use of source materials, and how well they followed the school's 'Safe Internet Use' guidelines. Children recorded their own narration onto the slides and added Tudor music sourced from the internet. One group of children embedded an extract from the recent BBC History series *The Tudors* into their presentation.

Heather's evaluation of the lesson showed that throughout the project the children remained engaged, motivated and on task. They made appropriate choices of content that demonstrated their understanding of the historical context, and combined and edited the content in creative ways to make their ideas clear. They presented their work to a high standard, demonstrating an awareness of the needs of their audience. Children shared technical expertise with each other as well as ideas related to the content.

The children's presentations were of such a high standard that Heather decided to share them at a school Open Evening. The enthusiastic response from parents encouraged her to seek a wider audience by posting the presentations on to the school's website. The children were thrilled to receive positive comments on their work from all over the world.

Two weeks later the head teacher of Heather's school received a letter from a photographer claiming that some images of a Tudor mansion included in the children's presentations were copyrighted material. She requested payment for the republication of these images on the school website. Heather explained to the head teacher that copyright law did not apply in this case as the original images were not marked with the copyright symbol, and that furthermore they were used by the children for non-profit, educational purposes only.

Unfortunately Heather was mistaken. She like many of us over-estimated her right to use materials in an educational context and believed that if materials were not marked by the copyright symbol ©, this meant that they were freely

/continued

CASE STUDY – continued

available for reuse or republishing without the permission of the owner. All originally created work *is* automatically subject to copyright and does not need to display a copyright notice to be protected in law. Educational, non-profit use is not excluded from the law.

By posting the presentations on a freely available website Heather had in effect become a publisher and so legally the photographer was correct to claim payment. The matter was resolved when Heather wrote to the photographer and apologised for her mistake. She immediately removed the copyrighted images from the website and the matter was dropped.

A BBC News report (2008) outlined the dangers facing schools republishing images and other media from the internet.

School websites are elaborate and highly professional notice boards packed full of text and images with content usually provided by staff, students and parents.

But if schools are tempted to include material from other internet sites, without prior permission, they could face unexpected bills.

Photographers and photo agencies can now trace their pictures with the help of specially designed software which alert them when their material appears on the internet.

If the publisher has not gained prior permission to use their material, they are breaching copyright laws and may be asked to reimburse the owner.

Jean-Louise Green who runs Picture Nation picture library said: 'The problem schools have is that while a lot of images are OK for them to use under the "education" umbrella, when they out those images on their websites or swap lesson plans with those images in, they are facilitating the free re-distribution of those images and that is where the problems are occurring.'

Copyright lawyer Linda Macpherson said there is a fairly common misconception that material can be freely copied if this is for educational purposes.

'A school that uses images taken from the internet on its own website will be infringing copyright unless the copyright owner consents.

'In theory, a school could end up with a large bill for using pictures from the internet without consent.
'The school could also end up in court if it refused to pay,' she said.

http://news.bbc.co.uk/1/hi/education/7283926.stm

Key idea: **New literacies and the remix culture**

> *Remix* describes the process of modifying or adapting an existing creative work in any media: music, text, image, video, etc. The remix may be subtle, or it may completely redefine how the work comes across. It may add new elements or include parts of other works, but generally it is focused on creating an alternative version of the original.

The American lawyer and academic Lawrence (Larry) Lessig argues that 'remix culture': the practice of incorporating existing texts (including audio-visual media, ideas and information) into new artefacts, is a significant mass literacy practice. Lessig believes that existing laws regarding copyright and intellectual property should be reformed as they stifle innovation and creative expression. *Remix in art is, of course, nothing new. What is new is the law's take on this remix* (Lessig, 2004, page 48).

'Remix' has a long history. Shakespeare based some of his plays on existing stories and borrowed freely from text written by others. Classical composers such as Brahms, Dvořák and Bartok 'sampled' folk music and popular songs of the time in their compositions. For an introduction to 'remix culture', and the impact of copyright and intellectual property laws, see the series of short online videos by Kirby Ferguson at **www.everythingisaremix.info/watch-the-series**/. These are clear, accessible and entertaining and provide plenty of examples of 'remix in action', showing how widespread it is in popular culture. Ferguson (2011) defines creativity as people's ability to *copy, transform and combine* existing artefacts and ideas, and he provides examples from the worlds of science, technology, art, music and film to show that almost all human achievement builds on what has gone before. In the words of Isaac Newton we are all 'standing on the shoulders of giants'.

From a New Literacies perspective there are strong educational arguments for considering 'remix' as a classroom activity. Through remixing digital assets to create new artefacts children develop skills and working habits relevant to the 21st century. Knowing how to select, edit and combine resources purposefully, and to share the new artefact with others for evaluation and further development are key workplace skills. New technology techniques and practices are developed almost as an incidental part of this process and not as an end in themselves. Consider how quickly and retentively you grasped how to operate technologies that had a purpose for you: your mobile phone, social network site or computer game; and compare this to a context where you needed to learn technology skills that held no immediate purpose or interest for you (spreadsheets are often an example of this!).

Remix can also be used as an opportunity to introduce children to new concepts: about the nature of art, about originality and creativity and, as will be explored later on in this chapter, about the ethical dilemmas associated with everyday activities such as downloading music or videos or republishing images on social networks and blogs.

A socio-cultural critique of school practice in literacy frequently suggests that it is remote from many children's actual experiences and interests. This can have the effect of marginalising children who are already at risk of failing. Teachers know that if pupils cannot see the relevance of activities then they will quickly become bored and frustrated and this has a negative impact on learning. Further, if what children are told in school – 'copying is always wrong!' – directly contradicts their experience of everyday life where artists such as 50 Cent and Kanye West make fortunes from sampling and remixing tracks, this can make school, and teachers, seem irrelevant and out of touch.

If, however, activities build on children's existing skills and interests then they are more likely to promote engagement and learning. Through acknowledging current, authentic literary practices alongside traditional print-based materials, teachers can provide children with opportunities to discover and articulate their own interpretations of texts and other media. Bryant (2007, page 18) believes that it makes good educational sense to engage with the digital technologies and social practices engaged in by many children today because *the fundamental pattern of learning and innovation using social tools: find » remix » share, seems ideally suited to the way most young people like to discover and make sense of the world around them.*

Critical thinking exercise 1: *Find » remix » share:* creativity or theft?

Consider the following examples where artists have 'appropriated' the work of others in order to create a new artwork.

Example 1
Use an internet image search engine to find an image of the artwork *Hymn,* by Damien Hirst. It is a 6-metre high bronze sculpture which has been described as an 'iconic, ironic visual statement'. Compare this to an image of the 'Young Scientist Anatomy Set' manufactured by *Humbrol Limited.*

Example 2
Use an internet image search to find a copy of 'Campbell's Soup Cans', a series of silk screen prints by Andy Warhol featuring the iconic Campbell's labels for condensed soup. You will probably be already familiar with the artwork as the images are amongst the most iconic of the 20th century. Compare with a 'real' Campbell's Soup Can label.

Example 3
Identify a work you value, from the field of literature, film, music or art, where the creator has clearly derived aspects of it from the work of another artist.
For all three examples, **list** the pros and cons of appropriation; it may be helpful to consider the issue first from the point of view of the original artist, and then of the remix artist. From your list identify which of your points relate to the law, and

/continued

'*Campbell's Soup Cans*' by Andy Warhol in the Museum of Modern Art, New York. Photo from palindrome6996's photostream.

'*Hymn*' by Damian Hirst.
Photo by Peter Bjork.

Both images licensed by Creative Commons through Flickr (by-nd)

Critical thinking exercise 1 – continued

which are based on ethical judgements about right and wrong. For example, it may be legal in some countries for an artist to profit from remixing, but do you think it is 'right'? Use your notes to help you to **articulate** your own view regarding 'artistic' appropriation. Is remix legitimate artistic activity or is it morally wrong? Are your conclusions the same for each of the examples above?

Discuss whether you would feel comfortable appropriating the work of someone else. How would you feel if your work was appropriated? It is interesting to note that some of the artists who regularly sample the work of others are often very quick to threaten legal action if their own work is remixed.

The legality and ethicality of the Hirst sculpture was widely debated in the media at the time of its first exhibition in 2000. A typical report can be found in the *Guardian* newspaper archives (**www.guardian.co.uk/uk/2000/may/19/claredyer1**). Hirst settled out of court with Humbrol, making a substantial payment to a children's charity to avoid legal action for breach of copyright.

Comment

Many children, by the time they reach Upper Primary, will have sufficient access to technology and the expertise to be engaging outside of school in some 'remixing' of their own. New technologies and a large number of web-based tools and downloadable applications (apps) for phones and tablets have made it simple, cheap and fun to find, remix and share text and audio-visual media, and children are likely to be familiar with some of the 'buzzwords' that have emerged to describe remix practices

---

such as *sampling*, *bricolage* and *mashup*. These terms are explored below; together with some ideas for including remix approaches in your classroom.

Sampling

Contemporary dance music makes extensive use of sampling techniques, incorporating previously recorded sounds in a new track. You will no doubt be able to think of many examples of music that includes sampling, such as 'SOS' by Rihanna (2006), which samples the song 'Tainted Love' by the 1980s band Soft Cell. Sampling can also be detected outside of the music world; T.S. Eliot's poem *The Waste Land* (1922) famously 'samples' more than 30 literary sources.

Sampling leverages the power of imitation as a learning tool. Children are avid 'samplers' of popular culture in their talk and in their play. Marsh and Willett (2010) found that children drew extensively on television sources such as talk shows and reality talent shows to inform their role-play games in the playground: noting that *media characters, texts and/or artefacts, seep into all aspects of their lives from a young age* (page 5). Children also draw inspiration from computer games (including Wii games) and internet sites such as YouTube. Sampling of music, text and video as a classroom activity can be used to provide 'building blocks' for children to use as a basis for their own creative compositions. This approach can be motivational through making links to children's everyday experience and interests, and through enabling a 'quick start' by bypassing the daunting 'blank sheet of paper'. It also provides a context to raise questions about the nature of composition. You could discuss with children why some artists, musical phrases or drum-breaks (or writers, texts and plot devices) are so frequently sampled, and explore what differentiates one interpretation from another.

The Department for Education website includes case studies of children sampling idioms (well-known phrases) from the King James Bible and using these as a basis to create and perform their own rhymes and raps. These were videoed by a local film company and shown at a community event. In another activity, children performed drama based on the biblical idioms 'an eye for an eye', 'spare the rod and spoil the child' and 'am I my brother's keeper?' which they applied to the modern-day setting of a storyline from *Coronation Street.*

www.education.gov.uk/schools/toolsandinitiatives/b00205257/king-james-bible/case-studies/king-james-school

Bricolage

Bricolage is a French word similar to the English term *Do It Yourself* (DIY), and refers to something created from whatever materials are at hand. Seymour Papert (1991) defined constructionist learning as 'bricolage': tinkering with whatever resources are available to invent and construct something new. Papert wrote extensively in the 1980s about the need for children to learn how to control and create with technology as well as being consumers of content, and he devised the programming language LOGO to help them achieve this. Today, there is renewed interest in Papert's ideas, with support from the

Department for Education and others for teaching children programming using applications such as *Scratch*, which can be downloaded free from **scratch.mit.edu** and installed on your school network.

The name *Scratch* comes from the technique used by hip hop DJs of spinning vinyl records to mix music clips together in creative ways. Similarly, Scratch programming enables children to create animations and games through mixing together a wide variety of media: graphics, photos, music, and sounds and sharing them online through the *Scratch* community at **scratch.mit.edu**. Anyone can play and comment on a project, or download, modify and re-upload it to their own profile. Currently more than 25 per cent of the projects are modifications or *'remixes'* of other projects, and 71 per cent participants say that they began learning Scratch through editing a project created by someone else.

In the Scratch community, as elsewhere, people care about how their projects are remixed. Most users expect to be credited in a remixed work for their original idea, and most also expect creative changes to have been made to the original before re-upload (i.e. not just a straight copy). The Scratch community website automatically adds a link back to the source project, so the original author gets credit. Each project includes links to its 'derivatives' (projects remixed from it), and the 'Top Remixed' projects are featured prominently on the Scratch homepage. This emerging culture can be a very useful way for children to combine learning to program while at the same time developing an awareness of ethical practice through participating in a remix community.

Mashup

A *mashup* combines digital information from two or more sources to create something not intended or even imagined by the original creators. Mashed up music videos are popular and there are hundreds of examples, good and bad, available to view on YouTube, not all of which are suitable for viewing in school. One that is, combines the Bee Gees with Pink Floyd, in a work called *'Stayin' Alive in the Wall'* **www.youtube. com/watch?v=U13xOvDa19U**. You will no doubt be able to find your own favourites.

Literary mashups enjoyed a brief spell of popularity a few years ago with *Pride and Prejudice and the Zombies* being the best-known example. Teachers have long made use of a similar genre-switching approach to develop literacy skills, rewriting *The Three Little Pigs* as a newspaper report for example, or taking two favourite fairy tales and mixing them up (*Cinderhood; The Gingerbread Beanstalk*). Rebranding this technique as 'mashup' and using digital media to bring the production to life might help inspire children's interest and creativity.

Your social networking page on Facebook, if you have one, is a form of 'mashup' as it probably combines digital media contributed by yourself and your friends with a range of services, games and other content including targeted advertising. Teachers can introduce the technique of combining original and sampled content on a digital platform to encourage children to present their own takes on a topic. The presentations created by the children in Heather's class in the case study above could be described as 'mashups', bringing together as they did text and images, video, audio and narration both original and derived from internet sources. Related terms include *collaging* or *digital scrapbooking/e-scrapbooking*. There are various online tools for creating collages, posters or project boards from media assembled from different sources. Examples include Photovisi **www.photovisi.com**, Pinterest **pinterest.com**, Glogster **edu.glogster.com**, Web Poster Wizard **poster.4teachers.org** or Prezi **prezi.com**. Alternatively, you could use any standard application which supports media mixing and editing, such as Microsoft PowerPoint, Microsoft Photostory 3 or iLife multimedia software on Apple systems.

Remix and the new literacies

Current educational thinking about 'remix culture' is ambivalent. In terms of the new literacies, as illustrated briefly in some of the examples above, 'sampling', merging sources, and building on existing media to create new work are regarded as legitimate approaches to teaching and learning. They are seen as a way of democratising culture by widening the scope of what is defined as creativity and breaking down barriers to literacy for children from disparate backgrounds. By engaging with remix practices learners also engage with questions about the distinctiveness of authorial voice: what makes a work of high quality, where an idea comes from, how it is put together and what makes it powerful; concepts which will be familiar from most traditional literacy teaching. Through participating in 'publish and share' sites such as the Scratch community, children feel proud, not upset, when their projects are adapted and remixed by others. They learn the value of collaboration, co-operation and co-teaching when developing projects; all core 21st-century skills for the workplace.

However, some educationalists would argue that sampled or remixed work is automatically inferior to 'original' work, and point out that 'copying', particularly without attribution, carries the social stigma of plagiarism. There is a sense that incorporating the work of others into one's own is a parasitic practice: a means of benefitting unfairly from someone else's effort. Furthermore, as we saw in the case study, there is often confusion about the legality of reusing materials from online sources. These questions of legality and ethicality are considered in later in this chapter, but first we examine children's attitudes to 'copying' from the web.

Key idea: **Ownership, authorship and the appropriation of ideas**

'I copy off the net because everyone else does it so why shouldn't I?'

Online, children and adults alike practise a culture of appropriation with regard to digital material enabled and encouraged by Web 2.0 tools. If you have a social

/continued

Key idea: **Ownership, authorship and the appropriation of ideas** – continued

networking site you will know how easy it is to share images and videos, and to embed material from the internet on to your home page to share with friends. From this perfectly legal activity it may seem a small step to downloading copyrighted materials and sharing these files with others. James et al. (2009) points out that many websites provide free, or a mix of free and paid for content, which can give rise to confusion among children about what is and is not legal to download. She identifies an 'infringing culture' where many children believe that if something can be copied and pasted, or downloaded then it is automatically OK to use it.

It is likely that you first met the term *plagiarism* during study skills sessions in the first year of your university course. The word *plagiarism* is derived from a Latin verb meaning 'to kidnap', and it refers to the practice of acquiring the work of others and passing it off as your own. At one time an aspiring plagiarist needed to laboriously rewrite or retype a passage from a printed book or journal and it must have been fairly clear to them that this was inappropriate behaviour. Digital technology, however, has made it easier to copy and paste chunks of text from one place to another, and unintentional plagiarism is much more likely if students do not keep careful track of the source of their notes. The internet has opened up a much wider variety of sources of information and this might lead students into the mistaken belief that the chances of detection are low. It may even tempt them into using one of the essay writing sites that offer downloadable assignments for a fee.

In recent research, Dan Rigby, an economics lecturer at Manchester University, found that half of university students would be prepared to submit assignments purchased from the internet. Rigby questioned 90 second and third year students at three universities and found they would be prepared to pay more than £300 for a first-class essay, £217 for a piece of work worth a 2:1 and £164 for a 2:2.

Most universities in the UK already use the software *Turnitin* to check assignments for plagiarism but higher education may be too late for learners to be first introduced to the importance of valuing other people's work and referencing appropriately. Some commentators, such as Dr Christine Urquhart of Aberystwyth University, believe that plagiarism begins in primary schools. Internet research involving cutting, pasting and printing from the web has become standard practice for projects and homework and Dr Urquhart points out that schoolchildren don't realise it's wrong to present someone else's work as their own. She also considers that some teachers value children's presentation of work above its content: *The computer work looked pretty and attractive and they got plus points. But printing things off the computer makes plagiarism easier... There is too much emphasis now on appearances.*

Critical thinking exercise 2

Read the following comments recorded by young teenagers (aged 11–15) on a BBC discussion forum. **Analyse** the comments for the reasons given for plagiarising work; do you have sympathy with any of the views expressed? Do the comments provide any hints for teachers keen to educate children to avoid plagiarism?

If I have to do a project I will normally copy and paste most of the work. I do research from books sometimes, and just copy big chunks out of them instead! It saves a lot of time and it's a quick and easy way of getting all the information you need.

I never use things from the internet for my homework, because it's just not fair. My friends do it, but I still tell them it's not right and then they say I'm right, but they started too late on their essay.

Yes I do it all the time, it's great! It helps me do it quicker so that I can get on with the more important thing of playing with my friends.

I only cheat if I forget to do my homework.

When I have eight subjects of homework at the weekend like last week, I don't really care if the homework is mine or not.

I copy off the net because everyone else does it why shouldn't I. And also after school is your free time so homework should be scrapped altogether except coursework and other important stuff, but if we have to do it you might as well do it quickly.

I sometimes do, I don't see the point in having homework after you've been at school all day, so I just rush it and get it over and done with by getting it off the net!

It gives me more spare time and the teachers don't notice.

What I do is copy off large chunks and print it off, then make it into bullet points and explain it in my own words. It is handy if you can't go to a library.

I never copy important stuff like coursework or essays but I use the internet for almost all my homework and often copy and paste without even reading it. But everyone does so it don't really matter.

You should be allowed to use the net for homework help, and I do admit to copy and pasting the odd sentence occasionally, but some people can be so lazy and it can be obvious they've not even read what they're handing in. It's also down to teachers to pick up on this, not to give people high marks for ICT skills in a history essay on WW1, for example.

/continued

> **Critical thinking exercise 2** – continued
> *I sometimes feel tempted to cheat because of the strain that my parents and teachers put on me. Cheating seems a good easy way to get brilliant marks.*
> **http://news.bbc.co.uk/cbbcnews/hi/chat/your_comments/newsid_3513000/3513234.stm**

Comment

As these comments illustrate there are a number of reasons why learners are tempted to plagiarise. They are aware that copying and pasting straight from the internet is disapproved of in schools but pressures of time and workload, competing priorities, the 'everyone does it' culture, high parental expectations and the simplicity of hoodwinking teachers all present temptations. However, if we agree that university, or even secondary school, is too late to tackle plagiarism, we need to help children to develop good study habits in primary schools.

Strategies for introducing ethical use of information

Even quite young children have strong feelings about the concept of 'fairness' and can begin to articulate reasons why it might be unfair to copy the work of others. Children can engage in role-playing everyday situations, discussing how they would feel for example if someone copied their answers to maths problems. You might encourage children to compare copying the work of a classmate to lifting ideas directly from the internet or other digital sources.

BBC Learning Zone

The BBC hosts a series of video clips and lesson materials to help teachers to introduce concepts of legal and ethical use of technology. You can find these on the *BBC Learning Zone* website at **bbc.co.uk/learningzone/clips/**. The short videos introduce characters in a band called *'The Alleyk@tz'* who encounter issues of copyright and plagiarism as they create music and market their band. Each clip is accompanied with ideas for its use in the classroom. Video Clip 9483 is a short animated cartoon suitable for children in Key Stage 2 that explains what plagiarism is and outlines appropriate ways of using digital sources. Clip 9484 introduces and explains the importance of copyright.

Cracking Ideas

The Intellectual Property Office (IPO) which is responsible for overseeing patents and trademarks has teamed up with Aardman Animations, the creators of *Wallace and Gromit,* to create a website aimed at introducing children to the world of innovation and creativity at **www.crackingideas.com**. To help children nurture their creativity and generate new ideas the website contains a wealth of educational resources and curriculum links that can be downloaded free. These aim to help teachers educate children to understand the personal and economic value of intellectual property, and explain how they can protect their own innovations and ideas. The education packs are designed for children aged 4–7 years, 8–11 years or 12–16 years.

Kids Britannica

Alongside learning cutting and pasting skills when researching topics, children can be taught to acknowledge the source of the information in simple ways, for example by pasting the source URL to indicate where content has been derived from online sources. The excellent Encyclopaedia Britannica for kids, **kids.britannica.com,** provides properly formatted references for all of its articles. Searching for 'penguins' and choosing an article link from the list provides information together with a choice of citation formats for copy and pasting.

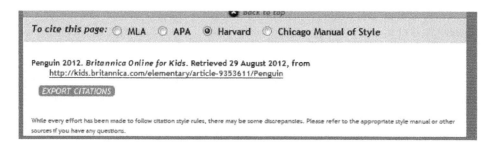

Example of citation panel from *Encyclopaedia Britannica Kids* online.

kids.britannica.com/elementary/article-353611/Penguin?.9353611.toc

Authors' Licensing and Collecting Society (ALCS)

The Authors' Licensing and Collecting Society (ALCS) produces a one-page summary of copyright that is suitable for posting in your classroom or computer room. It presents the key rules about copyright in an accessible way. Entitled *Copyright for young people* (192 kb), it is available for download from **www.alcs.co.uk/Resources/Document-library/ Other.** The poster explains that copyright is automatic for all written work and authors do not need to apply for it. It can be signalled by the copyright symbol , but whether or not this is present the work is still protected under the law.

Creative Commons

Children will learn to value the work of others if their own work is valued. Encourage them to use the copyright symbol on their written and creative work and to check with classmates for permission before sharing work. To type on a PC hold down the *Ctrl* and *Alt* keys and press 'c'; on a Mac hold down *Alt* and press 'g'. You might also invite children to label their work using the **Creative Commons** classifications. These are explained in more detail in the next section. Establishing a culture of collaboration, co-operation and sharing in your classroom can help children to recognise that the proper accreditation of sources is a compliment that they can both give and receive.

Key idea: **Legally blended?**

How can I ensure that I, and the children in my class, stay within the law?
In the case study at the beginning of this chapter Heather was prompted by the
enthusiasm of the children into seeking a wider audience through publishing their
work, containing third party images, to the school's website. By effectively
becoming a publisher herself she risked prosecution and a fine for copyright
infringement. She, and her school may well have felt that this was an extreme
penalty for re-using images for non-profit educational purposes and many people
would agree. A government commission looking into current UK copyright law
(2011) concluded that UK copyright law is over-complicated, fails to reflect the
digital age, and is likely to be a barrier to creativity and economic growth. The
commission has called for reform on the grounds that the current law blocks
valuable new technologies simply because those technologies were not imagined
when the law was formed. It also found that, like Heather, most people are
confused about what is allowed under copyright law and what is not.

Critical thinking exercise 3

Copyright law is based on the principle of protecting the rights of an author or
creator so that he or she can profit for a reasonable period by their investment of
time and effort. Bearing this principle in mind, **consider** the following questions of
copyright in school and **decide** which activities you think would be legal as they
are unlikely to have any impact on the creator, which activities may be restricted
in some way, and which may be against the law as they could cause harm or
loss to the original author.

1. Jane has an *Early Reading* book in her classroom that is only ten pages long.
   She scans it so that she can display it on her interactive whiteboard for whole
   class guided reading.
2. Tom uses some images from other websites on the school Learning Platform
   (VLE). He provides a link to the original source of the picture under each image.
3. Janet downloads a selection of Japanese fairy tales from **www.gutenberg.org/**
   for her Year 5 class to 'remix' to create their own versions. She then publishes
   the children's versions to the school website.
4. Iftikhar creates a resource file of art images from a CDROM owned by his
   school for printing and display in his classroom. He checks first that this is
   covered by his school's copyright licence. He then emails his resource file of
   images to a colleague in another school.

/continued

Critical thinking exercise 3 – continued

To help you decide how these teachers stand legally, see the following websites for guidance to the law regarding copyright in UK schools:

- http://copyrightandschools.org/
- http://schools.cla.co.uk/

Both sites are easy to use and have been written specifically for teachers and schools in the UK. You can if you wish post your individual copyright queries to the sites for legal experts to answer. You can also 'follow' the CLA 'Copyright Geek' on *Twitter*: *@CopyrightGeek* and tweet your questions to him.

Comment

The answers given below to the copyright questions above assume that your school is covered by the Copyright Licensing Agency (CLA) Schools' Licence, as is the case in most state maintained schools. If you are unsure whether this applies in your school, check with your Head teacher, administrator or librarian. Information about the CLA licence for schools can be found on the schools CLA website at **schools.cla.co.uk/**.

1. Jane's action does breach copyright. This is because the CLA only covers the reproduction of one chapter (or 5 per cent, whichever is greatest) of an original copy of a book owned by your school. This is regardless of the length of the book. Publishers often provide interactive digital resources to support such activities and it is recommended that these are used where available. This is so that the investment of the author and the publisher are protected.

2. Tom's action is legal if the website where the image is from is a digital publisher which has opted in to the CLA licence scheme. A list of these publishers together with the terms and conditions for reuse is available from the CLA website **schools.cla.co.uk/your-cla-schools-licence/what-can-be-copied/digital-material-publishers/**. If the publisher isn't included on this list then it is worth contacting the creator or copyright holder of the image directly to ask for permission to re-use their work. In either case, it's good practice to credit the creator of the image. If you can't find the name of the creator then a weblink to the source site is better than nothing. This ensures that the rights of the copyright holder are respected and due credit is given.

3. This is perfectly legal. The *Project Gutenberg* site contains ebooks that are free of copyright restrictions because they are in the **Public Domain**. These texts can be used with almost no restrictions whatsoever, i.e. copied, reused and republished. UK law considers that allowing a creator of an original text to profit from their efforts for the duration of their own lifetime and for their descendants to reap the benefits for a further 70 years represents a reasonable reward for effort. After that time, in most cases, the text is in the public domain and is not subject to copyright. Sound

---

recordings and films enter the public domain 50 years after release. For a selection of public domain children's books browse the Project Gutenberg *Children's Bookshelf* section.

4. Iftikhar is risking prosecution by emailing the copies of his file to a colleague. If you make any resource, which incorporates other material, such as text, images or audiovisual elements, you do not have the right to share this with other schools, even though you may be licensed to use it within your own school. This includes uploading copyright content to any externally accessible website including a Learning Platform or school website, or sharing via email or a blog.

Creative Commons

Thankfully, many digital publishers provide media materials that you and your class can reuse freely, and this will be specifically stated on the site. Check for an 'OK for education use' notice and read its terms and conditions. Additionally, there is an increasing amount of material that schools, and others, can use without having to pay or seek special permissions because it is labelled as '*Creative Commons*'. Creative Commons was founded by Larry Lessig whose ideas we met earlier in this chapter. It means that the creator of a work retains copyright, but gives others permission to use it in specified ways. There are several categories of creative commons, the main categories and their codes and conditions are listed below:

- (BY) Attribution – you must credit the creator of the work.
- (NC) Non-commercial – you may not use the work for commercial purposes.
- (ND) No derivative works – you may not alter, transform or build upon this work.
- (SA) Share alike – if you alter, transform or build upon the work, you may distribute the resulting work only under a licence identical to this one i.e. you must allow others to use your new work in the same way.

All CC licenses require attribution to the author (BY) but this basic permission can be extended by adding one or more of the other three conditions. For example, BY-NC means that you can use the work provided you credit the original creator and do not try to profit from the work. A short film that explains the system can be found at **creativecommons.org/videos/creative-commons-kiwi**.

Below are the creative commons logos that children can copy or draw on their own work.

 Attribution (BY)

 Non Derivative Works (ND)

Non-commercial (NC)

 Share Alike (SA)

Logos from **creativecommons.org**

Finding creative commons and public domain resources

Search engines such as *Google* or *Yahoo* and media sharing sites such as *Flickr* and *YouTube* now feature advanced search options, which return lists of resources with Creative Commons licenses. *Geograph* **geograph.org.uk/** features a collection of Creative Commons photographs from every part of the British Isles. *Openclipart* **openclipart.org** has a wide range of public domain images that can be used without restriction. *Ictopus* **ictopus.org.uk** is a free web-based support service for primary education that includes a copyright free picture gallery of high quality images linked to education. See the **Useful Resources** section at the end of this chapter for other sources.

What about YouTube?

YouTube has become an increasingly valuable resource and many teachers use YouTube video clips for teaching. Because some schools block YouTube from their networks, teachers sometimes download and convert YouTube clips for use offline. If you choose to do this caution is advised. Thousands of YouTube clips breach copyright as the site places the onus on people who post video clips to the site to honour copyright. Clips that are reported to YouTube as breaking copyright are promptly removed, but they may have been available for some time before this happens. Don't be tempted to put a downloaded YouTube clip on a school website without checking that it is in the public domain, is registered as creative commons, or has been otherwise cleared for educational use. If you are not sure, use the YouTube 'embed' tool or create a hyperlink back to the YouTube site. If you want to block comments and advertising from the YouTube site then the Quietube filter (**quietube.com**) will do this.

One simple action you could consider is to contact a copyright owner directly to ask for permission to use their materials. A polite email stating where you found the media, the purpose you wish to use it for and the extent to which you will be republishing it will usually suffice, provided you can find an email address or contact details. Most copyright holders are delighted that you find their work useful and are only too happy to give permission for you to use it, particularly for educational purposes. Do ask how they would like to be credited for their work. If you are likely to profit commercially from the reuse then you may be asked for, or might offer, a small payment.

Key idea: **Ethics in the classroom: What you do reflects on you**

How can teachers encourage children's ethical use of technology? Most teachers would agree that networked digital technologies offer tremendous potential for learning; however, many have concerns about children's vulnerability when engaging with a network where information is literally 'out of control'.

As information and communications technologies move from a peripheral to a central role in everyday life, attitudes are shifting from unrestrained optimism about the internet, which was described by the DFEE in 1997 as making *available to all learners the riches of the world's intellectual, cultural and scientific heritage* to a more measured recognition that with these riches come new challenges.

In the late 1990s many schools responded to concerns about children's use of technology by seeking to limit and control access. Most schools allowed children to use the internet only with adult supervision, and online access was restricted to so-called 'walled gardens' of pre-approved applications, content and media. Pupils were warned to communicate via the internet only with people that they already knew and with the permission of (and preferably in the presence of) a teacher or parent. More than a decade later adult concerns persist but children have many more opportunities for unrestricted and unsupervised access to the internet. Mobile phones and tablets, games consoles and TVs are connected to the internet as a matter of course, and young people are noticeably more proficient than many adults in using them to browse wherever they please and download any content that appeals to them. They can and do share information with each other about how to get round age and other restrictions on social networking, gaming and file-sharing sites.

Studies have shown that teachers in primary education still emphasise technical skills in ICT lessons. The social and ethical strands of ICT generally have a much lower priority (Tondeur *et al.*, 2007). Turvey (2006) argues that the current attitude in schools towards technology is highly risk averse, and while this stems from a duty of care towards children and a desire to protect them from potential dangers, the gap is widening *between schools that choose to ignore significant new forms of communication and the wider society which continues to embrace them* (no page number). The growing importance of technology in society suggests that we should pay more, not less, attention to our ethical responsibilities as educators.

We cannot supervise children all the time so we need to promote in them a safe and ethical approach to technology. This includes educating them to have a regard for the physical, mental, intellectual, reputational and economic welfare of themselves and others. Children usually have a pronounced interest in principles of fairness and unfairness, and can with guidance begin to develop ethical values of respecting the individual needs and rights of other people alongside their own wishes and desires.

CASE STUDY

File sharing in Year 6

In conversation with a Year 6 class recently I was struck by children's confidence as they explained how to locate, download and share music tracks, games and other files. They cited their favourite websites for sharing which included a

/continued

CASE STUDY – continued

number of well-known pirate (illegal) sites. Pupils had learned from their older siblings that as one website is closed down or blocked following copyright infringement, another will spring up to take its place. Their teacher shook her head and declared that there was no one in school with the necessary technical and legal knowledge to address these issues with the children. This was surprising, as this teacher had more than 20 years' experience of teaching Key Stage 2 children and she had dealt successfully with a huge range of behaviours and situations. Yet when confronted with a context involving the ethical use of networked technologies she immediately felt out of her depth. If the children had been sharing information about how to help oneself to goods from a local shop without paying, the teacher would have had no difficulty in knowing how to respond.

Some teachers' lack of confidence with technology and uncertainly about the law may indicate a need for targeted professional development; however, most teachers are competent to make judgements about the ethical use of technology, as it is inherently no different to ethical behaviour in any area of life. Our actions in the virtual world of information technology are equally subject to ethical principles as our actions in the 'real' world.

Critical thinking exercise 4: What is ethical behaviour?

The philosopher Immanuel Kant (1724–1804) argued that behaving ethically requires us to treat all people, including oneself, with respect. Kant believed that we should consider each individual person as an end in themselves and not as a stepping stone to achieve our own purposes and ambitions. So, for example, if we wish to use the work of someone else for any purpose of our own, simply to take it without acknowledgement is unethical because it treats the creator of the original work merely as the means by which we achieve our ends. Requesting permission and accrediting or paying them for the use of their work treats the creator as an individual worthy of respect; or as Kant would put it – as 'an end in themselves'.

This principle holds whether we know the creator personally or not, and whether an individual or a group of people is involved. 'File-sharing' a program or game on the internet to avoid paying for it breaks Kant's principle as it treats the creator(s) of the program with disrespect through depriving them of income which should

/continued

Critical thinking exercise 4 – continued

rightfully be theirs, just so that we can have the use or enjoyment of their work. It sets aside their individual rights and treats them as a means for us to get what we want. Another test of ethical behaviour is to consider what would happen if everyone behaved as we do, would the outcome be of general benefit to others or not?

Behaving ethically, therefore, invites us to consider whether our actions support the following outcomes:

- The general well-being of society.
- Individual rights and freedoms, including one's own.
- Treatment of others that respects their inherent value as individuals.
- Protection of oneself and others from harm.

Some primary schools' *Acceptable Use Policies* (AUP) for the Internet emphasise only the fourth of the above points: the protection of children. Frequently, policies fail to address the other three principles, although some schools are now beginning to address ethical issues. Locate a Primary School AUP, from a school you know or by entering the term *'Primary School Acceptable Use Policy'* into an internet search engine.

A **Evaluate** the extent to which the policy addresses the ethical dimension of technology use by children and teachers, as well as the e-safety aspects. Does the policy make it clear how children will be helped to understand how to behave ethically?

B **Decide** how you would respond to the children in the case study: *File sharing in Year 6* (above) if you were the teacher. What are the key issues that you would raise with them and how would you respond to the argument that 'Everyone does it!' What positive actions might you take to promote children's consideration of the impact of individual behaviour upon others?

C **Consider** your response to a colleague in school who copies an educational program without paying for it, or shares passwords to a site with subscription-only content. Does the justification that the action is taken for children's educational benefit outweigh the potential financial harm to the individual or company who own the copyright? What would you say to your colleague? Would you accept or refuse a copy of the program, or access to the password if it was offered to you?

Comment

Ethical education establishes the importance of children (and adults) taking their responsibilities seriously with regard to the well-being of others. Establishing clear guidelines for ethical behaviour within the school AUP is a good beginning but it is not sufficient on its own. Two further strategies include: focused teaching about information ethics; and yourself providing a positive role model of ethical behaviour.

Teaching ethical use of information and networked technologies should not take place in a one-off session but, like e-safety training, should be embedded throughout the teaching of ICT and also within other subjects where appropriate, such as Literacy, Citizenship or Religious Education lessons. ICT 'skills' development such as locating resources on the web, copy and pasting, image editing and multimedia work should always include some consideration of the legal and ethical implications of what children are learning. 'Babies' need to learn how to use their 'superpowers' legally, safely and responsibly.

So, as well as learning how to use search engines to find information, children should be encouraged to look for copyright information on websites. When your pupils download text, an image or some music to remix in a creative piece of their own, insist that a list of the sources and influences behind the piece is presented prominently alongside the work itself. Be on the alert for 'teachable moments', when news articles or incidents provide opportunities to debate online issues and ethical behaviour. Nancy Willard, author of *Cyber Safe Kids, Cyber Savvy Teens*, recommends working through the following questions with children when considering technology behaviours.

- Is this kind and respectful to others?
- How would I feel if someone did the same thing to me, or to my best friend?
- What would my parent or other trusted adult think or do?
- Would this violate any agreements, rules, or laws?
- How would I feel if my actions were reported in a newspaper?
- What would happen if everybody did this?
- Would it be OK if I did this in Real Life? How would this reflect on me?

The BBC Learning Zone materials at **bbc.co.uk/learningzone/clips/** mentioned in the previous section provide a resource for schools that addresses illegal file sharing and piracy (Clip 9485). It raises legal and ethical questions in a context suitable to raise awareness among Key Stage 2 children. The clip considers why it is unethical to download or share music, films and other files without permission.

Finally, teachers themselves need to model ethical technology use. If your pupils see you using pirated software or flouting copyright laws, then this will undermine any teaching you have provided about ethics. Conversely, the opposite is true. If, for example, you ensure that you display weblinks for images and information that you use in teaching presentations, or write to an author for permission to use their work in class; and if you talk about these actions with children as you engage in them, then this in itself will be a very powerful teaching tool.

Conclusion

In this chapter you have reflected on how technology empowers users to find, copy, edit and republish digital information quickly and easily. You have considered how drawing on the work of others can be seen as a legitimate and creative process, and that it can contribute to the widening of our understanding of what literacy is. Ways in which children's interest in 'remix culture' can be channelled to enrich their learning have been explored, together with some practical examples. The legal implications of reusing digital materials in your classroom have been raised and you have found out how to check if your intended use is permitted or not. You have also explored some sources of information about copyright and intellectual property that you can share with children in order to promote their good study habits. Finally, you have considered three crucial approaches to teaching ethical behaviour in school: providing clear and accurate guidelines, maximising opportunities to teach information ethics across the curriculum, and through being a good role model for the children.

Further Reading

For a very readable article on why teachers feel deskilled by technology when dealing with ethical issues see:

Johnson, D. (no date) Does technology change how schools teach ethical behaviors? Real Questions, Good Answers. *Knowledge Quest*, Vol 3 no. 2 Retrieved from www.doug-johnson.com/dougwri/does-technology-change-how-schools-teach-ethical-behaviors.html.

A great introduction to ethics written for Primary practitioners:

Knowles, G. and Lander, V. (2012). *Thinking Through Ethics and Values in Primary Education*. London: SAGE/Learning Matters.

For a discussion of participatory learning using Web 2.0 technologies, illustrated by real-world examples of educational practice see:

Merchant, G. (2009). Web 2.0, new literacies, and the idea of learning through participation. *English Teaching: Practice and Critique*, 8 (3): 8–20. Available from Sheffield Hallam University Research Archive (SHURA) at: http://shura.shu.ac.uk/1102/.

Useful Resources

Copyright in school

The Copyright Licensing Agency (CLA) **www.cla.co.uk**

The schools' section of the CLA **http://schools.cla.co.uk**

Consortium of licensing organisations provide clear advice about copyright in schools. You will find answers to most of your queries here: **http://copyrightandschools.org**

A Guide to schools and copyright **http://copyrightsandwrongs.e2bn.org/schools-a-copyright**

What is 'Creative Commons'?

www.creativecommons.org.uk/home/aboutCreativeCommons/ VideosaboutCreativeCommons.aspx

Copyright and intellectual property for children
Authors' Licensing and Collecting Society (ALCS) poster: **www.alcs.co.uk/Resources/ Document-library/Other.** *Copyright for young people* (192 kb)

ALCS/National Schools Partnership resources about copyright for the children. Includes lesson plans, teachers' notes and videos. Aimed at Key Stage 3 but also suitable for upper Key Stage 2: **www.copywrite.org.uk/resources.php**

BBC Learning Zone 'The Alleyk@tz' series for resources to inspire discussion about information ethics: **bbc.co.uk/learningzone/clips**

The *Intellectual Property Office (IPO)* and *Aardman Animations* **www.crackingideas.com**

Willard, Nancy. *Cyber-Safe Kids, Cyber-Savvy Teens: Helping Young People Learn to Make Safe and Responsible Choices Online.* Booklet available: **http://csriu.org/documents/ docs/cskcstreproduce.pdf**

Remix culture
The Artquest video case study and discussion of artistic expression and the law. See website for range of resources and advice for teachers and others, especially: 'When does artistic freedom become copyright infringement?' **www.artquest.org.uk/articles/ view/art-and-appropriation**.

Ferguson, Kirby. Introduction to 'remix culture', and the impact of copyright and intellectual property laws. A series of short online videos available at: **www.everythingisaremix.info/watch-the-series**.

Resources for remix
Search for creative commons media **http://search.creativecommons.org/**

Text
The Gutenberg Press **www.gutenberg.org/**

Images
Google advanced image search. Scroll to the foot of the page and choose your copyright option from the *usage rights* section **www.google.com/ advanced_image_search**

Flickr **www.flickr.com/commons**

Geograph **geograph.org.uk/**

Openclipart **openclipart.org**

Ictopus **ictopus.org.uk**

Stock Exchange **www.sxc.hu/rg/** not copyright free but very few restrictions apply to these images. Fine to reuse on school websites and in teaching resources.

Music and sounds
CCMixter **http://ccmixter.org/**

Jamendo **www.jamendo.com/en/**

PD Sounds **www.pdsounds.org/**

Video
YouTube lists the licence status of videos published on the site, where known. Look for videos that carry a *Creative Commons* licence. This guide shows how
www.youtube.com/t/creative_commons

SpinXpress media search **spinxpress.com/getmedia**

Software for remix
Scratch: Free software download, tutorials and remix community available at
scratch.mit.edu

Support for using Scratch with Year 5 and 6 children can be accessed via Code Club
codeclub.org.uk

Photovisi **www.photovisi.com**

Glogster **edu.glogster.com**

Web Poster Wizard **poster.4teachers.org**

Prezi **prezi.com**

References

Association of College and Research Libraries & American Library Association (2000) *Information Literacy Competency Standards for Higher Education*. Chicago, IL: ACRL.

Baker, E. A., Pearson, P. D. and Rozendal, M.S. (2010). Theoretical Perspectives and Literacy Studies: An exploration of roles and insights, in Baker, E.A. (Ed.) *The New Literacies: Multiple Perspectives on Research and Practice*. New York: The Guilford Press.

Bamford, A. (no date) The Visual Literacy White Paper. [Available online] wwwimages.adobe. com/www.adobe.com/content/dam/Adobe/en/education/pdfs/visual-literacy-wp.pdf. (Accessed 3 August 2012).

Barnes, D. (1992) The Role of Talk in Learning, in K. Norman, *Thinking Voices: The Work of the National Oracy Project*. London: Hodder and Stoughton.

Bax, S. (2003) CALL – Past, Present and Future. *System, 31*.

BECTA (2004) *Using ICT to Support Students who have English as an Additional Language*. V1 edn.

Begoray, D. (2001) Through a Class Darkly. Visual Literacy in the Classroom. *Canadian Journal of Education, 26*.

Bolduc, J. and Fleuret, C (2009) Placing Music at the Centre of Literacy Instruction. *Research Monograph #* 19, May 2009.

Boyd, D. (2007) Why Youth (Heart) Social Network Sites: The role of networked publics in teenage social life, in D. Buckingham) (Ed.) *MacArthur Foundation Series on Digital Learning – Youth, Identity, and Digital Media Volume* (pp. 1–26). Cambridge MA: MIT Press. Retrieved from http://scholar.google.com/scholar?hl=en&btnG=Search&q=intitle: Why+Youth+(+Heart+)+Social+Network+Sites+:+The+Role+of+Networked+Publics+in+ Teenage+Social+Life#0.

British Film Institute (BFI) (2003) *Look Again: A teaching guide to using film and television with three to eleven-year olds*. London: BFI Education.

British Film Institute (BFI) (2010) Using Film in Schools – A Practical Guide. [Available online] http://industry.bfi.org.uk/media/pdf/g/h/Using_Film_in_Schools_-_A_Practical_Guide-Dec 2010.pdf. (Accessed 15 August 2012).

Bruce, C., Edwards, S. and Lupton, M. (2006) *Six Frames for Information Literacy Education: A conceptual framework for interpreting the relationships between theory and practice*, in S. Andretta (Ed.) *Challenge and Change: Information literacy for the 21st century*. Adelaide: AUSLIB Press.

Bruckman, A. (1999) Can Educational be Fun? Retrieved from www.cc.gatech.edu/~asb/ papers/bruckman-gdc99.pdf.

Bryant, L. (2007) Emerging Trends in Social Software for Education. *Becta: Emerging Trends in Technology, 2.*

Catts, R. and Lau, J. (2008) *Towards Information Literacy Indicators Conceptual Framework paper.* Paris: United Nations Educational, Scientific and Cultural Organization (UNESCO).

Clark, C. and Dugdale, G. (2009) Young People's Writing Attitudes, behaviour and the Role of Technology. *Literacy,* (November).

Coiro, J. (2003) Exploring Literacy on the Internet. *The Reading Teacher,* 56 (5): 458–64.

Coiro, J. and Dobler E. (2007) Exploring the Online Reading Comprehension Strategies Used by Sixth Grade Skilled Readers to Search for and Locate Information on the Internet. *Reading Research Quarterly,* 42 (2): 214–57.

Connaway, L., White, D., Lanclos, D. and Le Cornu, A. (2011) Visitors and Residents: What motivates engagement with the digital information environment? *Proceedings of the 74th ASIS&T Annual Meeting,* 48: 1–7.

Connell, I. (1979) TV/Video: Television, News and the Social Contract. *Screen,* 20 (1): 87–108.

Davidson, C. (2009) Young Children's Engagement with Digital Texts and Literacies in the Home: Pressing matters for the teaching of English in the early years of schooling. *English Teaching: Practice and Critique,* December 2009, 8 (3): 36–54. Retrieved from: http://education.waikato.ac.nz/research/files/etpc/files/2009v8n3art3.pdf.

Davies, N. (2004) Not Just How But Why: EAL and ICT in the multilingual classroom. *NALDIC Quarterly,* 1 (4).

De Souza, Z. and Dick, G. (2008) Information Disclosure on MySpace – the what, the why and the implications. *Pastoral Care in Education,* 26: (3) 143–57.

De Vries, P. (2010) What We Want: The music preferences of upper primary school students and the ways they engage with music. *Australian Journal of Music Education,* 1, 3–16.

DES (Department of Education and Science) (1978) *Special Educational Needs* (Warnock Report). Cmnd 7271. London: DES.

DfE (2008) Talk for Writing. [Available online] http://education.gov.uk/publications. (Accessed 15 August 2012).

DfE (2010) The Importance of Teaching. [Available online] www.gov.uk/goernment/publicat ions. (Accessed 4 May 2013).

DfE (2012) *Teachers' Standards.* London: DfE.

DFEE (1997) Excellence in Schools. [Available online] http://education.gov.uk/publications (Accessed 4 May 2013).

DFEE (2001) English: The National Curriculum in England (Key Stages 1-4) [Available online] http://education.gov.uk/publications. (Accessed 15 August 2012).

DFES (2006) The Primary National Strategy [Available online] http://webarchive.national archives.gov.uk (Accessed 20 November 2012).

DFES (2007) Improving Speaking and Listening Skills. [Available online] http://education.gov. uk/publications. (Accessed 15 August 2012).

Dombey, H. (2006) How should we teach children to read? *Books for Keeps,* 156: 6–7. [Available online] http://booksforkeeps.co.uk/issue/156/childrens-books/articles/other-articles/how-should-we-teach-children-to-read (Accessed 28 November 2012).

Dyer, J. (2011) Musical Thought: Using Music to Enhance Literacy Instruction. *Illinois Reading*

Council Journal, 39 (4) Fall 2011.

Eaude, T. (2011) *Thinking Through Pedagogy for Primary and Early Years.* Exeter: Learning Matters.

Egan, K. (1990) *Romantic Understanding: The development of rationality and imagination, ages 8-15.* New York: Routledge.

Eisenberg, M. and Berkowitz, B. *Big 6 Skills.* [Available online] www.big6.com (Accessed 1 November 2012).

EU Kids Online Network (2011) *EU Kids Online, Final Report.* London: London School of Economics.

Faux, F. (2007) Multimodality: How students with special educational needs create multi-media stories. *Education, Communication and Information,* 5 (2): 167–81.

Ferguson, K. (no date) [Available online] www.everythingisaremix.info/ (Accessed 11 November 2012).

Frawley, T. J. (2008) Gender Schema and Prejudicial Recall. *Journal of Research in Childhood Education,* 22: 291–303.

Freebody, P. and Luke, A. (1990) 'Literacies' programs: Debates and demands in cultural context. *Prospect,* Vol. 5, No. 3, May 1990.

Freebody, P. (1992) A Socio-cultural Approach: Resourcing four roles as a literacy learner, in A. Watson and A. Badenhop (Eds) *Prevention of Reading Failure.* Sydney: Ashton-Scholastic.

Freire, P. (2000) *Pedagogy of the Oppressed.* New York: Continuum.

Gee, J.P. (1996) *Social Linguistics and Literacies: Ideology in Disclosures.* London: Taylor and Francis.

Gee, J. (2003) *What Video Games Have to Teach us About Learning and Literacy. Computers in Entertainment (CIE).* Basingstoke: Palgrave Macmillan. Retrieved from http://dl.acm.org/citation.cfm?id=950595.

Gee, J.P. (2004) *Situated Language and Learning.* London: Routledge.

Giorgis, C., Johnson N.J., Bonomo A., Colbert C., Conner A., Kauffman G. and Kulesza D. (1999) Children's Books: Visual Literacy. *The Reading Teacher,* 53 (2): 146–53.

Griffin, S.M. (2011) Through the Eyes of Children: Telling insights into music experiences. *Visions of Research in Music Education,* 18. Retrieved from http://www-usr.rider.edu/~vrme/v19n1/visions/Griffin.

Goldacre, B. (2012) *Bad Pharma: How drug companies mislead doctors and harm patients.* London: Fourth Estate.

Goularte, R. (2010) Visual Literacy and Descriptive Writing'. [Available online] http://share2 learn.com/cabe2010workshop.pdf. (Accessed 1 August 2012).

Groff, J., Howells, C. and Cranmer, S. (2010). *The Impact of Console Games in the Classroom: Evidence from schools in Scotland.* Bristol: FutureLab. Retrieved from http://scholar.google.com/scholar?hl=en&btnG=Search&q=intitle:The+impact+of+console+games+in+the+classroom+:+Evidence+from+schools+in+Scotland#0.

Hall, S. (1980) *Culture, Media, Language: Working papers in cultural studies, 1972-79.* [Centre for Contemporary Cultural Studies, University of Birmingham]. London: Hutchinson.

Hansen, D. and Bernstorf, E. (2002) Linking Music Learning to Reading Instruction. *Music Educators Journal*, 88 (5): 17–21.

Harrison, C., O'Rourke and M. Yelland, N. (2009) Maximising the Moment from Preschool to School: The place of multiliteracies and ICT in the transition to school. *The International Journal of Learning*, Volume 16, Number 11.

Henry, L. (2006) SEARCHing for an answer: The Critical Role of New Literacies on the Internet. *International Reading Association*, 59 (7): 614–27.

Hess, C. and Ostrom, E. (eds) (2007) *Understanding Knowledge as a Commons*. Cambridge, MA: The MIT Press.

Hobbs, R. (2001) Improving Reading Comprehension by Using Media Literacy Activities. [Available online] http://teachwithvisionml.files.wordpress.com/2009/04/medialit.readl.pdf. (Accessed 3 August 2012).

Hull, G.A. (2003) *Multiple Literacies: A compilation for adult educators*. Columbus, OH: Center on Education and Training for Employment, College of Education, the Ohio State University.

Hummell, L. (2011) Feel the Rhythm: Music technology. *Children's Technology and Engineering*, December 2011.

Jackson. L, Gauntlett, D. and Steemers, J. (2008) Children in Virtual Worlds: Adventure Rock users and producers study. Retrieved from www.bbc.co.uk/blogs/knowledgeexchange/westminsterone.pdf.

Jacobson, E. (2010) Music Remix in the Classroom, in M. Knobel and C. Lankshear (Eds) *DIY Media: Creating sharing and learning with new technologies*. Oxford, Peter Lang.

Jama, D. and Dugdale, G. (2012) *Literacy: State of the Nation. A picture of literacy in the UK today*. National Literacy Trust (January), 1–7.

James, C., Davis, K., Flores, A., Francis, J.M., Pettingill, L., Rundle, M. and Gardner, H. (2009) Young People, Ethics, and the New Digital Media. *Digital Media*. Retrieved from www.citeulike.org/group/10688/article/7664217.

Johnson, D. (no date) Does Technology Change how Schools Teach Ethical Behaviors? Real Questions, Good Answers. *Knowledge Quest*, 3 (2). Retrieved from www.doug-johnson.com/dougwri/does-technology-change-how-schools-teach-ethical-behaviors.html.

Kellner, D. and Share, J. (2005) Toward Critical Media Literacy: Core Concepts, Debates, Organizations, and Policy. *Discourse: Studies in the Cultural Politics of Education*, 26 (3): 369–86.

Kist, W. (2005) *New Literacies in Action: Teaching and learning in multiple media*. New York: Teachers College Press.

Knobel, M and Lankshear, C. (2008) Remix: The Art and Craft of Endless Hybridization. *Journal of Adolescent & Adult Literacy*, 52 (1) September 2008.

Knowles, G. and Lander, V. (2012) *Thinking Through Ethics and Values in Primary Education*. London: SAGE/Learning Matters.

Lankshear, C. and Knobel, M. (2006), *New Literacies: Everyday practices and classroom learning*, Maidenhead: Open University Press.

Lankshear, C and Knobel, M. (2007) Sampling 'the New' in New Literacies, in C. Lankshear and M. Knobel (Eds) *A New Literacies Sampler* (pp. 1–24). New York: Peter Lang.

Lankshear, C. and Knobel, M. (2007), Researching New Literacies: Web 2.0 Practices and Insider Perspectives. *E-learning*, 4 (3): 224–40.

Larson, L. (2009) Reader Response Meets New Literacies: Empowering readers in online learning communities. *The Reading Teacher*, 62 (8): 638–48.

Lessig, L. (2004) *Free Culture: How big media uses technology and the law to lock down culture and control creativity*. New York: Penguin.

Leu, D., Kinzer, C.K., Coiro, J.L. and Cammack, D.W. (2004). Toward a Theory of New Literacies Emerging From the Internet and Other Information and Communication Technologies. Retrieved from http://www.readingonline.org/newliteracies/leu/.

Lieberman, D., Bates, C. and So, J. (2009) Young Children's Learning With Digital Media. *Computers in the Schools*, 26: 271–83.

Livingstone, S.M. (2003) *The Changing Nature and Uses of Media Literacy*. London: Media @LSE, London School of Economics.

McIntire, J. (2007) Developing Literacy through Music. *Teaching Music*, Vol. 15, Issue 1.

Malone, T. (1981) Toward a Theory of Intrinsically Motivating Instruction. *Cognitive Science: A Multidisciplinary Journal*, 5 (4): 333–69. doi: 10.1207/s15516709cog0504_2.

Manfra, M. and Lee, J.K. (2011) Leveraging the Affordances of Educational Blogs to Teach Low-Achieving Students United States History. *Social Studies Research and Practicve*, 6 (2).

Marsh, J. (2004) The Techno-literacy Practices of Young Children. *Journal of Early Childhood Research*, 2(1): 51–66.

Marsh, J. (2005) Ritual, Performance and Identity Construction: Young children's engagement with popular cultural and media texts, in J. Marsh (Ed.) *Popular Culture, New Media and Digital Technology in Early Childhood*. London: RoutledgeFalmer.

Marsh, J., Brooks, G., Hughes, J., Ritchie, L., Roberts, S. and Wright, K. (2005) Digital Beginnings: Young children's use of popular culture, media and new technologies. Sheffield: University of Sheffield.

Marsh, J. and Hallet, E. (2008) *Desirable Literacies: Approaches to Language and Literacy in the Early Years* (2nd Edn). London: SAGE.

Marsh J. and Willett R. (2010) Mega Mash-ups and Remixes in the Cultural Borderlands: Emergent findings from the ethnographic studies of playground games and rhymes in two primary schools, Paper presented at '*Children's Playground Games and Songs in the New Media Age*: Interim Conference', 25th February 2010, London Knowledge Lab, London.

Merchant, G. (2005a) Digikids: cool dudes and the new writing. *E-Learning*, 2 (1): 50–60.

Merchant, G. (2005b) Barbie meets Bob the Builder at the Workstation, J. Marsh (Ed.) *Popular Culture, New Media and Digital Technology in Early Childhood* (pp. 183–218). London: RoutledgeFalmer.

Merchant, G. (2009) Web 2.0, new lLiteracies, and the idea of learning through participation. *English Teaching: practice and critique*, 8 (3): 8–20.

Merchant, G. (2010) 3D Virtual Worlds as Environments for Literacy Learning. *Educational Research*, 52 (2): 135–50. doi: 10.1080/00131881.2010.482739.

Milton Keynes Ethnic Minority Achievement Support Service (2004) *Supporting Pupils with*

English as an Additional Language. Milton Keynes Council.

Miners, Z. and Pascopella A. (2007) The New Literacies. *District Administrator* [Available online] http://reading rockets.org/article/21208 (Accessed 10 November 2012).

Mitchell, D. (2012) Quadblogging. [Available online] http://quadblogging.net (Accessed 12 November 2012).

Nixon, H. and Comber, B. (2005) Behind the Scenes, in J. Marsh (Ed.) *Popular Culture, New Media and Digital Technology in Early Childhood* (pp. 219–36). London: RoutledgeFalmer.

Ofsted (2011) Excellence in English. [Available online] http://ofsted.gov.uk/resources/excell ence-english. (Accessed 18 August 2012).

Ofsted (2012) Music in Schools: wider still, and wider. Ofsted.

O'Hara, M. (2011) Young Children's ICT Experiences in the Home: Some parental perspectives. *Journal of Early Childhood Research* 9 (3): 220–31.

O'Neill, B. (2010) Media Literacy and Communication Rights: Ethical Individualism in the New Media Environment. *International Communication Gazette,* 72 (4-5): 323–38.

Pagett, L. (2006) Mum and Dad Prefer Me to Speak Bengali at Home: Code switching and parallel speech in a primary school setting. *Literacy,* 40 (3).

Papert, S. and Harel, I. (1991) *Constructionism.* New York: Ablex Publishing Corporation.

Passey, D. (2011) *Internet Safety in the Context of Developing Aspects of Young Peoples Digital Citizenship* (p. 102). Lancaster. Retrieved from http://eprints.lancs.ac.uk/40916/1/40916.pdf.

Prensky, M. (2001) Digital Natives, Digital Immigrants Part 1. *On the Horizon,* 9 (5): 1–6. doi: 10.1108/10748120110424816.

QCA (2000) *Unit 6D Using the Internet to Search Large Databases and to Interpret Information.* UK: QCA.

Riddick, B. (2011) Dyslexia and Inclusion: time for a social model of disability perspective. *International Studies in Sociology and Education,* 11 (3): 223–36.

Rief, L. (1992) *Seeking Diversity: Language arts with adolescents.* Portsmouth, NH: Heinemann.

Roberts, J. (2000) Read any Good Films Lately? *Literacy Today,* 23.

Roberts, M. (27 March 2012) *Chocolate 'may help keep people slim'.* [Available online] www.bbc.co.uk/news/health-17511011 (Accessed 28 January 2012).

Rose, J. (2006) The Independent Review of the Teaching of Early Reading. [Available online] http://education.gov.uk/publications. (Accessed 15 August 2012).

Rose, J. (2009) The Independent Review of the Primary Curriculum. London: DCSF. [Available online] http://education.gov.uk/publications. (Accessed 15 August 2012).

Rowan, L., Knobel, M., Bigum, C. and Lankshear, C. (2002) Boys, Literacies and Schooling: The dangerous territories of gender-based literacy reform. *British Educational Research Journal.* Buckingham: Open University Press. Retrieved from www.tandfonline.com/doi/abs/10.1080/0141192032000161225.

Salmon, A. (2010) Using Music to Promote Children's Thinking and Enhance Their Literacy Development. *Early Child Development and Care,* 180 (7): 937–45.

Sandford, R. and Williamson, B. (2005) *Games and Learning: A handbook from Futurelab.* Bristol: FutureLab. Retrieved from http://archive.futurelab.org.uk/resources/documents/

handbooks/games_and_learning2.pdf.

Seymour, P.H.K., Duncan, L.G., Aro, M. and Baillie, S. (2005) Quantifying the Effect of Orthographic and Phonological Complexity on Foundation Literacy Acquisition: The English-Finnish contrast. Symposium on Direct Cross-linguistic Comparison Studies of Literacy Acquisition. *Conference of the Society for the Scientific Study of Reading,* Toronto, June 2005.

Schön, D.A. (1987) *Educating the Reflective Practitioner.* San Francisco, CA: Jossey-Bass.

Skelton, C., Francis, B. and Valkanova, Y. (2007) *Breaking Down the Stereotypes: Gender and achievement in schools.* Manchester: Equal Opportunities Commission.

Stafford, T. (2011) *Teaching Visual Literacy in the Primary Classroom* (1st Edn). Oxon: David Fulton.

Stone, J.C. (2007) Popular Websites in Adolescents' Out-of-School Lives: Critical lessons on literacy, in M. Knobel and C. Lankshear (Eds) *A New Literacies Sampler* (pp. 49–65). New York: Peter Lang.

The 2011 Skills for Life Survey: A Survey of Literacy, Numeracy and ICT Levels in England (2012). Retrieved from http://dera.ioe.ac.uk/16147/1/12-p168-2011-skills-for-life-survey. pdf.

The Report of the All-Party Parliamentary Literacy Group Commission (2012). *Boys' Reading Commission.* Retrieved from http://www.literacytrust.org.uk/assets/0001/4056/Boys _Commission_Report.pdf.

Tondeur, J., van, B.J.and Valcke, M. (2007) Curricula and the use of ICT in Education: Two worlds apart? *British Journal of Educational Technology,* 38 (6): 962–76.

Turvey, K. (2006) *The Ethical Challenges of Researching Primary School Children's Online Activities: A new ethical paradigm for the virtual ethnographer?* [Available online] www.leeds.ac.uk/educol/documents/157434.htm.

UK Literacy Association (UKLA) (2013) *Teaching Reading.* Leicester: UKLA.

Ulicsak, M and Williamson, B. (2010) *Computer Games and Learning.* Bristol: FutureLab. Retrieved from http://futurelab.org.uk/resources/computer-games-and-learning-hand book

UNESCO (1951) The Use of Vernacular Languages in Education: The Report of the UNESCO Meeting of Specialists, in J.A. Fishman (Ed.) *Readings in the Sociology of Language.* The Hague: Mouton Press.

Valentine, G. and Holloway, S.L. (2002) Cyberkids? Exploring Children's Identities and Social Networks in On-line and Off-line Worlds. *Annals of the Association of American Geographers,* 92 (2): 302–19. doi: 10.1111/1467-8306.00292.

Vygotsky, L. (1978) Interaction Between Learning and Development. [Available online] http:// psy.cmu.edu/siegler/vygotsky78.pdf. (Accessed 15 August 2012).

Walinsky, L. (2011) Utilizing Music to Help Teach Literacy. *Based on a Workshop Presented through Young Audiences of Pennsylvania.*

Waller, M. (2010) Using Twitter in the Classroom. [Available online] http://changinghorizons. net (Accessed 12 November 2012).

Whitaker, J.L. and Bushman, B.J. (2009). Online Dangers: Keeping children and adolescents safe. *Washington and Lee Law Review,* 66, 1053. Retrieved from http://heinonlineback

up.com/hol-cgi-bin/get_pdf.cgi?handle=hein.journals/waslee66section=31.

Whitworth, A. (2009) *Information Obesity*. Oxford: Chandos.

Willard, N.E. (2007) *Cyber-Safe Kids, Cyber-Savvy Teens: Helping young people learn to use the Internet safely and responsibly*. John Wiley & Sons, Inc.

Williams, R. (2010) *Internet Plagiarism Rising in Schools*. Retrieved from www.guardian.co.uk/education/2010/jun/20/internet-plagiarism-rising-in-schools.

Wohlwend, K.E. (2009) Damsels in Discourse: Girls consuming and producing identity texts through Disney Princess play. *Reading Research Quarterly*, 44 (1): 57–83. doi:10.1598/RRQ.44.1.3.

www.fanfiction.net (no date) (Accessed 12 November 2012).

www.flatstanley.com (no date) (Accessed 12 November 2012).

www.learner.org/journeynorth (no date) (Accessed 12 November 2012).

Yenawine, P. (1997) Thoughts on Visual Literacy. [Available online] http://vtshome.org/system/resources/0000/0005/Thoughts_Visual_Literacy.pdf. (Accessed 1 August 2012).

Young, S. (2007) Digital Technologies, Young Children, and Music Education Practice, in K. Smithrim and R. Upitis. *Listen to Their Voices*. Waterloo, Ontario: Canadian Music Educators Association (pp. 330–43). [Available online] www.academia.edu/352647/Digital_Technologies_Young_Children_and_Educational_Practice.

Zimmermann, S. and Hutchins, C. (2008) *7 Keys to Comprehension: How to Help Your Kids Read It and Get It!* Crown Publishing Group.

Index

Added to a page number 'f' denotes a figure.

Thinking Through New Literacies from Primary and Early Years